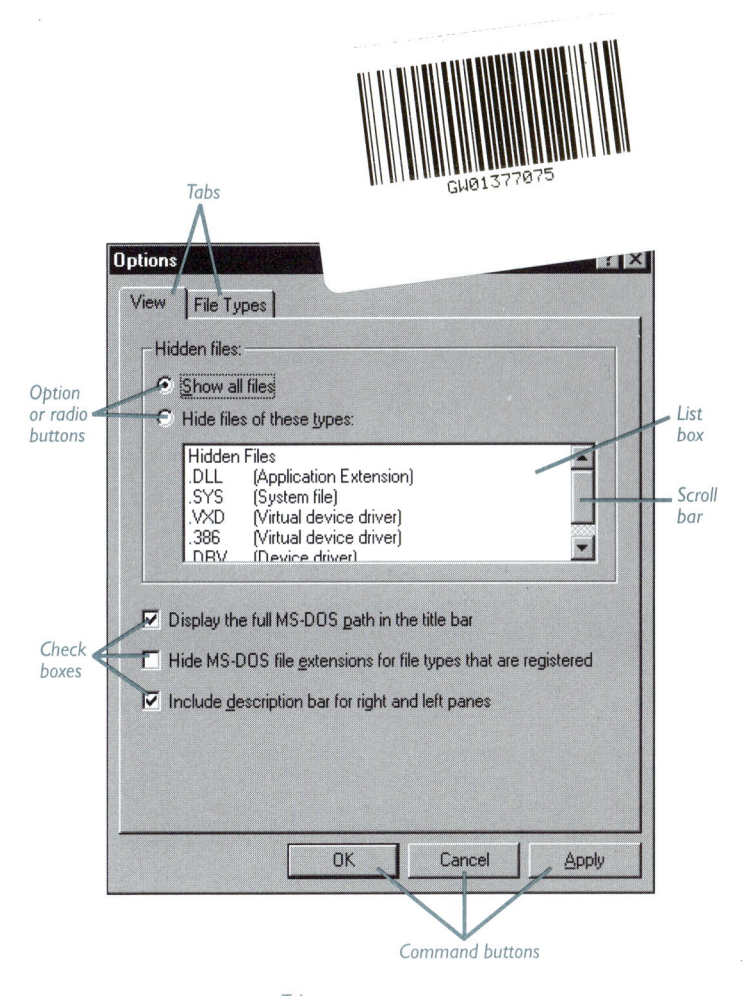

Tabs

Options ❔ ✖

| View | File Types |

Hidden files:
- ⦿ **Show all files**
- ○ Hide files of these types:

  Hidden Files
  .DLL (Application Extension)
  .SYS (System file)
  .VXD (Virtual device driver)
  .386 (Virtual device driver)
  .DRV (Device driver)

Option or radio buttons

List box

Scroll bar

☑ Display the full MS-DOS path in the title bar
☐ Hide MS-DOS file extensions for file types that are registered
☑ Include description bar for right and left panes

Check boxes

[OK] [Cancel] [Apply]

Command buttons

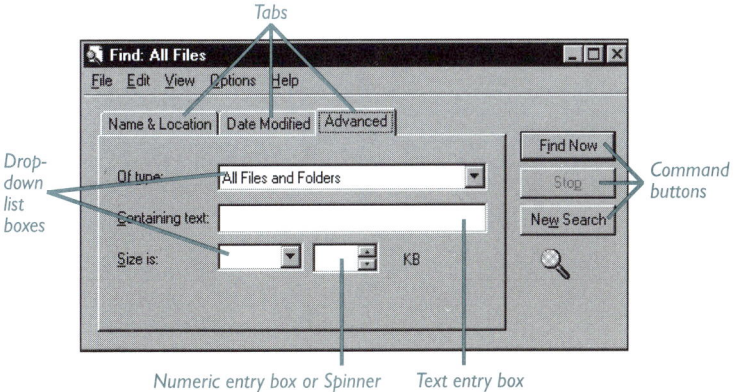

Tabs

Find: All Files ▁ ☐ ✖

File Edit View Options Help

| Name & Location | Date Modified | **Advanced** |

Of type: [All Files and Folders ▼]

Containing text: [   ]

Size is: [▼] [▲▼] KB

[Find Now]
[Stop]
[New Search]
🔍

Drop-down list boxes

Command buttons

Numeric entry box or Spinner   *Text entry box*

WINDOWS® 95

INSTANT REFERENCE

**Carole Boggs Matthews and
Martin Matthews**

SYBEX®

San Francisco • Paris • Düsseldorf • Soest

Acquisitions Manager: Kristine Plachy

Developmental Editor: Gary Masters

Editor: Kristen Vanberg-Wolff

Technical Editor: Tanya Strub

Desktop Publishing Specialist: Molly Sharp

Book Designer: Seventeenth Street Studios

Production Coordinator: Dave Nash

Indexer: Nancy Guenther

Cover Designer: Design Site

Cover Photographer: Mark Johann

SYBEX is a registered trademark of SYBEX Inc.

TRADEMARKS: SYBEX has attempted throughout this book to distinguish proprietary trademarks from descriptive terms by following the capitalization style used by the manufacturer.

Every effort has been made to supply complete and accurate information. However, SYBEX assumes no responsibility for its use, nor for any infringement of the intellectual property rights of third parties which would result from such use.

Copyright ©1995 SYBEX Inc., 2021 Challenger Drive, Alameda, CA 94501. World rights reserved. No part of this publication may be stored in a retrieval system, transmitted, or reproduced in any way, including but not limited to photocopy, photograph, magnetic or other record, without the prior agreement and written permission of the publisher.

Library of Congress Card Number: 95-69859

ISBN: 0-7821-1489-X

Manufactured in the United States of America

10 9 8 7 6 5 4 3 2

*To James E. Boggs, father, father-in-law,
and good friend, who is always there!*

Acknowledgments

A book requires a tremendous effort to produce. We would like to thank the many folks at Sybex who have made this book possible: Gary Masters, developmental editor, for giving the book a chance; Kris Vanberg-Wolff, editor, for excellence in editing and for being such a pleasure to work with; Tanya Strub, technical editor, for keeping us honest and accurate; and others who made a difference—desktop publisher Molly Sharp, production coordinator Dave Nash, and indexer Nancy Guenther.

In addition, we would like to thank Microsoft's Windows 95 product manager, Brent Ethington, who repeatedly answered our questions clearly and generously, with technical knowledge and patience.

Contents

Introduction xi

PART ONE:
An Orientation to Windows 95 1

PART TWO:
Command and Feature Reference
(listed alphabetically) 23

Index 329

Introduction

Windows 95 is an entirely new operating system that enhances the Windows graphical environment and the DOS operating system. It includes a user interface with many new and improved features and capabilities. In many ways, it is easier, more intuitive, and more fun to use than earlier versions of Windows. Regardless of the extent of your technical knowledge, Windows 95 is a powerful new tool for PC users. Although you probably will want to, you don't have to convert all at once to the new interface. Since it is compatible with previous versions of Windows *and* DOS, you can still run your favorite old programs.

How This Book Is Organized

This book contains both an overview of Windows 95 and a detailed guide to its commands and features. Part One gives you an overview of the new Windows 95 interface and features. After reading it, you'll understand the key differences between Windows 95 and previous versions, and you'll be able to navigate your way around it. Just reading Part One will enable you to use many features on your own—Windows 95 is that easy to use! (With the aid of this book, of course!)

Part Two contains descriptions of the many features and commands in Windows 95. For each subject, it describes the screens, menus, and toolbars, and lists the steps needed to complete related tasks. The contents of Part Two are ordered alphabetically so that you can look up a subject by function, feature name, or just a guess. Most topics contain multiple references so you can find what you need one way or another, and references are given to other topics that give additional, related information. All major components and features are addressed, and

INTRODUCTION

graphic images are included to illustrate the subjects being discussed.

You'll also find some handy information inside the front and back covers. Inside the front cover on the left is a screen image of a window, with labels for its standard components. Beneath it and on the right are three dialog box images, which show the kinds of buttons, check boxes, lists, and other elements you'll see in Windows 95. Inside the back cover, you'll find many shortcut keys that will enable you to perform tasks without going through the menu systems.

Who Should Read This Book and Why?

Windows 95 Instant Reference was written for both Windows 3.1 users upgrading to Windows 95 and users buying Windows for the first time. You do not have to be technically oriented to use this book, but you should read Part One to get a general understanding of the interface and features of Windows 95 before you delve into Part Two.

For those upgrading from a previous Windows product, you will find that this book eases your transition into Windows 95. It allows you to grasp the essential points without getting bogged down in details. With a quick reference to the book when needed, you'll find that the intuitive approach used by Windows 95 will make heavy reading unnecessary.

New users will find Part One to be essential to gaining a basic level of knowledge about Windows 95. The graphics and step-by-step approach used to explain how to perform tasks will lead the user through most complex situations. Once you have gained familiarity with the book's organization, you

INTRODUCTION

will be able to quickly find what you need. And since it's small in size, you can carry the book with you in your briefcase or pocket. You'll find that it becomes your most commonly used reference—easy to use, thorough, and complete.

What Conventions Are Used?

As you thumb through this book, you'll find some consistently used conventions to help you find the information you need. Graphic images or icons being described or used in a procedure are included next to the topic to help you clearly identify what is being discussed. Occasionally, Windows 95 has changed the name of a feature or function, but you can still look up the old name, and the entry will point you to the new name and entry. You'll also find cross-references at the end of some entries pointing you to other entries. Sometimes the information is required to use the feature; sometimes the information is simply related and useful for gaining familiarity with the product.

Additional information is also given in the form of Notes, Tips, and Warnings, as described here:

NOTE: *Notes provide additional information about the topic being discussed.*

TIP: *Tips give handy clues to making better use of the feature, or shorter methods for obtaining the same results.*

WARNING: *Warnings alert you to potential pitfalls when using a feature.*

INTRODUCTION

Terms Used in This Book

The following specific terms are used to represent commonly used actions or screen components:

Point
Move the mouse pointer until it is on top of an object. Point on a menu option in a menu to select it.

Click or click on
Point on an object and then press and release the left mouse button. This is the most common way to select an object.

Double-click
Point on an object and then press and release the left mouse button twice in rapid succession. This activates a program or opens a folder. If you double-click on a file or document, you will both activate its program and open the document.

Drag across an object
Point to one end of an object, press and hold down the left mouse button, and then drag the mouse pointer to the opposite end before releasing it. This will select the object.

Drag an object
Point on an object, press and hold down the left mouse button, and then drag the object where you want it. For example, if you drag the title bar, you will move the entire window. Dragging one of the sides of a window will change its size.

Right-click
Point to an object and click the right mouse button. This displays a popup or context menu appropriate to the object.

PART ONE

An Orientation to Windows 95

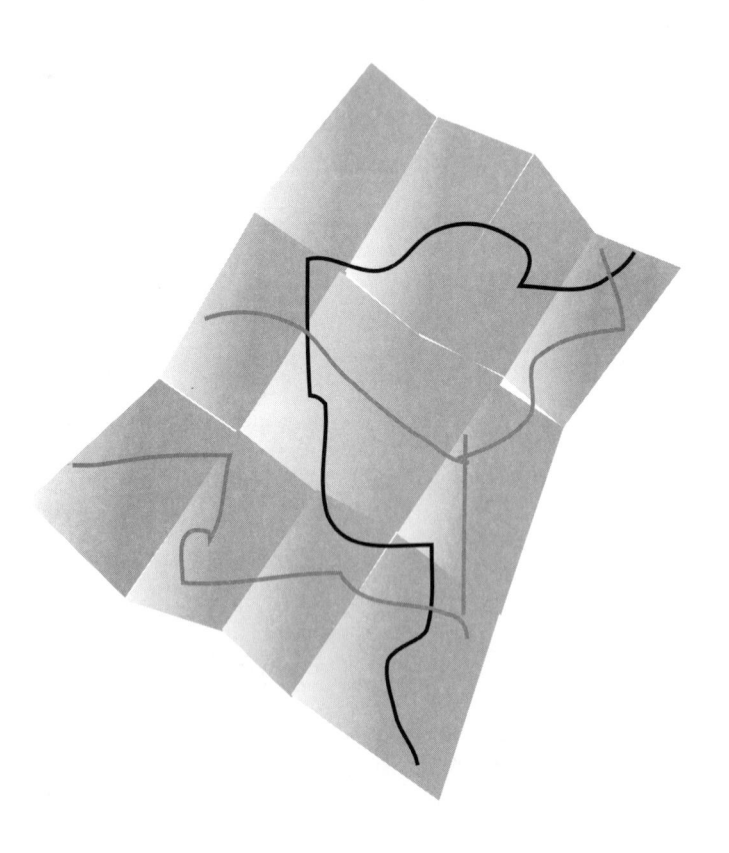

THE WINDOWS 95 SCREEN

Windows 95 is a completely new, self-contained operating system built to replace the combination of the MS- or PC-DOS operating system and the Windows graphical user interface. In addition to providing networking and communications capability, it also introduces many new features, functions, and applications. It does all of this with a new user interface that looks and feels different, but retains enough similarities to previous versions to make you feel somewhat at home.

The good news is that Windows 95 is easier to use. Once you get used to seeing and using the new Windows 95 screens, you'll never look back.

Let's take a look at this exciting new tool!

The Windows 95 Screen

The new user interface is immediately apparent when you look at the initial Windows 95 screen shown below. "Where's the Program Manager?" you ask. The Program Manager that appeared in prior versions of Windows is nowhere to be seen. (If you want it back, it is still available. See *Program Manager* in Part Two.) In place of the Program Manager, Windows 95 gives you an empty screen with several icons on the left (yours may differ depending on the components installed on your computer) and a bar on the bottom with a button and a clock.

AN ORIENTATION TO WINDOWS 95

The Windows 95 screen does not have to remain empty, it just starts out that way. Unlike prior versions of Windows, even if you have a lot of applications, they do not have to be visible to get quick access to them. The objects visible on the initial screen provide several quick ways to start your applications and use Windows.

The Taskbar

The bar at the bottom of the screen is the *Taskbar*. In addition to the Start button and the clock, it contains a variable-sized button for each application you have running. It also includes a notification area where icons alert you to incoming mail and faxes, your online status, accessibility selections, and where you can set the volume of your sound system or check on your printer status. You can switch to another application that is running by simply clicking on one of the buttons. (See *Taskbar* in Part Two for additional information.)

THE WINDOWS 95 SCREEN

The Start Button

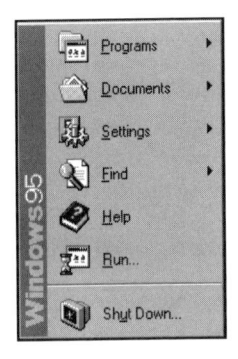

The Start button, which appears on the left of the Taskbar, is the primary means of accessing your applications and data files. If you place the pointer over the Start button, a popup label identifies it with the words, *Click here to begin*. You can also use it to change the settings on your computer, and it is the only way that you can gracefully shut down and leave Windows 95. When you click on the Start button, a menu appears with seven entries or *options*. The first four of the options have a right-pointing triangle on the right side. This triangle means that when you select that option by moving the mouse pointer to it, a submenu will open. The last two options have an ellipsis (...) after them. This tells you that a dialog box where you can enter or select information will open when you select that option.

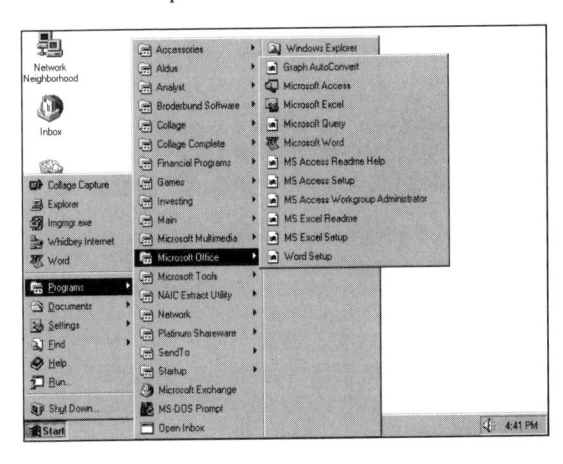

Moving the mouse to one of the first four options on the Start menu opens that option. You don't have to click the mouse button. Depending on the option, you may be able to move the mouse and open another submenu several times, all without clicking. A series of submenus is shown here. To select the final option you have chosen, you must click the left mouse button.

AN ORIENTATION TO WINDOWS 95

The options on the Start menu and their functions are as follows:

Programs provides the primary means of starting an application. To select a program group and then an application within the group, move the mouse pointer until the application you want is highlighted and then click the left mouse button.

Documents provides a list of the last 15 documents that you have opened directly from Windows (not from an application). By selecting (clicking on) one of these, you first start the application that is associated with the document and then load the document so you can work on it.

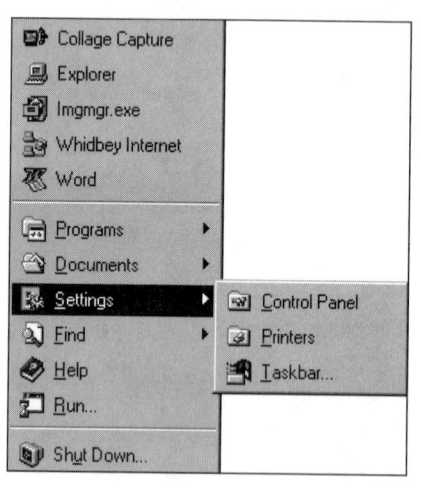

Settings provides the means to adjust many aspects of your system through special control panel windows. You can also open a window to add, delete, and manage printers; and open the Taskbar Properties dialog box.

Find allows you to locate files, folders, and computers on your network by their name and location. You can also locate files and folders by date modified, type, size, and whether they contain certain text. For your online use, Find locates Microsoft Network services for you, such as Internet newsgroups, bulletin boards, and so on.

Help opens the Windows 95 Help system, where you can look up words in an index or a topic in a table of contents and get an explanation of what you have selected.

Run provides a command line in which you type a path and program or folder name to run the program or open the folder. For example, typing **a:\setup** and then pressing ↵ or clicking OK will run the Setup program on the A drive.

Shut Down allows you to leave Windows 95 and either shut down or restart your computer (in MS-DOS perhaps), or simply log off and on to the network. You should always use Shut Down in the Start menu to gracefully leave Windows 95. Turning off your computer without using Shut Down may cause you to lose information that should have been written to your disk.

Adding to the Start Menu

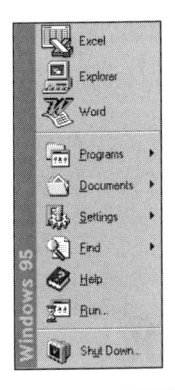

To bypass the menu system, you can add frequently-used programs directly to the top of the Start menu rather than within the Programs option. You must be selective, of course, in the programs you add to the menu, since it is limited to twelve options. (See *Arranging Applications* and *Start Button* in Part Two for instructions on how to add to the Start Menu.) An example of a Start Menu with three added programs is shown here.

The Desktop, Windows, and Dialog Boxes

The initial Windows 95 screen, outside of the Taskbar, is called the *Desktop*. The objects on the Desktop take one of three forms: an icon, a window, or a dialog box.

An icon represents an application or a document that is not in use at the moment but is available if you simply double-click on it.

Windows and dialog boxes are both defined areas on the screen with a border around them. There are important differences, however. The purpose of a

AN ORIENTATION TO WINDOWS 95

dialog box is to gather or give information so a task can be completed. For example, to save a file, you must enter the name of the file in a dialog box. A dialog box is a fixed size and does not have a menu bar with a set of menus. A *window*, on the other hand, contains objects that you can manipulate in some way. For example, the window shown inside the front cover of this book contains icons for files that you can open, close, copy, move, rename, and delete. A window can be resized and, in most instances, contains a menu bar with a set of menus in it. A window that contains an application like WordPerfect for Windows fits the classic definition of a window with a menu bar. An application window may also contain one or more windows within it that contain data files. This is called a *document window*, and does not have a menu bar.

Parts of a Window

The following graphic shows the parts of a typical window. Following it is a list of these parts and a description of each of their functions.

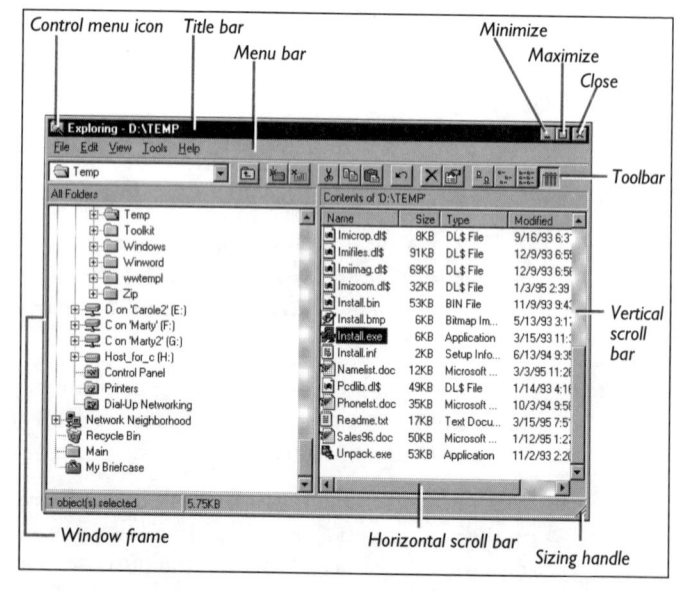

THE WINDOWS 95 SCREEN

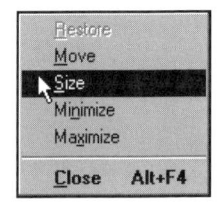

Control menu The control menu is opened by clicking on the control menu icon or by pressing Alt+Spacebar. The Control menu allows you to control the window's physical characteristics. You can select an option either by clicking on it or by typing the underlined letter. If you double-click on the Control menu icon, you will close the window.

Minimize button This button reduces the size of the window so that it is just an entry on the Taskbar.

Maximize button This button enlarges the window so it fills the screen or is as large as the window containing it will allow. After a window has been maximized, the Maximize button becomes a Restore button, which will return the window to its previous size.

Close button This button closes the window.

Window frame You can adjust the size of the window by dragging the window frame in one direction. When the mouse is on the frame, the mouse pointer becomes a two-headed arrow.

Vertical scroll bar Clicking on the scroll arrows at either end of the vertical scroll bar scrolls the contents of the window up or down one line at a time. Dragging on the raised scroll box, which indicates the relative position of the window's contents, moves the contents in the direction you are dragging. Clicking on the scroll bar outside of the scroll box moves the contents in greater increments—about one screen at a time.

Sizing handle You can adjust the size of the window in two dimensions by dragging the sizing handle diagonally. The sizing handle in the lower-right corner provides a larger area to drag, but you can

AN ORIENTATION TO WINDOWS 95

drag any corner of a window diagonally and get the same effect.

Horizontal scroll bar You can scroll the contents of the window left or right in the same manner as the vertical scroll bar.

Menu bar You can open a menu by clicking on it. Using the keyboard, you can press Alt or F10 for the menu bar and then press the ← or → key, and then press the ↵ key or the ↓ key.

Title bar The title bar contains the title of the window. You can move the window by dragging on the title bar.

Toolbar The toolbar contains buttons or icons that are shortcuts for performing many common tasks. If a toolbar is not visible, select it from the View menu.

Parts of a dialog box

Three dialog boxes containing examples of typical controls are displayed inside the front cover for your convenience. A desciption of each control and its function is listed below.

Tabs allow you to select from among several "pages" in a dialog box by clicking on the tab you want to use. Each page presents a separate set of controls.

Option buttons allow you to select one, and only one, option from among several that are presented in a group by clicking on the button. These are also called "radio buttons" because they operate like the buttons on a car radio. The option that is selected has a black dot in it.

Check boxes To turn a particular feature on or off, click in its check box. You may select as many check

THE WINDOWS 95 SCREEN

boxes in a group as you want. When the check box is on or selected, a check mark appears in the box.

List boxes allow you to choose an option from among several that are presented in a list. There may or may not be a scroll bar on the right. Click on an option to select it.

Drop-down list box is the same as a list box except that you must click on the down arrow on the right to open the list. The currently selected option is displayed when the list is closed.

Text box allows you to enter text such as a file name. If there is no existing text in the box, simply click in the box and type the text you want. If you want to replace existing text, drag across the existing text and type the replacement. To add and/or replace selected characters, click where you want the change, use Del or Backspace to remove characters to the right or left respectively, and type the new text.

Numeric entry box This is the same as a text box except that it only accepts numbers.

Spinner Often associated with a numeric entry box, a spinner allows you to increase or decrease a number by clicking on the up or down arrows respectively.

Slider You can change a value by dragging the slider left or right.

Command buttons allow you to perform a command such as closing and leaving a dialog box. Two common command buttons are OK and Cancel. OK accepts the changes you have made to the dialog box and then closes it. Cancel ignores any changes you have made and then closes the dialog box.

Help button This button adds a question mark to the mouse pointer, and then provides a context-sensitive

AN ORIENTATION TO WINDOWS 95

help window containing information on whatever you have clicked on in the dialog box.

Close button Clicking on this button closes the dialog box and ignores any changes you have made, just as if you had clicked on Cancel.

The Mouse and the Keyboard

In order to communicate with Windows, you must use the mouse and the keyboard.

Selecting and Moving with the Mouse

The mouse (a term which includes trackballs and other pointing devices) performs three important functions: selecting, activating, and moving objects on the screen.

Usually, when an object is selected it is *highlighted* in some way. For example, selecting an icon reverses the color of its name. If it was black on white, it becomes white on blue in the default color scheme. The highlighting is usually obvious, as shown here:

As described in the Introduction, you select an object by pointing on it, and then clicking it, encircling it, or dragging across it while pressing the left mouse button. To activate or open an object, you usually double-click on it, which both selects and then activates it. However, if you are choosing a menu option, you simply click on it to activate it. To move an object, you simply drag it.

The left mouse button is the one used to select, activate, and move objects. In most instances in this book and in many others, you will not see a reference to the left button. This is because the left is considered the main or primary mouse button, and the one inferred if no reference is given. However, if you are left-handed or have some other reason, you can use the Mouse control panel to switch your right and left buttons so the right mouse button takes on the primary role (See *Mouse Tab Options* in *Accessibility Options*, and *Right Clicking* in Part Two). When the secondary button (normally the right button) is referenced, it is always called the "right mouse button."

Using the Keyboard

Windows 95 assumes that you are using the mouse to perform such tasks as opening the Start menu, using the Taskbar, or selecting an object. The user interface was designed to be used with the mouse; it is the easiest and most intuitive way to work in Windows 95. The keyboard, however, can be handy for accessing the Start menu and the Taskbar, and using it can be preferable when you don't want to remove your hands from the keyboard. These special key combinations and their functions are shown inside the back cover.

Of course, these keystrokes work only in circumstances in which they make sense. For example, if you are in a window without subdivisions like the one shown inside the front cover, Tab does nothing. However, in the Explorer window described in the next section, Tab moves the active area from one part of the screen to the next. The best way to understand these keystrokes is to try them out.

Oh No! Not the File Manager, Too!

Yes, it's true. The File Manager is gone too, replaced by the Explorer.

AN ORIENTATION TO WINDOWS 95

Although it is still available, the File Manager is no longer part of the default Windows 95 environment. The goal of Windows 95 file management is to be more intuitive, more powerful, and to address information in a way that did not easily fit into the old hierarchical file structure. As a result, Windows 95 includes two new schemes for accessing information: the first separates it into logical types of information, and the second looks at all information as a single continuum. Both schemes share the same file structure.

Directories Become Folders

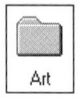

Windows 95 has replaced the concept of a directory as a container for files and subdirectories with a very intuitive container called a *folder*, and given it a manila file folder for an icon. The folder to the left has been named "Art."

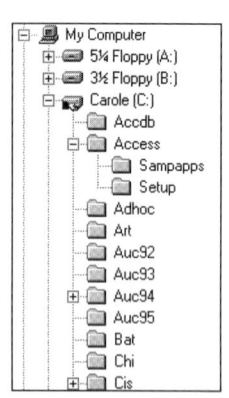

A folder can do everything a directory can do and more. A folder can contain other folders as well as files and other objects, such as e-mail messages and faxes. The Windows 95 file structure, then, consists of computers containing disks, containing folders, containing other folders, containing files as shown here. The concept expands to include the network with its shared disks and folders all displayed on the same continuum.

Types of Information

In order to simplify access to information and make it more intuitive, Windows 95 provides a separate facility to access each of three different types of information. These facilities and the types of information they access are My Computer, Network Neighborhood, Microsoft Exchange (Inbox), and Explorer.

OH NO! NOT THE FILE MANAGER, TOO!

My Computer

Use this facility to access information that is stored in the classical file structure on your computer. When you open My Computer, a window like this appears on your screen:

```
My Computer
File  Edit  View  Help

5¼ Floppy (A:)   3½ Floppy (B:)   C (C:)   (D:)

C on 'Carole'   C on 'Marty2'   D on 'Marty'   C on 'Marty'
    (E:)            (F:)            (G:)          (H:)

Wgpo on        Control Panel    Printers    Dial-Up
'Marty2' (M:)                                Networking

12 object(s)
```

The My Computer window contains icons for all of the disk drives that you can access from your computer, as well as the Control Panel, Printers, and Dial-Up Networking folders that allow you to adjust the settings of various objects on your computer. The window shown above contains two floppy drives (A and B), a local hard disk (C) that is shared with other network users (in the icon, the hand underneath the drive tells you it is shared), a local shared CD-ROM drive (D), and four hard disk drives that are on other computers on the network (in the icon, the cable underneath indicates the drives are on the network). These network drives are mapped to, or identified as, drives E through H on my computer. Your computer may have a different number of drives. The network drives on other computers are available in My Computer because they have been *mapped* to drive letters on this

AN ORIENTATION TO WINDOWS 95

computer. For example, drive C on the computer Marty2 is mapped to drive F on this computer. As a result, an application running on this computer can access the drive on Marty2 by using drive F. (See *Mapping Network Drives* in Part Two.)

You can open any of these drives by double-clicking on the one you want. A new window will appear displaying the contents of the drive. If the new window contains a folder, you can double-click on it to open it. If you do that several times, you will have a series of windows, each of which displays one object in the window above it (its *parent*). Eventually you will reach a point where you no longer have any folders—only files like this:

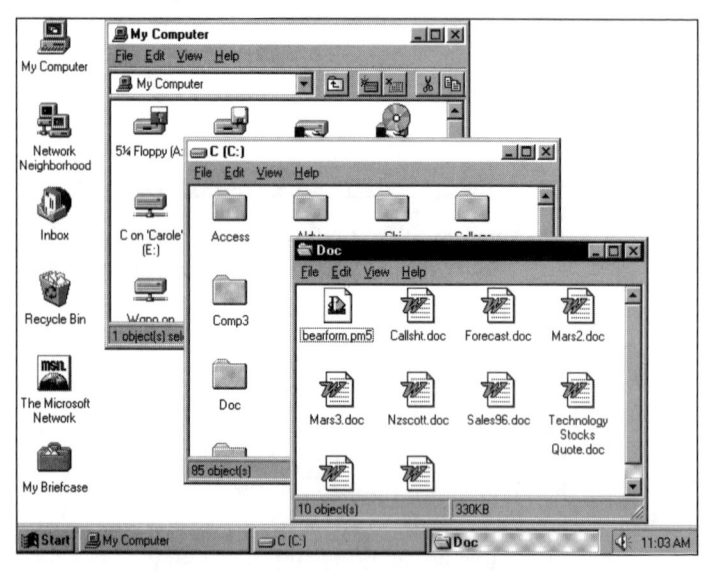

If the file you want is an application, you can start the application in its own window by double-clicking on it. If the file is associated with an application, for example a Word for Windows document, you can double-click on the file and the associated application will open along with the file (see *My Computer* in Part Two).

OH NO! NOT THE FILE MANAGER, TOO!

Network Neighborhood

This facility is used to access information that is stored on other computers across a network. If you are not connected to a network, you will not see a Network Neighborhood icon. If you do have a Network Neighborhood icon and you open it, you will see a set of icons similar to those shown here.

Your Network Neighborhood icons will include a computer icon for each computer in your immediate work group (Carole, Carole2, Marty, and Marty2 in the illustration). These identify the people and network servers you work with on a day-to-day basis. There is an additional icon that represents the entire network to which you are connected, including all the other workgroups and servers that are available to you. Double-clicking on one of these icons will display the workgroups and the central servers or the drives and printers that are shared on the computer (see *Network Neighborhood* in Part Two).

Microsoft Exchange (Inbox)

Microsoft Exchange, available from the Inbox icon on the Desktop, provides access to messages, forms, and documents that you send and receive with electronic mail (e-mail), information services like CompuServe, the Internet, faxes, and workgroup applications such as Lotus Notes. Microsoft Exchange provides a common interface to send, receive, read, access, and move all of the objects it handles as well as providing a common address book. Depending on what is installed on your computer, such as modems, faxes, information services, and mail systems, what you do with your Microsoft

AN ORIENTATION TO WINDOWS 95

Exchange can vary greatly. The benefit, though, is that all information independent of its source or destination is stored and managed by Microsoft Exchange (see *Microsoft Exchange* in Part Two).

Explorer

Windows Explorer

Windows 95 also provides a single facility called *Explorer* to view all of the information to which you have access. Explorer will probably become your most frequently used file management tool. Although it may seem to resemble the Windows 3.1 File Manager, you'll find that a greater depth of information is available.

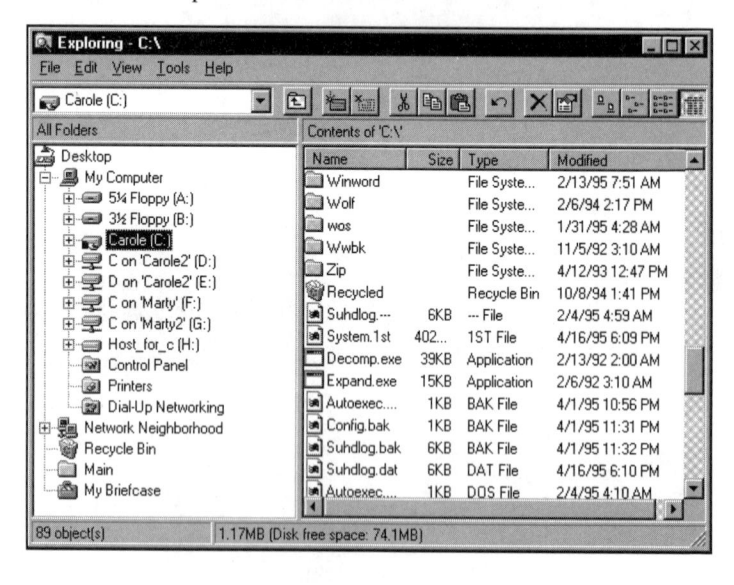

The hierarchical structure represents all of the information to which you have access—not just a single disk, as in the File Manager. If you select a disk or folder on the left, its contents will be revealed on the right.

You can scroll down and see the other objects to which you have access so that the left side of the

OH NO! NOT THE FILE MANAGER, TOO!

Explorer becomes a scrollable continuum spanning all of your information, and the right side displays the contents of one disk or folder (see *Explorer* in Part Two).

My Briefcase

My Briefcase provides a means of synchronizing files between two computers so that the most up-to-date file is on the computer you are currently using. For example, if you have a computer at home and one at the office, and you work on the same files on both computers, you can use My Briefcase to make sure that the files remain the same on both computers, as shown here:

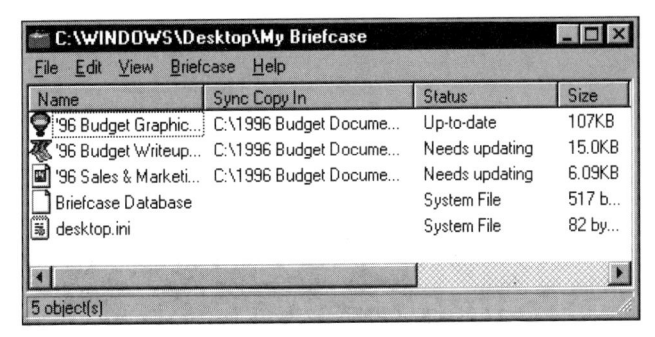

Name	Sync Copy In	Status	Size
'96 Budget Graphic...	C:\1996 Budget Docume...	Up-to-date	107KB
'96 Budget Writeup...	C:\1996 Budget Docume...	Needs updating	15.0KB
'96 Sales & Marketi...	C:\1996 Budget Docume...	Needs updating	6.09KB
Briefcase Database		System File	517 b...
desktop.ini		System File	82 by...

5 object(s)

See *My Briefcase* in Part Two.

Working with Files and Folders

Within Explorer, My Computer, or Network Neighborhood, you can perform many file operations, including copying, deleting, and renaming both files and folders by clicking the right mouse button on them and using the popup menu that appears. You can also perform many file operations directly on the files. You can:

- *Move and copy* files and folders by dragging them between any two open windows or the left and right panes in Explorer (press Ctrl while dragging to copy)

- *Delete* files and folders by clicking on them and pressing Delete
- *Open* files and folders by double-clicking on them or selecting them and pressing ↵.
- *Rename* files and folders by slowly clicking twice (not double-clicking) on the name, typing the new one, and then pressing Enter.

Long File Names

The name of a file or folder in Windows 95 can contain up to 255 characters, including spaces and other special characters. Prior to Windows 95, file names were limited to an eight character name and a three character extension. To maintain compatibility with older systems, Windows 95 will automatically create an additional "8.3" file name out of the long file name you create. In DOS listings, you'll see both the short name and the long name (see also *Naming Files and Folders* in Part Two).

Shortcuts

Windows 95 has added a powerful new type of file called a *shortcut*, which provides a link to another file or folder. When you double-click on a shortcut to activate it, you really activate the file or folder to which it is linked.

When you install a new application, the application files are normally placed in a folder dedicated to that application. Word for Windows, for example, stores all of your Word for Windows files in a folder it creates named \Winword. A second folder is created to store shortcuts for selected files. Word, for example, creates a second folder called Microsoft Office (if it doesn't already exist) in the \Windows\

OH NO! NOT THE FILE MANAGER, TOO!

Start Menu\Programs folder, and places shortcuts in it for some Word programs, including Word itself and Word Setup. These folders were known in Windows 3.x as program groups. Excel and Access also place their shortcuts in this same folder, as shown here:

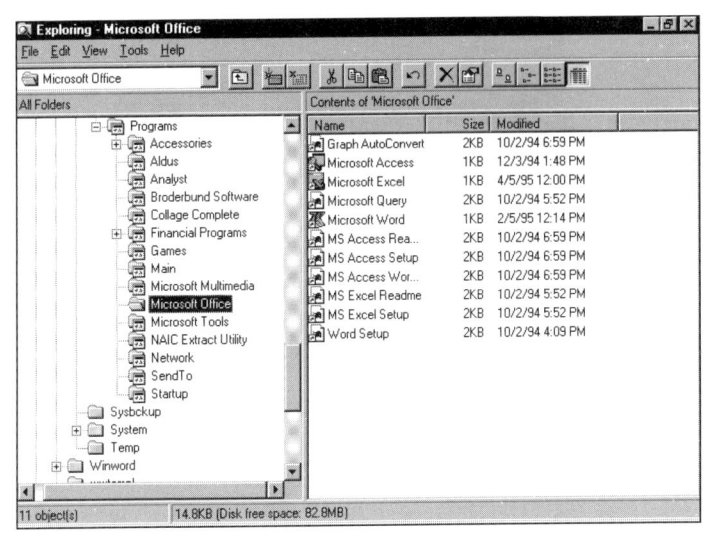

Name	Size	Modified
Graph AutoConvert	2KB	10/2/94 6:59 PM
Microsoft Access	1KB	12/3/94 1:48 PM
Microsoft Excel	1KB	4/5/95 12:00 PM
Microsoft Query	2KB	10/2/94 5:52 PM
Microsoft Word	1KB	2/5/95 12:14 PM
MS Access Rea...	2KB	10/2/94 6:59 PM
MS Access Setup	2KB	10/2/94 6:59 PM
MS Access Wor...	2KB	10/2/94 6:59 PM
MS Excel Readme	2KB	10/2/94 5:52 PM
MS Excel Setup	2KB	10/2/94 5:52 PM
Word Setup	2KB	10/2/94 4:09 PM

When you select a program to run from the Programs option in the Start Menu, you are selecting a shortcut placed in the \Windows\Start Menu\Program folder. Starting a program this way is obviously much easier than searching for the \Winword folder and then double-clicking on the Word application program file itself. You can create your own shortcuts to provide other ways of starting applications. (See *Shortcuts* and *Arranging Windows* in Part Two.)

Associating Files

You have already read that another way to start an application is to double-click on a document file that is *associated* with the application. This starts the

AN ORIENTATION TO WINDOWS 95

application and then loads the document you double-clicked on. For example, if you have a file named budget96.wk3 and double-click on it, the Lotus 1-2-3 application will start and then load the budget96.wk3 spreadsheet. Windows has been told to associate this type of file (one having a .WK3 extension) with the Lotus 1-2-3 application. Normally the application's installation or setup program is responsible for giving Windows the information about what types of files to associate with the application, although you can associate files yourself. (See *Associating Files* in Part Two.)

Deleting Files and the Recycle Bin

You can delete a file or folder by either selecting the object and pressing Delete, dragging it to the Recycle Bin, or selecting it and choosing File ➤ Delete. No matter how you delete the file or folder, under normal circumstances in Windows 95, the file or folder goes into the Recycle Bin, where you can still undelete it. This is a great safety feature to prevent you from mistakenly deleting something you want. The deleted item will take up space on your hard disk until you empty your recycle bin. To do this, right-click on Recycle Bin and choose Empty Recycle Bin. (See *Recycle Bin* in Part Two.)

Starting Applications and Arranging Your Screen

We have already described at least five ways to start an application. They are as follows:

- Double-click on an application icon in a folder accessible from a window such as Explorer or My Computer. The application was placed in the folder by either an installation program or the application itself.

- Double-click on a document icon associated with an application. The document was placed in the folder by either an installation program or by saving the document within the application itself.

- Click on an entry in the Programs submenu of the Start menu. This first requires that a shortcut be placed in the \Windows\Start Menu\Programs folder.

- Click on an entry on the Start menu itself, which first requires that a shortcut be placed in the Windows\Start Menu\Programs\Startup folder.

- Click on an entry in the Documents submenu of the Start menu. This requires that you have previously opened the document by double-clicking on its icon.

There are three other ways you can start applications: You can place shortcuts on the Desktop or in a new folder that is left on the Desktop, or you can use the Program Manager. (See *Arranging Applications*, *Shortcuts*, and *Startup Applications* in Part Two.)

This mixture provides alternatives that cover almost every situation. When all else fails, use Find in either the Start or Explorer menus (under Tools) to find the application file you want to run, and then double-click.

New and Enhanced Accessories

Many of the old Windows 3.x accessories are still in Windows 95, including Calculator, Character Map, Notepad, Paintbrush (now Paint), and, of course, Games. Most of them have been enhanced substantially. So, you will want to check for details in Part Two.

AN ORIENTATION TO WINDOWS 95

The new accessories, also described in Part Two, are as follows:

WordPad provides a capable word processor that you can use to edit unformatted files such as .TXT, .INF or .INI files, as well as files formatted in Word for Windows. WordPad replaces Write in Windows 3.x.

HyperTerminal provides a full-featured communications package for accessing communications services and bulletin boards, and for transferring files through your modem to and from other computers. It replaces the Windows 3.x Terminal accessory.

Phone Dialer allows you to use your modem to dial a phone number to a party that you then talk to on a regular phone. Calls made in this way can be logged to create a record.

Fax allows you to send and receive faxes. Faxes can be created in any of a number of applications including word processors, Desktop publishers, spreadsheets, and drawing packages. Received faxes can be viewed, printed, and saved.

CD Player controls the playing of CDs. This includes being able to fast-forward or back up through a CD-ROM, play only specific tracks, record the playing time in various ways, and play the tracks in various orders, as you decide.

Sound Recorder allows you to record via a microphone attached to your computer.

Now that you have an overview of what Windows 95 can offer, it's time to look at the details in Part Two. Happy Windowing!

PART TWO

COMMAND AND FEATURE REFERENCE

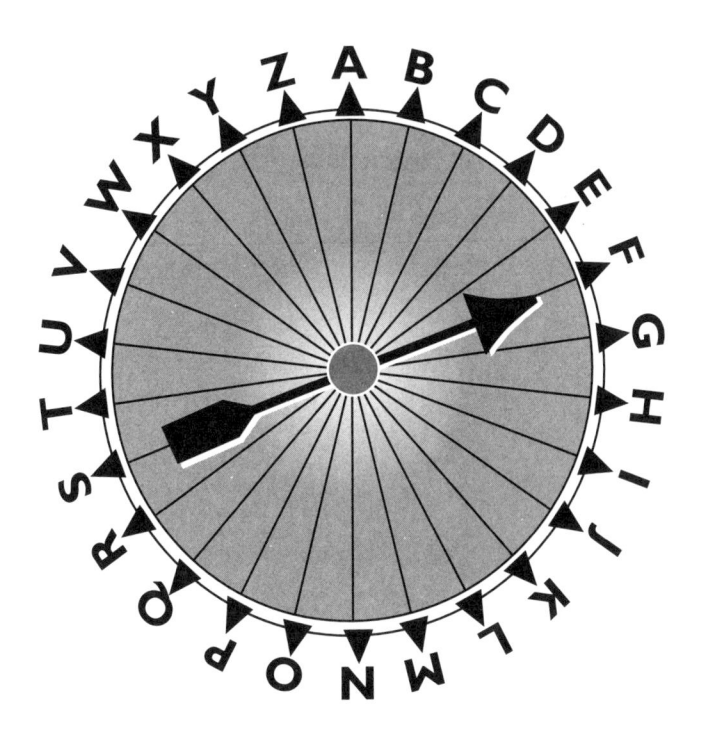

COMMAND AND FEATURE REFERENCE

Accessibility Options

The Accessibility options provide a way of making computers easier to use by people who are physically challenged. These features can help persons with reduced vision or hearing impairment, as well as those who have difficulty using the keyboard and the mouse. The table below shows each of these features and their functions:

Feature	Description
FilterKeys	Reduces double keystrokes, slows down key repetition, and reduces accidentally hit keys
High Contrast	Provides a high contrast on the screen for easier viewing
MouseKeys	Performs mouse functions with the numeric keypad
SerialKey Devices	Allows connection of an alternative input device
ShowSounds	Tells applications to display a visual sign that a sound is occurring on the screen
SoundSentry	Flashes a visual warning on the screen in addition to making a sound
StickyKeys	Allows one to press Alt, Ctrl, or Shift plus another key one at a time instead of simultaneously
ToggleKeys	Creates a sound when Caps Lock, Num Lock, or Scroll Lock are turned on or off

NOTE: *When you turn on an accessibility feature, an icon appears in the notification area of the Taskbar, as shown below for StickyKeys and MouseKeys.*

ACCESSIBILITY OPTIONS

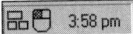

To access the accessibility options and their settings, select Start ➤ Settings ➤ Control Panel, and then double-click on the Accessibility Options icon. The Accessibility Properties dialog box, shown below, will be displayed.

TIP: *Many of the Accessibilities options have a shortcut key that allows you to turn them on and off from the keyboard. They are noted in the sections in which they apply.*

Five tabs are shown along the top of the Accessibility Properties dialog box. They are: Keyboard, Sound, Display, Mouse, and General.

Keyboard Tab Options

The Keyboard tab offers three accessibility options: StickyKeys, FilterKeys, and ToggleKeys.

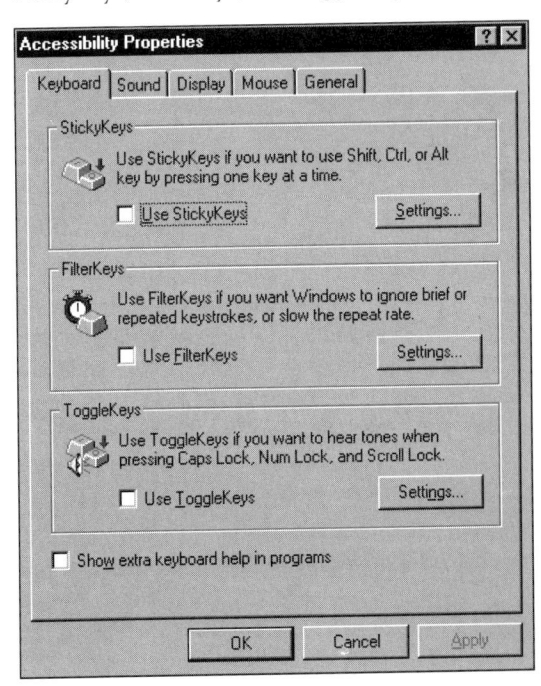

COMMAND AND FEATURE REFERENCE

StickyKeys allows you to press one of the modifier keys—Alt, Ctrl, or Shift—and another key one at a time instead of simultaneously. This allows those who cannot press two or three keys at a time to handle these keystrokes. You turn on StickyKeys either by clicking on Use StickyKeys or by using the shortcut key. To set the characteristics options for the StickyKeys, click on the Settings button for Use StickyKeys.

SHORTCUT KEY: *Press either Shift key five times*

FilterKeys is a set of features that desensitize the keyboard so that it is less likely to give you unwanted keystrokes. It does this by ignoring repeated or short duration keystrokes, or by slowing the rate at which a keystroke can be repeated. These features are valuable for persons with tremors or a tendency to "bounce" keys. FilterKeys are enabled and controlled together with the shortcut key or from the FilterKeys option on the Keyboard tab.

SHORTCUT KEY: *Hold Right-Shift for eight seconds*

ToggleKeys allows you to hear when you turn on and off the Caps Lock, Num Lock, or Scroll Lock "toggle" keys. You get a higher pitched beep when you turn one of them on and a lower pitched beep when you turn one of them off. Use ToggleKeys enables and disables the ToggleKeys options. Click on Settings to enable or disable the shortcut for ToggleKeys.

SHORTCUT KEY: *Hold Num Lock for 5 seconds*

Sound Tab Options

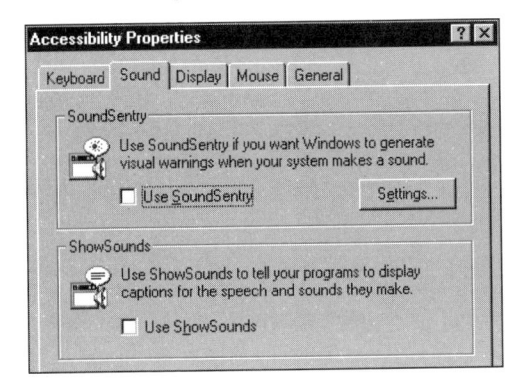

The Sound tab options, SoundSentry and ShowSound, are primarily for persons with hearing impairment. Both provide visual aids when sounds are generated by the keyboard.

SoundSentry allows you to see when Windows is beeping at you. In place of the audible cue, Windows will flash the part of the screen that you specify in Settings.

ShowSounds switches on and off a visual cue that applications can provide in addition to the audible cue. To select the option, place a check mark in the check box for Use ShowSounds.

Display Tab Options

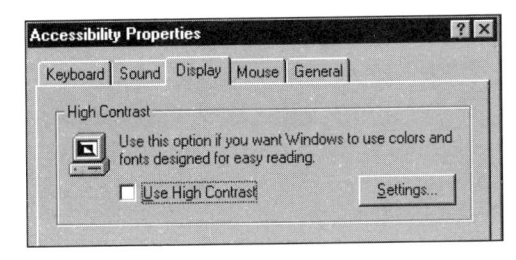

The Display tab options allow you to display alternative colors and fonts to make the screens more readable for vision impaired users. Use High Contrast, which when checked, allows a choice of colors and fonts to be used.

SHORTCUT KEY: *Left-Alt+Left-Shift+Print Screen*

COMMAND AND FEATURE REFERENCE

Mouse Tab Options

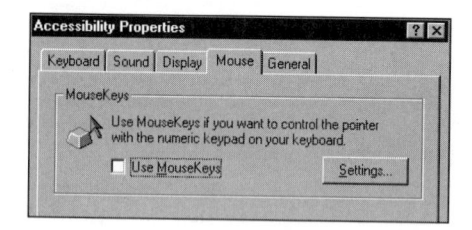

The Mouse tab is used to enable or disable MouseKeys. When MouseKeys is active, the numeric keypad on the right of most keyboards can be used to perform all of the functions that can be performed with a mouse. MouseKeys, which can be used at the same time you are using a mouse, is not only useful for those that have problems using the mouse, but it is also valuable when you are trying to position the pointer very precisely.

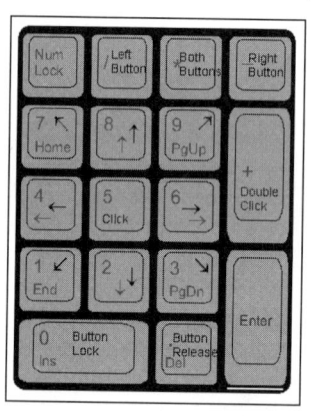

MouseKeys redefines the numeric keypad as follows:

The 5 key is the same as clicking the left mouse button once. Pressing 5 twice is the same as right-clicking the mouse.

The other number keys move the mouse pointer in the direction indicated.

Home, End, Page Up, Page Down move the pointer diagonally, as positioned on the keypad.

The – (minus) key pressed first, and then the 5, is the same as a right-click. The – key pressed first, and then the + (plus) key, is the same as double-clicking the right mouse button.

The + (plus) key performs the same function as double-clicking the left mouse button.

ACCESSIBILITY OPTIONS

The Ins key locks down the left mouse button for dragging. Press it and then an arrow key to drag a file or folder.

The Del key releases the left mouse button after dragging.

Ctrl and any number key except 5 jumps the pointer in large increments.

Shift and any number key except 5 moves the pointer one pixel at a time.

Num Lock switches between MouseKeys and the standard numeric keypad in whatever state (numeric entry or cursor movement) it was before MouseKeys was started.

SHORTCUT KEY: *Left-Alt+Left-Shift+Num Lock (press these three keys together)*

General Tab Options

The General tab options provide further definition of how and when the Accessibilities Options will be available.

Automatic Reset options allow you to set the length of time that your computer can be idle before the Access features are turned off. This enables two people with different access needs to use the same computer.

Notification allows you to choose whether the system is to give either a visual or an audio warning or both when a feature is turned on or off.

SerialKey Devices allows you to connect an alternative input device to your computer using a serial port. The serial port, substituting as a keyboard and mouse, sends information to the computer, which is then treated as keystrokes and mouse events. Click on Support SerialKey devices to allow devices other than mouse and keyboard

COMMAND AND FEATURE REFERENCE

devices to be used. Click on Settings to select the serial port and baud rates.

SEE ALSO: *Display Control Panel*

Accessing Disks, Folders, and Files

Locating and displaying or loading disks, folders, and files can be done with one of these Windows 95 tools: the Start button (the Programs or Documents options), My Computer, Network Neighborhood, Explorer and Find.

Add New Hardware

The Add New Hardware feature guides you through the process of adding new hardware using an interface called the New Hardware Wizard, which can detect most new standard hardware on your computer. It makes the appropriate changes to the Registry and to the appropriate configuration files so that Windows 95 can recognize and support your new hardware. Follow these steps to add a device:

1. Select Start ➤ Settings ➤ Control Panel, and then double-click on the Add New Hardware icon. The Add New Hardware Wizard will appear. Click on Next to begin installing the new hardware.

You must first decide whether you want Windows to automatically detect your hardware, or if you want to identify the hardware yourself. If you have already installed the hardware, it is recommended that you select Yes, the default choice, to have Windows search for the new hardware. However, if the new hardware is nonstandard, or not already physically installed, Windows may not be able to detect it. (The best first approach is to physically install the hardware and

ADD NEW HARDWARE

then run the New Hardware Wizard.)

2. If you choose Yes (recommended), you will be warned that Windows will spend several minutes searching for the new hardware and that your machine could quit functioning during the search. Click on Next.

A status indicator will appear to indicate the progress of the search. As long as the status indicator continues to mark progress or your disk light is flashing, all is well. Depending on the amount and type of hardware you have, the detection process could take five to seven minutes. If your computer should quit functioning, restart your computer and manually select the new hardware to install. When the search is completed, you will either be presented with the new hardware that Windows 95 has detected, or you will have to manually install the device, as described in Step 3.

3. If you don't want Windows 95 to try to detect the device, click on No, and then click on Next. A dialog box will prompt you to select the new device from a list. Click on the hardware type you are installing, and then click on Next.

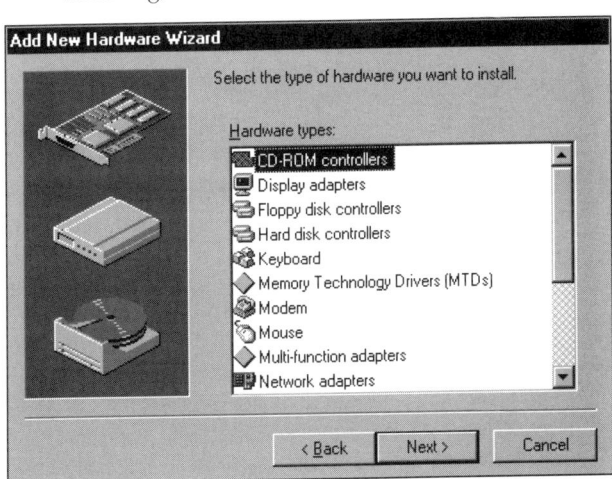

COMMAND AND FEATURE REFERENCE

4. From here on, you will be lead through the process of installing the new hardware. The screens will differ depending on the hardware type. Just follow the instructions as you are prompted.

Adding Printers

SEE: *Add New Hardware; Printers Folder*

Adding Programs

SEE: *Add/Remove Programs; Arranging Applications*

Add/Remove Programs

The Add/Remove Programs feature allows you to add programs to Windows 95, or remove them. Adding or removing application software with this feature enables Windows 95 to modify system files to support the addition or removal of the program. With this feature, you can also create a startup disk or add or remove Windows 95 components.

Start Add/Remove Programs by selecting Start ➤ Settings ➤ Control Panel and then double-clicking on Add/Remove Programs. The Add/Remove Programs Properties dialog box will be displayed, containing three tabs.

Install/Uninstall Tab

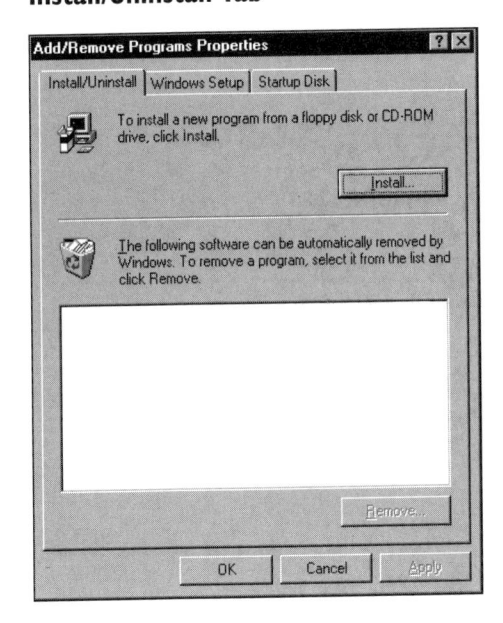

To install a new program from the Add/Remove Programs dialog box, follow these steps:

1. Click on the Install/Uninstall tab if it isn't already selected, and then click on Install.

2. Place the program's first disk or CD in the appropriate drive, and click on Next. A setup or install message will be displayed, informing you of the program to be installed.

3. To continue with the installation process, click on Finish. To make any changes, click on Back and repeat the procedure.

To uninstall a program previously installed under Windows 95, you must follow a different process. The list of programs that have uninstall capability (not all of them do) will be listed in the display box of the Install/Uninstall tab. Click on the program you want to uninstall, and then click on Remove. You will be to told when the uninstall is finished.

WARNING: *Uninstalling a program removes all references to the program throughout Windows. If you try to simply delete a folder or individual files, you may leave hanging references. Use the Uninstall Programs feature when it is available.*

COMMAND AND FEATURE REFERENCE

Windows Setup Tab

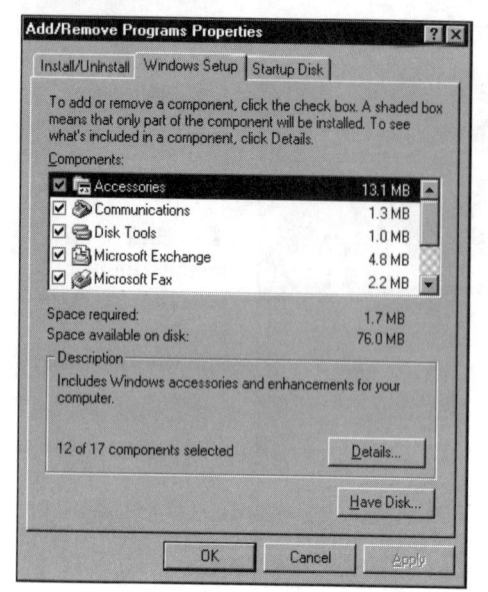

Some components of the Windows 95 operating system are optional and can be added or removed as you wish. If you click on the Windows Setup tab in the Add/Remove Programs Properties dialog box, you will see a list of such components with check boxes on the left of them. If the check box has a check mark in it, it means the component is currently installed. If the check box is gray, only some of the components of that type have been installed. Follow these steps to add or remove Windows components to your computer:

- *To add uninstalled components* to the system, click on the check box to add a check mark. Click on Details, and then select the components you want to add. Click on Apply and then OK.

- *To remove a component* click on Details for a list of components installed. Remove the check mark by clicking on the checkbox. Click on Apply and then OK.

NOTE: *Clicking on an empty check box adds a check mark, and clicking again on the check box removes it.*

Create a Startup Disk

A startup disk is a floppy disk that allows you to start or "boot" your computer and run diagnostic programs if something happens to your hard drive. When you installed Windows 95 you were asked if you wanted to create a startup disk. If you didn't do it at that time, or if the disk you created then is not usable, you can create another using the Startup Disk tab. Simply insert a disk into the appropriate drive and click on Create Disk. You will be informed of the progress as the disk is created.

Address Book

The address book found in the Tools menu within Microsoft Exchange (accessed from the Inbox icon on the Desktop) identifies the computers and individuals to which you may send and receive files and messages. Use it for sending e-mail or faxes, for telephone dialing, or for other communication functions using your computer.

The Address Book contains several address lists, which may vary depending on whether you are on a network or not. You may see these address lists:

Postoffice Address List contains the names from your LAN (Local Area Network).

Personal Address Book contains the names and addresses of individuals to with whom you might want to send or receive messages or files over a network such as The Internet.

Microsoft Network contains the names of persons with whom you want to connect using Microsoft Network.

COMMAND AND FEATURE REFERENCE

Finding the Address Book

Follow these steps to find the Address Book lists:

1. From the Desktop, double-click on the Inbox icon. You may be asked for a profile ID. Select the profile you want, and the Inbox window will be displayed.

2. Select Tools ➤ Address Book. The Address Book window will be displayed.

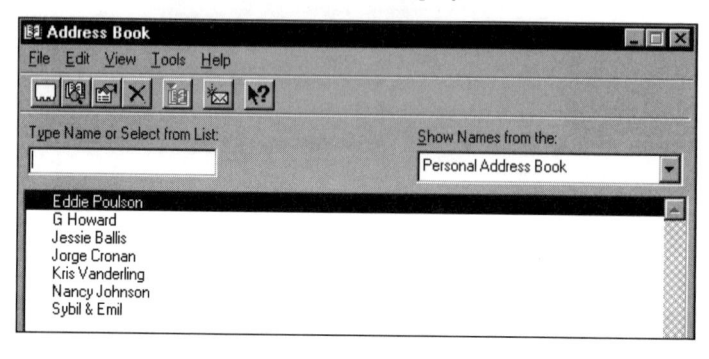

The Address Book Window

The Address Book window contains a text entry box for typing a name with which you want to work. You can type the name or select an entry from the list. A drop-down list box, Show Names from the:, identifies the current active address list. The names contained in the selected address list will be displayed.

The Address Book Menus and Toolbar

Four menus offer choices for working with the Address Book. Only the File and Tools menus offer options unique to the Address Book, however.

The **File menu** contains these unique options:

- **New Entry** allows you to create a new entry in one of the address lists. See below for how to do this.

ADDRESS BOOK

- **New Message** creates an e-mail message to send to a network destination.
- **Add to Personal Address Book** copies a selected entry from the current active address list into the Personal Address Book.

The **Tools menu** contains these two options:

- **Find** opens a Find dialog box so that you can find a name containing a sequence of letters. This should help you locate a name that you may not remember exactly how to spell.
- **Options** prioritizes your address lists. You can choose which of your address lists will be shown first, searched first when sending mail, and where your personal addresses are to be kept.

The toolbar in the Address Book window contains these buttons:

- **New Entry** allows you to create a new address entry.
- **Find** lets you locate a name containing a sequence of letters.
- **Properties** displays the Properties dialog box for a given entry.
- **Delete** deletes an entry from the current address list.
- **Add to Personal Address List** adds the current entry to the Personal Address Book.
- **New Message** allows you to create and send an e-mail message to an address listed.
- **Help** offers context-sensitive Help messages.

COMMAND AND FEATURE REFERENCE

Adding a New Entry to an Address List

You can easily add an entry to an address list by following these steps:

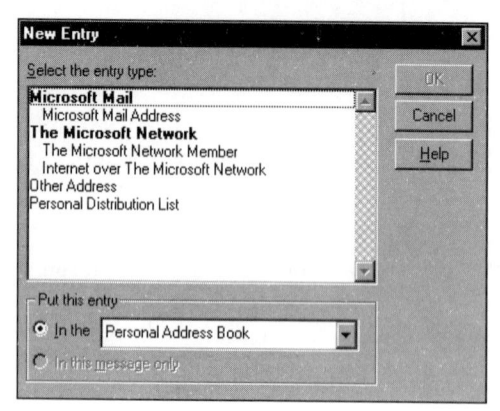

1. After finding the address list you want, select File ➤ New Entry, or click on the New Entry icon. The New Entry dialog box will be displayed.

2. Select the type of entry you will be creating: Microsoft Mail for an addressee on your own LAN; The Microsoft Network (MSN)—either an MSN addressee or one for the Internet; Other Address for other networks and communications; or a Personal Distribution List for members of your workgroup. (You may have others, such as a Fax entry.)

3. Specify in which address list you want to place the entry and then click OK. A data entry dialog box unique to the type of entry you are creating will be displayed.

4. Fill in the information needed. The address information will be unique to the type of entry you are creating, as listed here:

Microsoft Mail	Alias (User ID), Mailbox, Postoffice, Network, text format needed (Microsoft Exchange rich text or Gateway)
Microsoft Network Member	Member ID, Name

Internet from the Microsoft Network	E-mail address (*UserID@DomainName*), Domain name, Name of individual
Other Address	Name, E-mail address, E-mail type, whether Microsoft Exchange rich-text forms is important
Personal Distribu- tion List	Name of networked work- group

5. When you are finished, click on OK.

SEE ALSO: *Microsoft Exchange*

Arranging Applications

Arranging your applications involves organizing them so they can be accessed quickly and conveniently. There are several techniques for arranging applications, and all require creating shortcuts so that the application can be started by double-clicking on an icon or name (see *Shortcuts*). You can arrange access to your applications by placing the shortcuts:

- On the Start menu itself
- In the Programs option of the Start menu
- On the Desktop
- In a special purpose folder
- In the Startup folder

Follow one or more of the following procedures to organize your applications.

COMMAND AND FEATURE REFERENCE

Changing the Start Menu

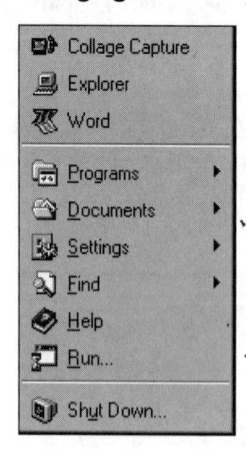

You can display the applications you use most frequently on the Start menu in order to have quicker access to them. The easiest way to do this is to drag an application icon from its folder to the Start button on the Taskbar. This automatically places the application name on the top of the Start menu. See below for how to remove them.

There is another way to place applications on the top of the Start menu that also allows you to add applications to the Programs submenu and to delete items from either place. Follow these steps:

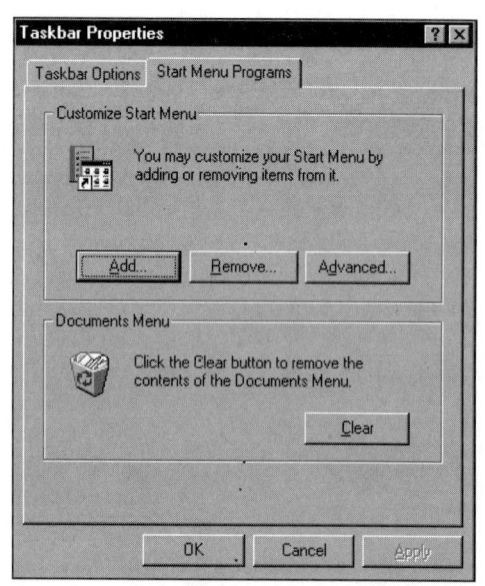

1. Select Start ➤ Settings ➤ Taskbar. The Taskbar Properties box will be displayed.

2. Select the Start Menu Programs tab if it is not already selected.

3. Click Add to add a shortcut to the Start menu. A Create Shortcut dialog box will be displayed.

4. Type in the path and name of the file to be added to the Start menu or use Browse to find it, and then click on Next.

ARRANGING APPLICATIONS

5. Select the name of the folder in which the file name will be added. Select Start Menu to place the added program on top of it, or select one of the folders under the Programs folder. You can also create a new folder. Click on Next.

6. Type in the name you would like the Shortcut to have. Click Finish. Click OK on the Start Menus Programs tab.

TIP: *To delete a shortcut that is currently displayed on the Start menu, click Remove on the Start Menu Programs tab. Select the program folder you want to delete, and then click on Remove. Click on Close.*

NOTE: *To have access to Explorer while you are working with the Start Menu, click on Advanced.*

Changing the Programs Submenu

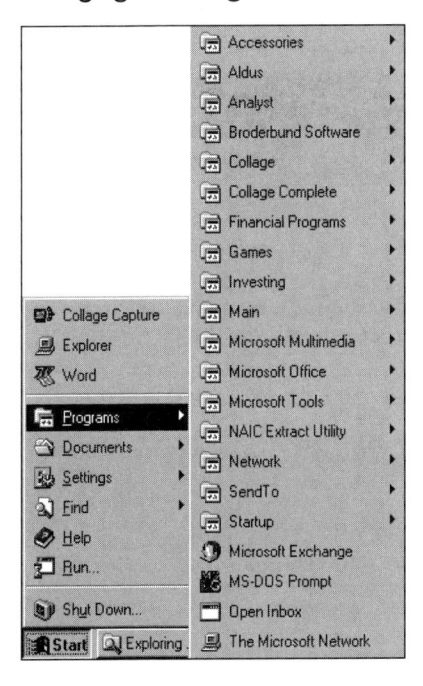

Placing the program name within a folder (Program group) in the Programs submenu of the Start menu is another approach to organizing your programs. When Windows applications are installed, shortcuts are automatically added to the appropriate folders in the Programs submenu. Non-Windows applications can be added by following the same steps outlined for adding programs to the Start menu, placing the program in a Program folder rather than the Start Menu folder.

COMMAND AND FEATURE REFERENCE

However, the easiest way to place a program in the Programs folder is to drag it there (to the Windows\Start Menu\Programs*folder*) using Explorer. When a program file is dragged to another folder, a shortcut is automatically created and placed in the destination folder.

TIP: *To delete a shortcut from the Program menu, use Explorer to select the name displayed in the open folder and press delete. The program will be removed from the menu.*

SEE ALSO: *Programs Groups, Adding to the Programs Menu; Shortcuts*

Placing Applications on the Desktop

Application shortcuts can be placed on the Desktop. Since these shortcuts will be immediately available as soon as Windows 95 is loaded, they can be used for frequently-used programs. However, you should note that Desktop shortcuts get covered when you open windows for folders and applications. To see the Desktop you must either close the windows or minimize them.

Follow these steps for placing applications on the Desktop:

1. Using Explorer or My Computer, find and select the program file whose shortcut you want to place on the Desktop.

2. Drag the program icon to the Desktop. Its shortcut will be automatically created and placed on the Desktop.

3. If it is necessary to see the new application shortcut, clear the open windows from the Desktop

ARRANGING APPLICATIONS

by right clicking on the Taskbar and choosing Minimize All Windows. When you are ready, restore the open windows by right-clicking on the Taskbar and choosing Undo Minimize All.

TIP: *You can also create a shortcut by pressing Ctrl+Shift while you drag the file to the Desktop. A popup menu will be displayed when you finish the drag operation. Choose Create Shortcut(s) Here. With this method, you do not have to use the menu or right mouse button at all.*

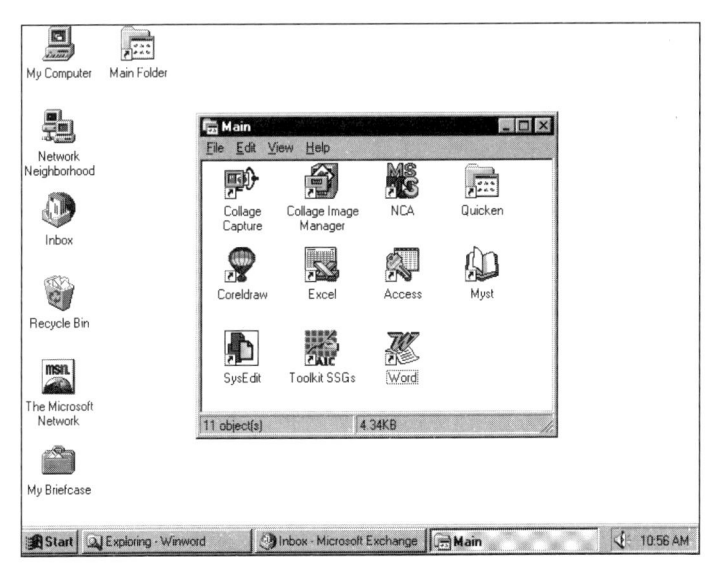

SEE ALSO: *Closing Files or Windows; Maximize/Minimize Windows*

Placing Applications in a Special Folder

One of the most efficient ways to access frequently-used applications is with a special folder. You create

COMMAND AND FEATURE REFERENCE

a special folder to contain shortcuts to these programs. The folder's windows will be displayed when Windows 95 is booted—as long as the window was open when the computer was shut down. If the folder is not open when the computer is shut down, it will appear as a folder on the Desktop, which can be opened with a double-click. Then, this folder can be accessed when other windows hide it by clicking on the folder's button in the Taskbar.

Follow these steps to create a special folder:

1. Right click on the Desktop and choose New ➤ Folder. A new folder will be displayed with the name New Folder highlighted.

2. Type in a new name over the words New Folder and then press Enter. You now have a new empty folder.

3. Open the new folder by double-clicking on it and then open Explorer or My Computer.

4. To place programs in the folder, you may do one of the following:

- If any of the desired shortcuts are on the Desktop, drag them to the folder.

- From Explorer or My Computer, drag a program file (a file that has an .exe extension) to the folder. A shortcut will be automatically created.

5. If you leave the new folder open when you shut down your computer, it will be opened and available on the Desktop when you next start Windows 95. In any case, you will be able to open the folder from the Desktop.

SEE ALSO: *Shortcuts; Startup Applications*

Placing Applications in the Startup Folder

You can place shortcuts to applications in the \Windows\Start Menu\Programs\Startup folder, a special folder that will cause the programs within it to be loaded and active when Windows is started. You should use this technique for applications you want to immediately access upon booting your computer.

NOTE: *If you have a shortcut of a folder in the Startup folder, and leave the folder open on the Desktop when you shut down Windows, you will get two open copies of the folder the next time you start Windows. Of course, you need only click on the close button to get rid of one copy.*

SEE ALSO: Startup Applications

Arranging Folders

You may want to create special purpose folders to contain applications or frequently-used documents. For instance, if you have several similar programs, you may want to place them in one folder—for example, an investments program folder, or a folder containing your most frequently-used programs. Then, by creating a shortcut to the folder, and placing it in an accessible location, you will be able to get to it easily.

Folders can be placed anywhere applications can be, although the most logical sites are on the Desktop, Programs submenu, or in the Startup folder.

SEE ALSO: *Arranging Applications; Shortcuts*

COMMAND AND FEATURE REFERENCE

Arranging Icons

In Explorer and My Computer, you can change the way files and folders are displayed with these commands: Large Icons, Small Icons, List, or Details. You can also sort the files and folders by name, file size, date last modified, or file type with the Arrange Icons option in the View menu.

SEE ALSO: *Explorer; Folder Window; My Computer*

Arranging Windows

To reposition Windows on your screen, choose one of the following methods.

- You can drag a window from one place on the screen to another by placing the pointer on the title bar and dragging the window. If you select Move from the Control menu, the pointer will turn into a four-headed icon which you can use to drag the window.

- By clicking on the Taskbar with the right mouse button, you will be able to arrange the windows by selecting one of these options from the popup menu:

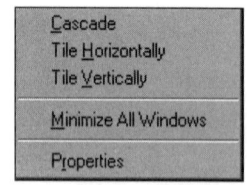

```
Cascade
Tile Horizontally
Tile Vertically

Minimize All Windows

Properties
```

Cascade places windows one behind the other beginning in the upper-left corner of your screen and working to the lower-right. In this position, the windows overlap so that you can see a portion including the Title Bar of each window.

Tile Horizontally stacks all the windows on the screen horizontally, one on top of the other, with a horizontal section of the window displayed.

Tile Vertically places the windows next to each other vertically, with vertical sections of the windows displayed.

SEE ALSO: *Moving Windows, Moving/Arranging Icons*

ASCII Files, Working With

SEE: *Notepad*

Associating Files

Associating files allows you to identify a relationship between an application and a document file. This enables you to open a document file and its associated application by merely double-clicking on the document file. Normally an application's installation or setup program is responsible for giving Windows the information about what types of files to associate with the application.

For files that are not automatically associated with an application—for instance, DOS files—you can create an association. For example, if you have several .zip files that you want to associate with the program PKUNZIP so that when you double-click on a .zip file it will begin to decompress or unzip automatically, follow these steps:

1. Double-click on an unassociated file to open the Open With dialog box.

2. Enter the description of the file type that you want to appear in the Explorer detail listing.

3. Select the application program that you want to use to open the file from the list below the

COMMAND AND FEATURE REFERENCE

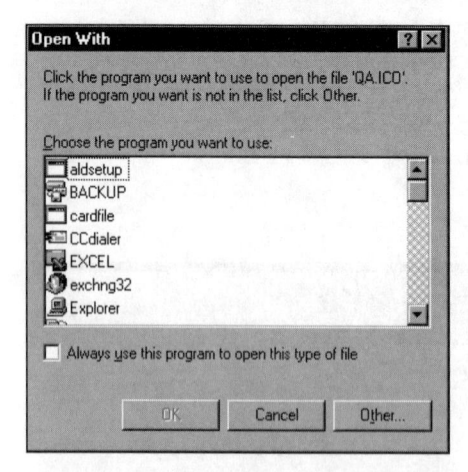

description, or click on the Other button and find the folder containing the program you want. Double-click on the folder and then on the file name of the application used to open the file.

4. Click on OK to register that file type and close the dialog box.

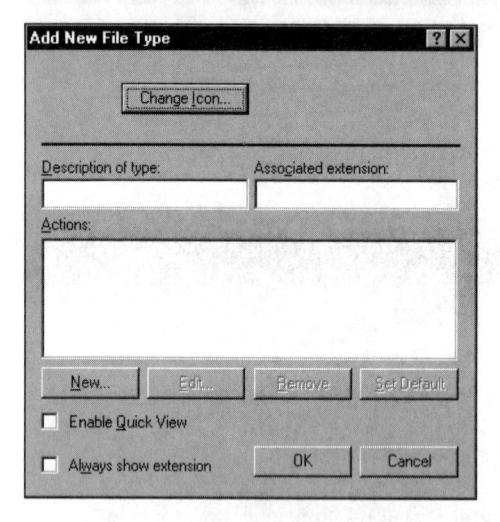

Another more general way to associate files is available from the Explorer. If you select View ➤ Options, the Options dialog box will open. Select the File Types tab. To add a new file association, click on New Type to open the Add New File Type dialog box, shown here. Enter a description of the file type, identify the extension of the associated file, and then click on New to identify the action (commands such as Print or Open), path, and name of the application which is to be initiated when you double-click on the file. You can also edit or remove existing file types, or change the icon representing the file type.

TIP: *A file's icon can help you figure out whether it is associated with a program. A file having an application-specific icon, such as for Microsoft Word, or Access, has been associated with that program. If a file has a general-purpose icon, such as the one on the left, then it may not be associated with a program. Double-click on it to find out if an associated program is loaded.*

SEE ALSO: Explorer; Associating Files

Automatic Phone Calling

SEE: Phone Dialer

Backing Up Files and Folders

Windows 95 provides a Backup program that helps prevent loss of data from accidents or power and disk failures. It allows you to perform both simple and sophisticated backups. Among the choices you have are:

- To back up all of your computer system or only some of the files. (See "Performing a Full Backup" and "Performing a Partial Backup," below.)

- To define and save a file set. (See "File Sets" and "Performing a Partial Backup," below.)

- To back up all files in a file set or just those that have changed (see the Options menu).

- To set up an accelerated drag and drop procedure for saving your most frequently backed-up files. (See "Creating a Drag and Drop Procedure," below.)

COMMAND AND FEATURE REFERENCE

> **TIP:** *Program files can be recreated from the original disks, so these files do not have to be backed up.*

The Backup Menus

Follow these steps to access Backup.

1. Select Start ➤ Programs ➤ Accessories ➤ System Tools ➤ Backup.

Two introductory screens will be displayed, which you only need to see once.

2. Once you have read the message on each screen, click on OK and the Microsoft Backup window will be displayed with three tabs:

- ◆ **Backup** enables you to select the files and folders to be backed up onto another device.

- ◆ **Restore** allows you to restore backed up files onto a selected device.

- ◆ **Compare** allows you to compare two or more files to verify the contents of a backup.

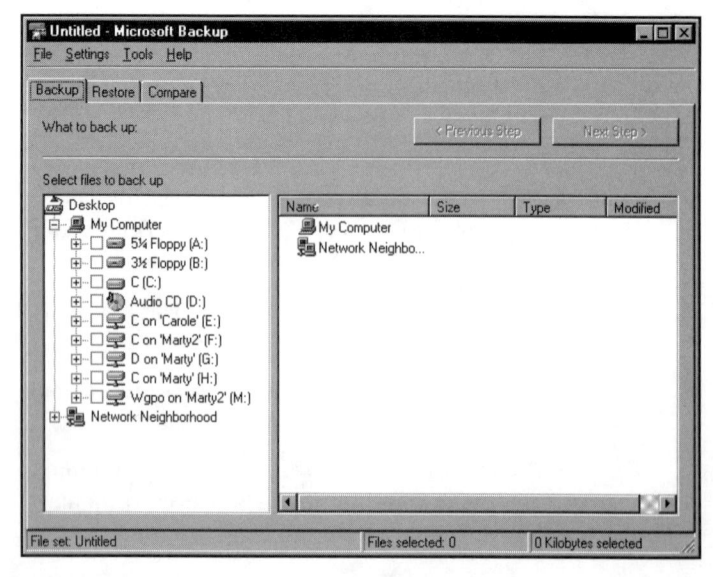

BACKING UP FILES AND FOLDERS

3. Click on the Backup tab, if it is not displayed.

The menus in the Backup tab have some unique options to enhance the way you perform backups.

File Menu

The File menu contains the following specialized options:

Open File Set allows you to choose a specific file set to be backed up. As explained in the introductory welcome window, one file set (in addition to the Log and HyperTerminal file sets used in other applications) is automatically defined for you—the Full System Backup. (See "File Sets" below.)

Print allows you to print the files selected for backup. You can double-check your choices.

Refresh redisplays the files listed in the left and right pages.

Settings Menu

The Settings menu contains four options for defining the way you perform backups:

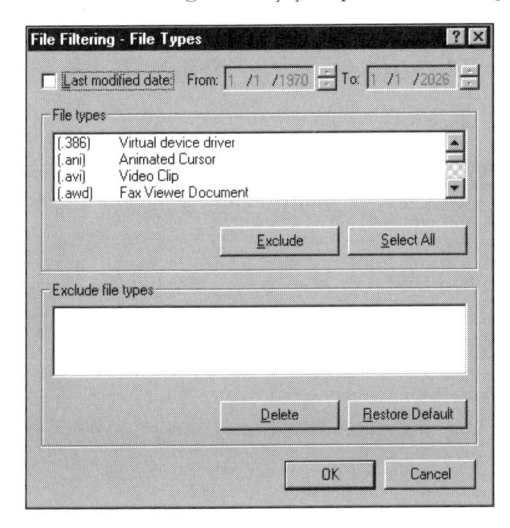

File Filtering enables you to select file types to be included or excluded from a backup.

Last Modified Date includes files last modified within the From and To dates, when checked.

File Types lists the file types that

can be included or excluded from a backup. Click on the file you want to exclude and then click Exclude. Or, when you want to include only a few of the many file types, select all files by using Select All, and then deselect the files to include in the backup and click on Exclude.

Exclude File Types displays a list of the file types to be excluded from the backup. You can remove file types from the list by selecting them and clicking Delete. To remove all excluded file types from the list, click Restore Default.

Drag and Drop offers you three options when you initiate a backup (see "Creating a Drag and Drop Procedure," below):

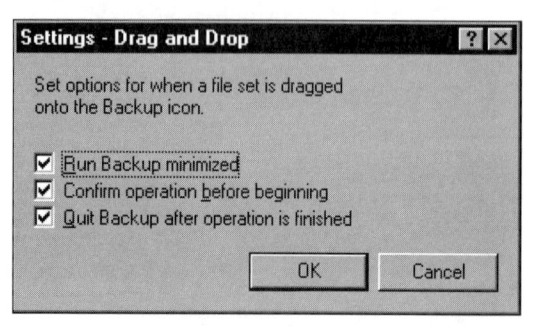

- **Run Backup Minimized** ensures that the backup window is minimized during the backup operation.

- **Confirm operation before beginning** allows you to confirm your choice of files to be backed up.

- **Quit Backup after operation is finished** closes the Backup window when the backup has been completed.

Options offers especially powerful Backup options. Click on the Backup tab to see them:

BACKING UP FILES AND FOLDERS

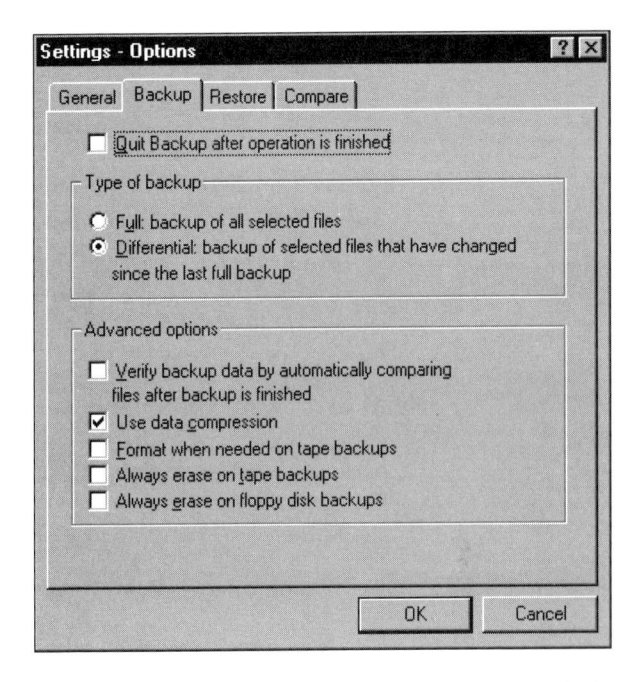

- **Quit Backup after operation is finished** closes the Backup window when the backup is completed. This is useful unless you want to Restore, Compare, or perform another backup after completing one backup.

- **Full: backup of all selected files** will cause all files in a file set to be backed up whether or not they have changed since the last backup.

- **Differential: backup of select files that have changed since the last backup** only backs up files in a file set that have changed.

- **Verify backup data by automatically comparing files after backup is finished** ensures that the backup has not erred when backing up files.

COMMAND AND FEATURE REFERENCE

- **Use data compression** compresses data as it is being backed up onto a tape drive in order to conserve space.

- **Format when needed on tape backups** automatically formats unformatted tapes before backing up.

- **Always erase on tape backups** erases an unformatted or nonstandard tape, when checked. Otherwise, the backup is added to the contents of the tape, if there is space on it.

- **Always erase on floppy disk backups** erases the contents on a floppy disk before backing up, when checked. Otherwise, the backup is added to the contents of the disk when there is space for it.

Tools Menu

The Tools menu allows you to manage your tape drive with the following options:

Format Tape allows you to format a tape. It may take several hours for larger tapes. Tapes must be QIC-compatible in order to be used for backing up.

Erase Tape erases the entire contents of a tape.

Redetect Tape Drive directs the Backup program to read the tape drive again (used, for example, when a new tape has been inserted and needs to be verified).

> **SEE ALSO:** *Comparing Files; Restoring Files*

File Sets

When you backup, you can create a *file set* to be used again to back up the same files. A file set is

BACKING UP FILES AND FOLDERS

simply a definition of a group of files that are saved. This helps substantially in creating a backup procedure or routine. Windows 95 automatically creates a file set for you called Full System Backup which will backup all the files you'll need for recovery from a disaster. To find out how to create a file set, see "Performing a Partial Backup" below.

Performing a Full Backup

A full backup is used for disaster recovery. It backs up all the files, folders, and special sets of data on your disk, including the system registry files. Follow these steps to perform a full system backup:

1. Select File ➤ Open File Set. The Open dialog box will be displayed.

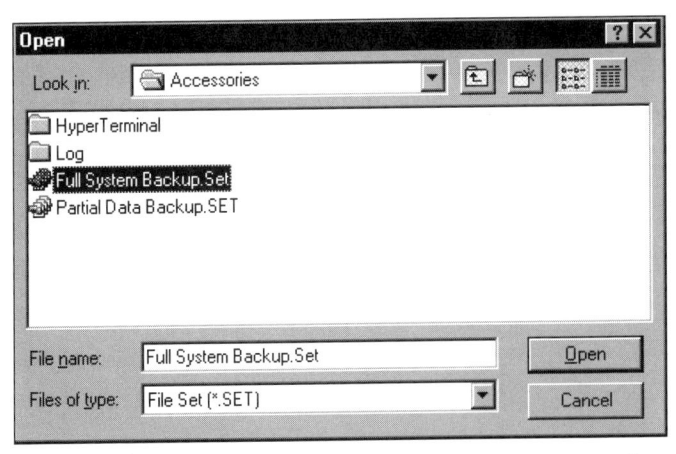

2. Click on Full System Backup.Set. Backup will take a few minutes to copy the Registry setting, and then the Backup window will select the system files to be backed up, as shown in the Files Selection status box. Click on Next Step.

3. Click on the destination of the backed up data, and then click on Start Backup.

COMMAND AND FEATURE REFERENCE

4. Type a name or label for the full system backup. To have the disk password protected, click on Password Protect. Click OK to start the backup.

The backup may take several hours to complete. Its progress will be displayed on screen.

Performing a Partial Backup

A partial backup will back up only those files you select—usually just data files. You can define a file set that contains those files you want to back up on a regular basis. Follow these steps:

1. From the Backup tab, click on the plus sign next to the disk containing the data you want to back up. A list of all folders and files on the disk will be displayed beneath the disk name in the left pane.

TIP: *Click on the drive itself to see the folders in the right pane rather than in the left pane. To select all the files and folders on a disk, place a check mark in the check box beside it. If you want to back up most of the drive, you can click on the check box and then in a later step deselect the folders and files you do not want to back up.*

2. Select the files and folders you want:

- To select all the files in a folder, place a check mark in the box next to the file or folder name.

- To select some of the files in a folder, click on the folder icon for the files to be listed in the right pane. Then select only those files you want backed up. If a folder is to be partially backed up, it will appear to be gray on the screen, as shown below.

3. Click on Next Step.

BACKING UP FILES AND FOLDERS

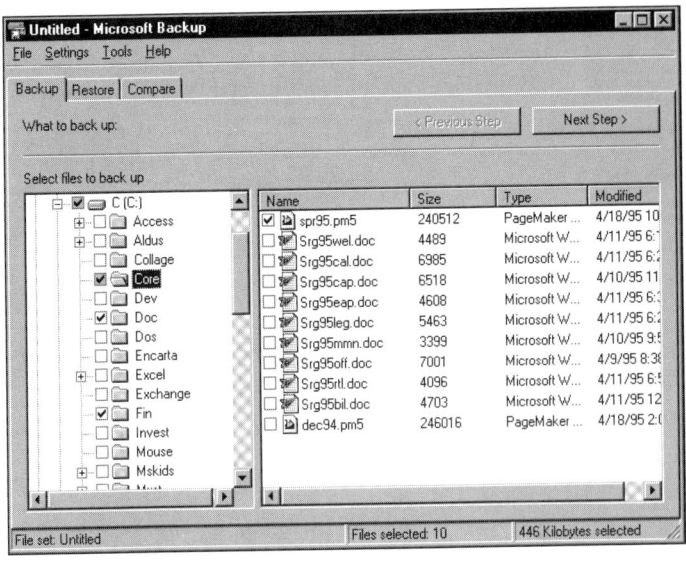

4. Click on the disk device containing the files or folders to be backed up.

5. Select Settings ➤ Options. On the Backup tab, verify that the options are set as you want them. Click OK.

6. Select File ➤ Save As. Type in a file set name and click on Save.

7. Click on Start Backup.

8. Type in a descriptive name for the file set. If you want to protect the backed-up data with a password, click on Password Protect and complete the dialog box. Click on OK.

As the backup begins, a window showing the progress of the backup will be displayed. If you are using a tape or disk that contains previous backup data, you will be asked if you want to erase it. After the backup has been completed, click on OK. You will see an *Operation complete* message, and will be

57

COMMAND AND FEATURE REFERENCE

informed of the number and size of the files you have just backed up. The Status Bar will indicate any errors encountered. Click OK to indicate that you recognize when the backup is complete.

Creating a Drag and Drop Backup Procedure

You can create a quick and simple backup by dragging the icon of an established file set to a Backup icon. Follow these steps:

1. Place a shortcut of Backup on the Desktop.

2. Set the Drag and Drop options in the Settings menu. (See "The Backup Menus," above.)

3. Create a file set to be used for the routine backup. (See "Performing a Partial Backup," above.)

4. Now all you need to do to perform a backup is to use Explorer to find the file set (a file with the .Set extension, usually located in C:\Program Files\Accessories), and drag its icon onto the Backup icon on the Desktop.

TIP: *You can also start a backup by double-clicking on the file set name, since it is a file type associated with Backup.*

SEE ALSO: *Shortcuts*

Background

"Background" applies to both the background of the screen display and to background printing.

SEE ALSO: *Display Control Panel; Printers Folder*

Boot Disk

SEE: Add/Remove Programs (Create a Startup Disk)

Booting Your Computer

SEE: Shut Down

Briefcase

SEE: My Briefcase

Broadcasting

Broadcasting allows you to send messages to multiple people on your network. You can use WinPopup to broadcast quick pop-up messages or Microsoft Exchange to broadcast e-mail or faxes.

SEE ALSO: Microsoft Exchange; WinPopup

Browsing Files

Browsing files allows you to look through the files in a folder, disk, computer, or network to find a specific file. Windows 95 offers several tools for browsing through files: Explorer, Find, My Computer, and Network Neighborhood. In addition to these tools,

COMMAND AND FEATURE REFERENCE

you may see a Browse or Find File button in some dialog boxes when you are trying to open, search, or import a file. If you click on the Browse or Find File button, you will see a dialog box like the one shown here:

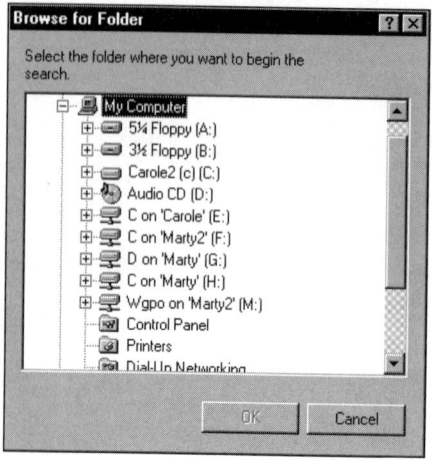

You can look through folders and files on any disk on any shared computer on the network to find the file you want by clicking on the selected path. When you find the file, folder, or computer, double-click on it and it will be opened, imported, or entered in a text box.

SEE ALSO: *Explorer; Finding Files and Folders; My Computer; Network Neighborhood*

Calculator

The Calculator is used to perform standard arithmetic as well as scientific or statistical calculations. The procedures used during the calculations and the keys available are slightly different depending on whether you are doing standard math or scientific math, as described below.

The Calculator Window

Access the Calculator by selecting Start ➤ Programs ➤ Accessories ➤ Calculator. The Calculator window

CALCULATOR

will be displayed in either Standard or Scientific mode, depending on which mode was selected when the window was last closed. In either mode, it contains these special keys:

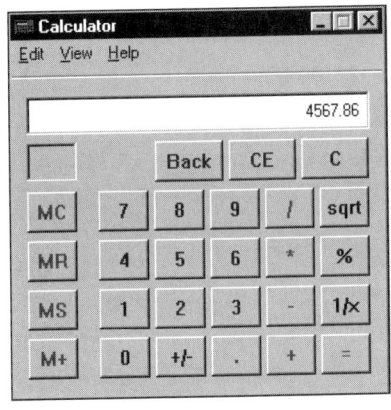

Back (or **Backspace** on the keyboard) to delete a single digit

CE (or **Delete** on the keyboard) to erase the last entry

C (or **Esc** on the keyboard) to clear a calculation altogether

MC to clear a number from the calculator's memory

MR to recall the number from the calculator's memory

MS to store a number in the calculator's memory, erasing whatever else was in memory (an "M" will appear in the box on the left below the display area)

M+ to add a number to the number in the calculator's memory

Copy and **Paste (Ctrl–C or Ctrl–V)** in the Edit menu to copy or paste a number or result to or from the clipboard

NUMLOCK (on the keyboard) to use the numeric keypad for entering numbers and operators

TIP: *When you store one number in the calculator's memory it replaces any number currently there.*

The two menus contain simple options:

Edit allows you to copy and paste.

View determines whether the standard or scientific calculator is displayed.

COMMAND AND FEATURE REFERENCE

To Perform a Standard Arithmetic Calculation

To add, subtract, multiply, divide, and perform other standard arithmetic operations, follow these steps:

1. Enter the first number to be used in the calculation.

2. Click on the operator: + to add, - to subtract, * to multiply, / to divide, Sqrt to take a square root, % for a percentage of another number, or 1/X to calculate the reciprocal.

3. Enter the next number.

4. Continue to enter operators and numbers in the order you want them entered.

5. Press = to get the final answer.

If you want to store a number while you are doing another calculation you may do so using the calculator's memory functions. After entering or calculating the first number you want to store, click on MS. Do whatever intermediate calculations you want, and then click on M+ to add it to the contents of the calculator's memory. When you are ready to look at the result in the calculator's memory, click on MR. You can then clear the calculator's memory by clicking on MC.

TIP: *To subtract a number from the current contents of the calculator's memory, enter the number, click on the +/- button to make the number negative, and then click on M+.*

To Perform a Scientific Calculation

To perform scientific calculations such as logarithms, follow these steps:

1. Select View ➤ Scientific. The Calculator will expand to include additional buttons for scientific expressions.

CALCULATOR

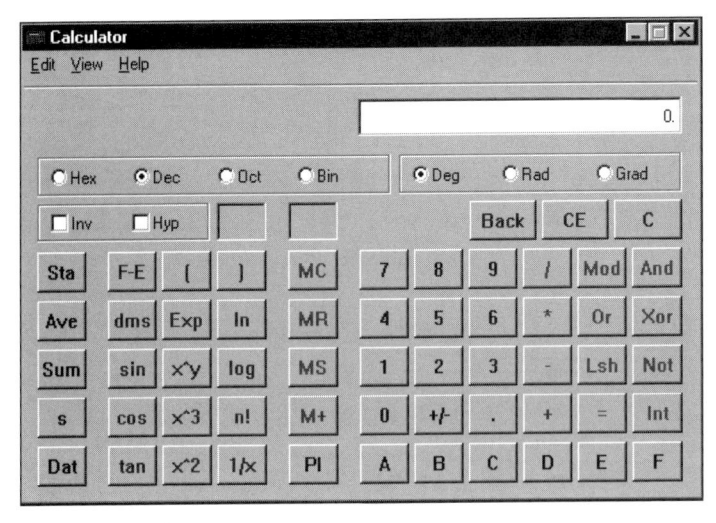

2. If entering a scientific calculation, choose a number system in the upper-left: hexadecimal, decimal, octal, or binary.

3. Enter the first number and then click on an operator.

4. Continue to enter numbers and operators.

5. Click on = for the final result.

TIP: *To get help on a Calculator key, click on it with the right mouse button for a Help submenu, and then click on What's This.*

To Perform a Statistical Calculation

Statistical functions, such as Average (Ave), Sum, and Standard Deviation (s), can be applied to a set of numbers entered in the Scientific view with the Sta and Dat buttons. The Sta button opens the Statistics Box, which contains the set of numbers entered with Dat. Follow these steps to enter a set

COMMAND AND FEATURE REFERENCE

of numbers which you can then use with the statistical functions:

1. Select View ➤ Scientific. The calculator will expand to include the additional statistical buttons. Enter your first number into the calculator display area.

2. Click on Sta to open the Statistics Box, and then click on Dat to enter the data.

3. Enter the rest of the numbers on top of the first number, clicking Dat after each entry.

4. Click Sta to see the list of statistical data being entered, and then click on RET to return to the calculator.

5. When you are finished entering your number set, click on the statistics functions you want.

The results will be displayed in the calculator display area.

The keys in the Statistics Box perform the following functions. Press:

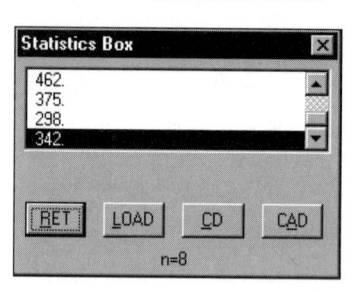

RET to exit the Statistic Box

LOAD to display the selected number from the Statistics Box in the Calculator display area

CD to clear the selected number

CAD to clear all numbers in the Statistic Box

Calling A Computer

SEE: *Dial-up Networking; HyperTerminal; Networks and Networking; Phone Dialer*

Calling Card

You may prefer to use a telephone calling or credit card for some or all of the phone calls you make via your computer. These phone calls will be billed to your calling card instead of the local telephone company.

To use a calling card on your system, follow these steps:

1. Select Start ➤ Programs ➤ Accessories ➤ Phone Dialer. The Phone Dialer dialog box will be displayed.

2. Select Tools ➤ Dialing Properties to display the Dialing Properties dialog box.

3. Under How I dial from this location:, place a check mark in the Dial using Calling Card check box. A Change Calling Card dialog box will be displayed.

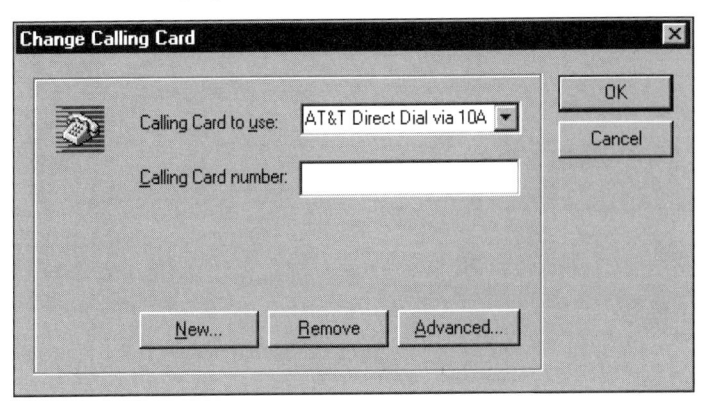

4. Under Calling Card to use, select from AT&T, MCI, or US Sprint options. If your card is different from one of these, click on New and then enter the name of your new card.

COMMAND AND FEATURE REFERENCE

5. Type your own number in the Calling Card number text entry box.

6. For a new card, enter differences in calling card numbers for local, long distance, and international calls by clicking on Advanced and then typing in the rules for dialing calls (available by clicking on the Help? button), as shown in the following illustration:

> Provides a space for you to type the rules for dialing calls.
> You can use the following characters to specify the rules for dialing calls:
>
> | Enter | To specify |
> |-------|------------|
> | 0-9 | Dialable digits |
> | ABCD | Dialable digits (tone dialing only; used for special control on some systems) |
> | E | Country code |
> | F | Area code (city code) |
> | G | Local number |
> | H | Card number |
> | *,# | Dialable digits (tone dialing only) |
> | T | Following digits are to be tone dialed |
> | P | Following digits are to be pulse dialed |
> | , | Pause for a fixed time |
> | ! | Hookflash (1/2 second on-hook, 1/2 second off-hook) |
> | W | Wait for second dial tone |
> | @ | Wait for quiet answer (ringback followed by five seconds of silence) |
> | $ | Wait for calling-card prompt ("bong") |
> | ? | Ask for input before dialing continues |

NOTE: *You can delete a calling card name by clicking on Remove. You will be asked if you are sure you want to do this.*

SEE ALSO: *Phone Dialer*

Canceling Last Action

To cancel or undo your last action, select Edit ➤ Undo or press Ctrl–Z. This will restore the results prior to the last action. Sometimes you can undo more than one action. If Undo is not available to you, you cannot cancel your last action.

Some actions where data has not been changed–such as calling up a menu–can be cancelled with Esc. Esc usually does not restore data, as Undo does.

Canceling Printing

SEE: *Printing*

Capturing a Screen Image

You can capture screen images—either the entire screen or just the active window—by copying the image to the Clipboard and then pasting it into a document you are creating. Use the following techniques:

- To capture the image of the active window and place it on the Clipboard, press Alt+Print Screen.

- To capture the image of the whole screen, press Print Screen.

- To paste the captured image, open the document where you want it to reside, move the insertion point to the desired location and choose Edit ➤ Paste or press Ctrl-V.

CD Player

The CD Player allows you to play audio compact discs on your CD-ROM drive. You must install it using the custom installation procedure. To use the CD Player, choose Start ➤ Programs ➤ Accessories ➤

COMMAND AND FEATURE REFERENCE

Multimedia ➤ CD Player. The CD Player window will be displayed.

The CD Player Window

You can choose among these toolbar options immediately beneath the menu bar:

Edit Play List creates a list defining which tracks of one or more CDs will be played. Use this list to play the tracks you like, and avoid those you don't.

Track Time Elapsed causes the elapsed time to be displayed in the CD Player window.

Track Time Remaining causes the time remaining to be displayed in the CD Player window.

Disc Time Remaining displays the remaining time the disc is to play.

Random Track Order plays the CD tracks in a random order. Normally the tracks are played in sequential order, starting with the first track. If you have a multidisc CD-ROM drive, the Random Track Order option will allow you to play tracks from each CD in random order.

Continuous Play plays the CD continuously. Normally, it will stop when the last track is over.

CD PLAYER

Intro Play plays the first segments of tracks. This can be used to search for specific tracks or songs.

The CD Player window has three menus that present another way to access the functions offered by the toolbar. The menus and their options are as follows:

Disc Menu

The Disc menu offers the **Edit Play List** option. When selected, a Disc Settings dialog box is displayed, which allows you to build a play list from the available tracks on the identified CD. After selecting a track from **Available Tracks**, click on **Add** to add a track to the Play List or **Remove** to delete a track. **Clear All** clears all tracks from the Play List. **Reset** restores the Play List to match the Available List. With the **Set Name** option, you can name the tracks with a descriptive title that will be easy to remember.

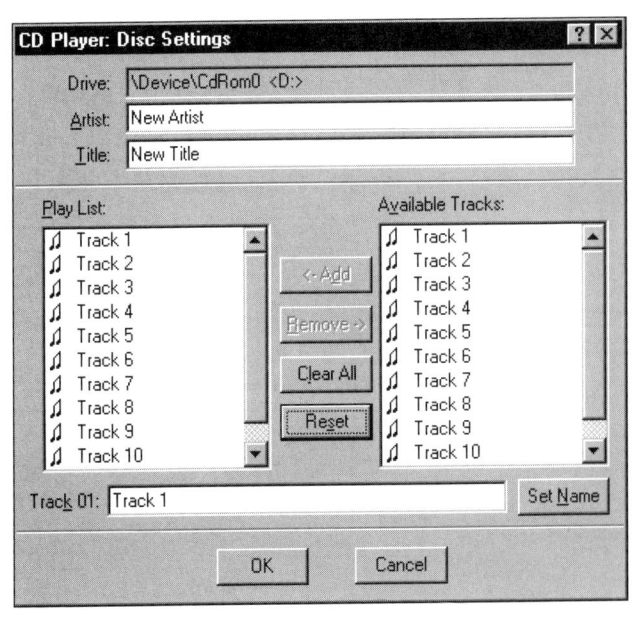

COMMAND AND FEATURE REFERENCE

View Menu

The View menu allows you to display the **Toolbar**, **Disc/Track Info** (which identifies the CD name, title and track currently being played), and the **Status bar** at the bottom of the dialog box. From the View menu, you can choose to display the **Track Time Elapsed, Track Time Remaining**, or **Disc Time Remaining**. You can also set the **Volume control**.

Options Menu

The options menu allows you to choose whether to play the CD in **Random Order, Continuous Play,** or **Intro Play**. You can also set the following **Preferences**:

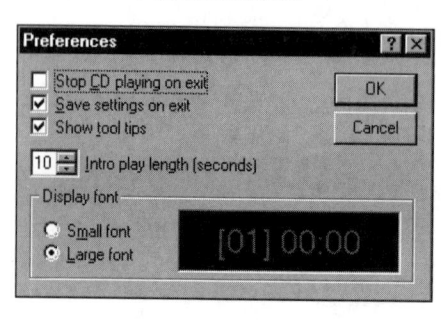

+ **Stop CD playing on exit** will stop the playing of the current CD when the CD Player is closed.

+ **Save settings on exit** saves the CD settings when CD Player is closed.

+ **Show tool tips** shows the popup description of the toolbar buttons when you place the pointer over them.

+ **Intro play length (seconds)** specifies how long the intro play will last.

+ **Display font** determines whether the display will use a large or small font to show the track or disc time remaining or elapsed.

Playing the CD

The CD Player provides several tools for manipulating the actual playing of the CD. You can stop, start,

CD PLAYER

skip, or pause the playing by clicking on the following buttons:

Play causes the CD to start playing.

Pause pauses the playing of the CD until Play is pressed again.

Stop interrupts the playing of the CD.

Previous Track plays the previous track again.

Skip Backwards skips backwards through the current track bit by bit.

Skip Forwards skips forward through the current track bit by bit.

Next Track plays the next track.

Eject causes the CD drive to eject the CD.

Setting the Volume for CDs

To set the default volume for listening to CDs through headphones, follow these steps:

1. Select Start ➤ Settings ➤ Control Panel and double-click on Multimedia.

2. Select the CD Music tab.

3. Slide the volume control for the Headphones to the position you want.

To set the volume during the playing of a CD:

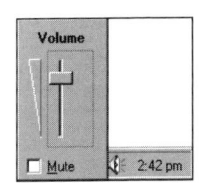

1. Click on the speaker icon for a Volume control popup.

2. Adjust the volume control by moving the slider up or down, and then click anywhere on the screen for it to disappear.

COMMAND AND FEATURE REFERENCE

TIP: *If you double-click on the speaker icon, the Volume Control window will be displayed from which you can control volumes for all multimedia equipment.*

NOTE: *To display the speaker icon in the notification area, Show volume control on taskbar must be selected in the Audio tab of the Multimedia Properties dialog box.*

SEE ALSO: *Volume Control*

Changing Display Colors, Patterns, and Wallpaper

SEE: *Display Control Panel*

Character Map

The Character Map displays the set of characters available with a given font. It must be installed using the custom installation procedure. Using the Character Map feature, you can copy special characters not available on a regular keyboard and then paste them into a document.

Follow these steps to copy characters from a given map:

1. To access the Character Map, select Start ➤ Programs ➤ Accessories ➤ Character Map. The Character Map dialog box will be displayed. (This assumes you have installed the program in the Accessories folder.)

CHARACTER MAP

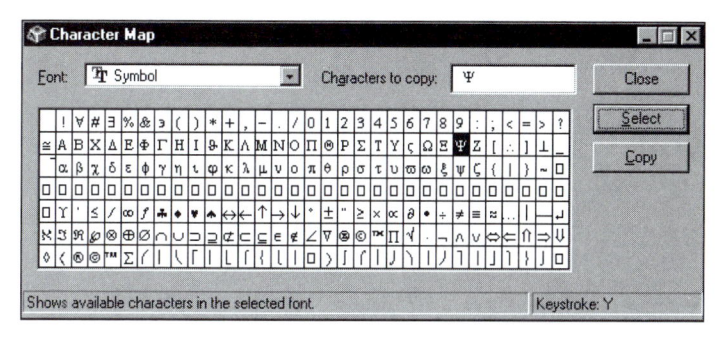

2. Click on the Font text box to see a list of available fonts. Select the font you want. When you select it, the characters it contains will be displayed.

3. Select the individual characters to be copied by clicking on a character and then clicking on Select (or double-clicking on the character). The selected characters will appear in the Characters to copy box. Repeat this for all characters to be selected.

4. After you have finished selecting all the characters you want to copy, click on Copy.

5. Bring up the document into which the characters are to be inserted, move the insertion point to the correct location, and select Edit ➤ Paste or press Ctrl–V to insert the characters into the document.

TIP: To see the characters more clearly, you can enlarge the individual characters in the map by clicking and holding the mouse button down. Do this to make sure that the small character is really the one you want.

NOTE: *Character Map characters can only be inserted into Windows-based programs or a DOS program running in a window.*

COMMAND AND FEATURE REFERENCE

Character Size and Font

You can change the size of the characters displayed on the screen. Select Start ➤ Settings ➤ Control Panel and double-click on Display. In the Settings tab, select Font Size. If the size you want is not displayed, select Custom to specify the exact size you want.

WARNING: *Do not use the large fonts a on smaller VGA monitors or the size of some dialog boxes may extend beyond the screen limits, and you will not be able to access all options.*

TIP: *If the Font size is unavailable (gray in appearance), you must move the Desktop area slider from Less toward More.*

SEE ALSO: *Display Control Panel*

Characters, Special

SEE: *Character Map*

Clipboard

The Clipboard is a temporary storage place where data may be held. Using the Cut and Copy commands as well as the Windows screen capture commands cause data to be stored on the Clipboard. The Paste command then copies the data from the Clipboard to a receiving document, perhaps in another application. You may not edit the

Clipboard contents; however, you can view and save the information stored in the Clipboard using the Clipboard Viewer, Clipbook Viewer, or by pasting the contents of the Clipboard into Notepad.

WARNING: *The Clipboard only holds one piece of information at a time, so when you cut or copy onto the Clipboard it overwrites the previous contents.*

SEE ALSO: *Clipboard Viewer; Notepad*

Clipboard Viewer

The Clipboard Viewer provides a way to view and save the contents of the Clipboard. It can be installed with Add/Remove Programs but not during the Windows 95 installation. It would normally be placed in the Accessories folder.

The Clipboard Viewer Window

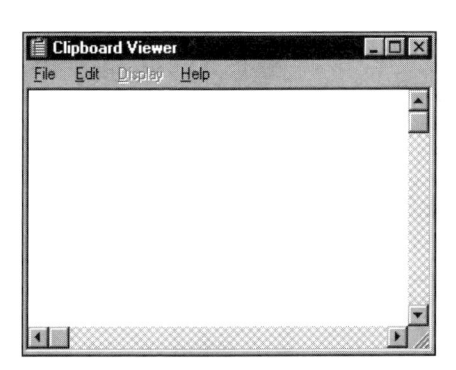

After installing the Clipboard Viewer, you access it by selecting Start ➤ Programs ➤ Accessories ➤ Clipboard Viewer. When you first open it, the Clipboard Viewer window shows the contents of the Clipboard. There are no toolbars, and the menus offer few options:

File allows you to save and open a Clipboard file. Files are saved as .clp files, which cannot be easily read by other applications, such as NotePad.

Edit allows you to clear the contents of the Clipboard with the Delete command.

Display lets you define the current clipboard contents as text, picture, graphics, or other objects.

Clock (Taskbar and Date/Time)

SEE: *Date Format; Date/Time, Setting; Regional Settings Control Panel; Time Format; Time Zone Default Settings*

Closing Files or Windows

Closing a file or a window causes you to terminate the operations of a program or the viewing of a file. Choose one of the methods below:

- Click on Close in the upper-right of the title bar.

- Select Control ➤ Close (identified by the icon to the left of the program name in the title bar) or simply double-click on the Control menu icon.

- Choose File ➤ Close or File ➤ Exit.

- Choose Start ➤ Shut Down. (You may have to close a program before using Shut Down.)

- With the right mouse button, click on the window's button on the Taskbar. Then click on Close or press Alt+F4.

Colors in Windows and Screens

SEE: *Display Control Panel*

Command Line (Run)

Select Start ➤ Run to start a program or open a folder without navigating through the menus. This command is often used to install software.

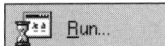

When you click on Run, the Run dialog box will be displayed. Type the path and file name of the program, folder, or document you want to use, and it will be loaded or opened for you. If you don't know the name, or where the program or folder is located, you can click on the Browse button to scan a network, computer, or disk to find it.

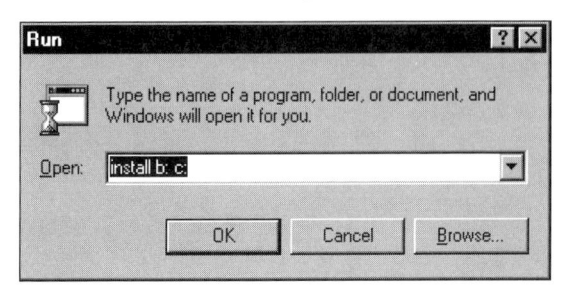

SEE ALSO: *Browse*

Communications on a Network

SEE: *Networks and Networking*

Compact Discs

SEE: *CD Player*

COMMAND AND FEATURE REFERENCE

Comparing Files

There are two ways to compare files in Windows 95. Backup provides a way to compare what you backed up with the original files. My Briefcase compares a file in the Briefcase with an identically named file on the hard disk so they can be synchronized.

Comparing Files with Backup

Follow these steps to verify that the contents of a file match the backup:

1. Select Start ➤ Programs ➤ Accessories ➤ System Tools ➤ Backup. Click OK twice to bypass the Welcome screen and the Full System Backup informational screen.

2. Click on the Compare tab in the Microsoft Backup dialog box.

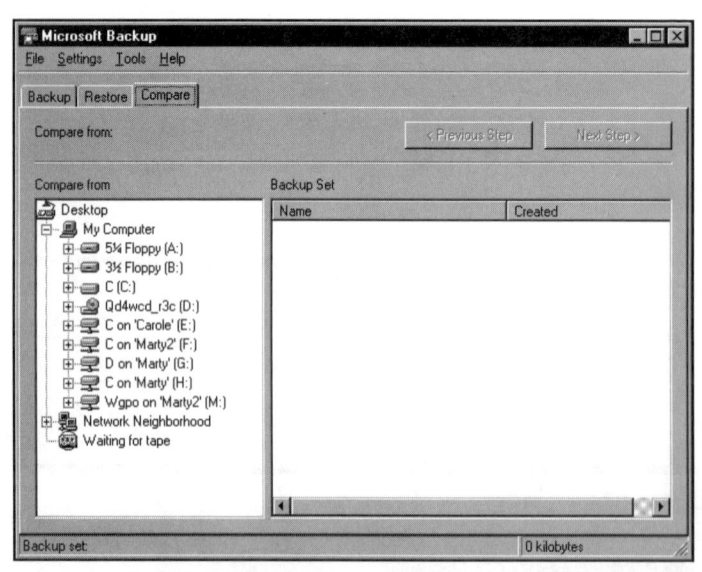

3. Insert the disk or tape containing the backup, and select the drive from the Compare from list on the left of the window. The name or label of the

COMPARING FILES

backup set will be displayed. If it is the one you want, select it and click on Next Step.

4. The folders and files on the backup file set will be displayed on the left. Place a check mark in the box of the folders or files you want to compare. If you want to see which files are contained in a folder, click on the folder name and the list of files in the actual folder will be displayed on the right. Place a check mark in the box next to the file names you want to compare.

5. Select Settings ➤ Options ➤ Compare. Set the specifications for the Location of Compare. Select Original locations if the files to be compared to the backup are where they were when the backup was performed. Select Alternative location if the files are now located in other folders or a disk. Select Alternate location, Single directory if the files to be compared are now in one directory, different from the original.

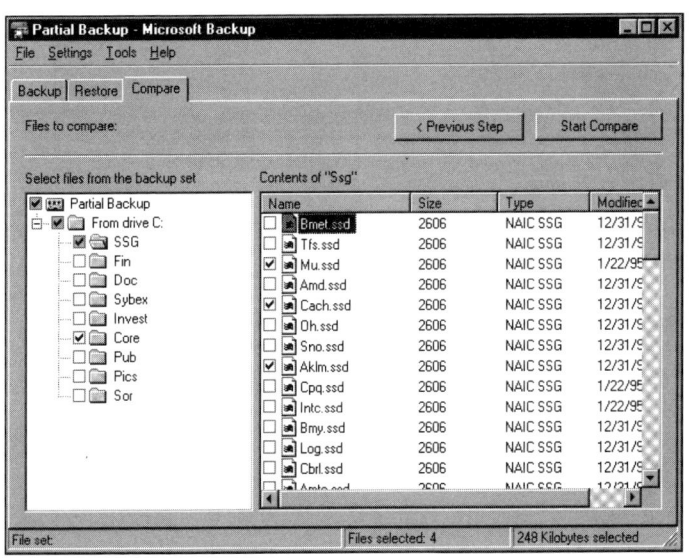

6. Click on Start Compare. A report of the progress will be displayed as the compare is made.

COMMAND AND FEATURE REFERENCE

When the compare is complete, an *Operation complete* message will be displayed. Click OK. The Compare dialog box will tell you the number of files compared, the size of the files, the elapsed time, and the errors encountered.

7. Click on OK to clear the compare messages. You will be returned to the Backup dialog box.

SEE ALSO: *Backing Up Files and Folders; My Briefcase*

Compression

Compression is the reduction in the amount of disk space taken up by a file. Windows 95 uses an application called DriveSpace to do this for ordinary files, and special routines called CODECs to do this for digital audio and video files.

SEE: *DriveSpace*

Configuration Settings for System Properties

SEE: *System Control Panel*

Connecting to Other Computers

There are three ways to connect to other computers:

- You can connect to another computer and transfer files with a parallel or serial cable, using the Direct Cable Connection program.

- You can connect to a remote computer, information service, or bulletin board using a modem, phone lines, and HyperTerminal to download or transfer files. You can also use Dial-Up Networking or Microsoft Network to communicate with others (through e-mail, for instance).

- You can use networking cards, cables, and Windows 95 networking capability to share files or hardware devices (such as a printer), or communicate over a network.

Each of these requires a different method for setting up the connection.

SEE ALSO: *Dial-Up Networking; Direct Cable Connection; HyperTerminal; Microsoft Network; Networks and Networking*

Control Panel

Control Panel provides a way to establish settings and defaults for many features. To access Control Panel, select Start ➤ Settings ➤ Control Panel. A window with the most commonly used control panels will be displayed. To open a control panel, either double-click on the icon you want or click once on an icon to select it, and then select File ➤ Open.

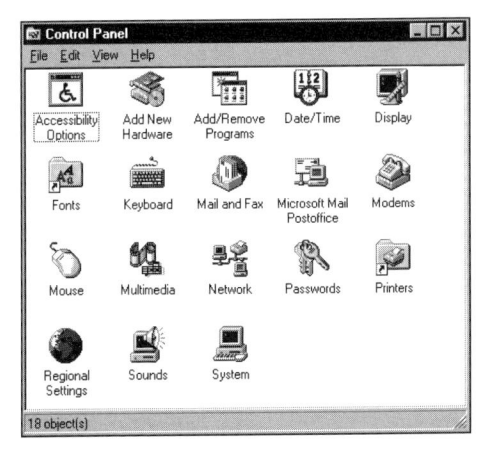

The Control Panel window is similar to all folder windows, and can be modified through the View menu.

Refer to the individual item to see the details about a particular control panel.

COMMAND AND FEATURE REFERENCE

Copying Disks

Copying disks can be accomplished with either the Backup application or the Copy Disk command. You can also use Diskcopy in a DOS window.

Copying Floppy Disks

To copy a floppy disk, use the Copy Disk command. The disks used must be of the same type—for example, a 3½" high-density disk must be copied to another 3½" high-density disk. Any information on the receiving disk will be replaced with the data from the source disk. Follow these steps:

1. Open Explorer or My Computer, and find the floppy disk drives you want to copy to and from.

TIP: *You can copy to and from the same drive. You will be prompted when you must change from the source to the destination disks.*

2. Place the pointer on the floppy disk icon and press the right mouse button. A popup menu will appear.

3. Select Copy Disk. A Copy Disk dialog box will be displayed.

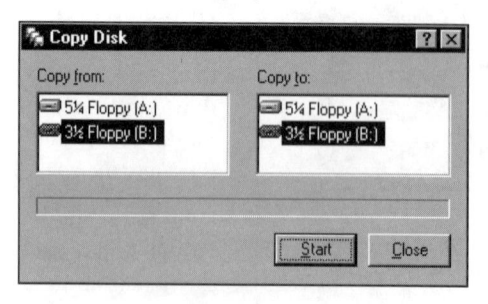

4. On the left, select the disk to copy from. On the right, select the disk to copy to.

5. Press Start. The program will begin reading and writing to the source disk.

6. If asked, insert the disk you want to copy to. Click OK.

You will be informed when the program has completed copying.

SEE ALSO: Backing Up Files and Folders

Copying Files and Folders

When you copy a file or folder, you duplicate it and move the copy to another location while leaving the original in place. Windows 95 offers three ways to copy files and folders: You can use the drag and drop method, the Edit menu's Copy and Paste commands, or you can use the right mouse button.

To Copy Using Drag and Drop

To use the Drag and Drop method, you must have both the source and destination folders in view. Press and hold Ctrl while holding down the left mouse button, and drag the file or folder from one location to another. When the file or folder is in the correct destination folder, release the mouse button and *then* release Ctrl.

NOTE: *Unless you are moving the file to a different disk, you must hold down Ctrl, or the file or folder will be moved rather than copied.*

To Copy Using the Edit Menu

The Edit menu in My Computer, Explorer, or any folder window provides a Copy and Paste feature.

1. Select the file or folder you want to copy.
2. Choose Edit ➤ Copy.
3. Find the destination file or folder and open it.
4. Choose Edit ➤ Paste.

COMMAND AND FEATURE REFERENCE

> **TIP:** You can select multiple files or folders to be copied by holding down Ctrl and clicking on the objects you want. If the files are contiguous, you can also use Shift to select files to copy.

To Copy Using the Right Mouse Button

Clicking the right mouse button on a file or folder causes a popup menu to appear, which can be used to perform a number of functions, including copying. To copy using the right mouse button, follow these steps:

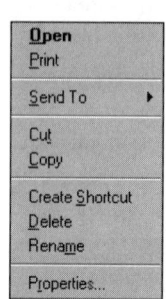

1. Locate the file or folder you want to copy and click the right mouse button on it. A menu will be displayed. Select Copy.

2. Open the destination folder, click the right mouse button, and select Paste.

Country Settings

SEE: *Regional Settings Control Panel*

Creating/Adding Folders

New folders can be added to a disk or another folder in My Computer or Explorer. Follow these steps:

1. In My Computer or Explorer, select the disk or folder in which you want to place a new folder.

2. Select File ➤ New ➤ Folder.

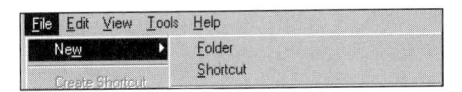

A new folder will be added to the disk or folder with the name New Folder highlighted.

3. Type in a new folder name, overwriting the temporary New Folder name, and press Enter.

Currency Format

You may want to change the way your currency is formatted. For example, you may want to vary the number of decimal points or the display of negative numbers. You can do this from the Currency tab on the Regional Settings Properties dialog box. Follow these steps:

1. Select Start ➤ Settings ➤ Control Panel, and then double-click on Regional Settings. Select the Currency tab.

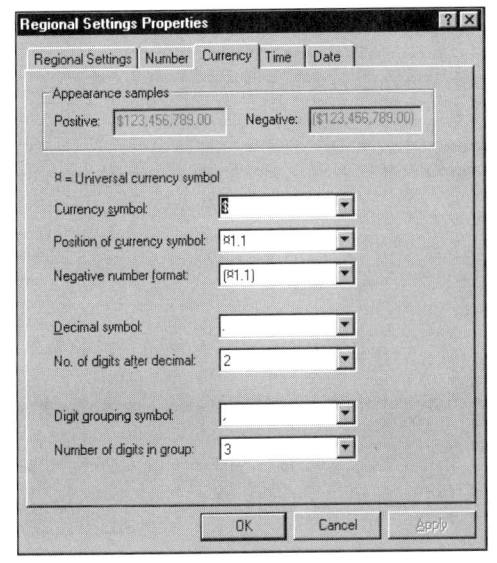

2. Choose from the following:

Currency symbol displays the symbol of the currency, such as the dollar sign.

Position of currency symbol shows where the currency symbol is displayed in the number—usually in front of a number.

COMMAND AND FEATURE REFERENCE

Negative number format sets how negative numbers will be displayed.

Decimal symbol determines which symbol separates the whole from the fractional parts of a number, such as the period.

No. of digits after decimal determines how many digits are by default shown after the decimal–usually two.

Digit grouping symbol shows which symbol—usually a comma—separates the number groups, such as thousands, millions, etc.

Number of digits in group determines how many digits determine a number group, such as 3 for thousands, millions, etc.

SEE ALSO: *Regional Settings Control Panel*

Cursor Properties and Speed

SEE: *Keyboard Control Panel; Mouse Control Panel*

Cut and Paste

SEE: *Copying Files and Folders; Moving Files and Folders*

Date Format

The defaults for how Date and Time are formatted and displayed are established in the Regional Settings control panel.

To Set Date Defaults

1. Select Start ➤ Settings ➤ Control Panel, and then double-click on Regional Settings. Select the Date tab. The following options will be available to you:

   Calendar type displays the types of calendars that might exist in your culture. The Gregorian Calendar, with U.S. English settings, will be the default and should not be changed thoughtlessly, as it will affect the naming and calculation of days, months, and years. In fact, this is so important that you cannot change the calendar from the Gregorian Calendar unless you alter the country and language settings.

   Short date sample displays an example of the current style.

   Short date style lists the formats available for displaying the date.

   Date separator lists the symbols that can be used to separate the month, day, and year.

   Long date sample shows an example of the Long date style.

   Long date style lists the formats available for displaying a formal date notation.

2. Select the choices you want and click on OK.

SEE ALSO: *Currency Format; Date/Time, Setting; Number Format; Regional Settings Control Panel; Time Format; Time Zone Default Settings*

Date/Time, Setting

The clock that appears in the right corner of the Taskbar displays the system clock. This is what is

COMMAND AND FEATURE REFERENCE

used to indicate the time and date on files you are creating or modifying. to set the clock, follow these steps:

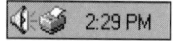

1. Double-click on the time in the Taskbar. Or, select Start ➤ Settings ➤ Control Panel and double-click on Date/Time. The Date/Time Properties will be displayed.

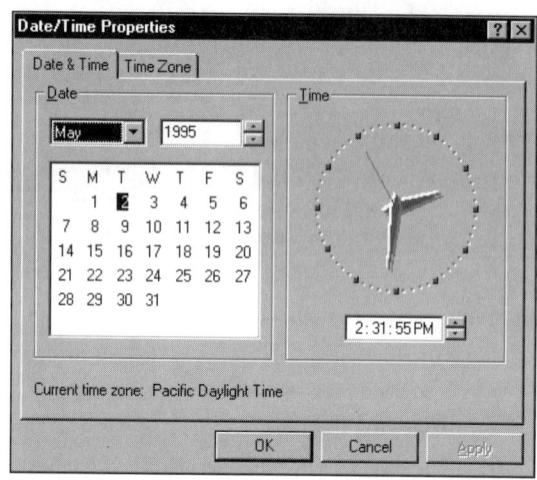

2. Select the Date & Time tab to set the date or time.

3. To change the time, either drag across the numbers you want to change beneath the clock and type in the new time, or highlight the numbers and use the up and down arrows to increase or decrease the values.

4. To change the date, click on the drop-down arrow to select the month, use the spinner arrows to change the year, and click on the appropriate day of the month.

TIP: *To see the date, place your pointer on the time in the Taskbar.*

NOTE: *To vary the format of the date and time in the Taskbar, select Start ➤ Settings ➤ Control Panel and double-click on Regional Settings. Use the Time and Date tabs to change formats.*

SEE ALSO: *Date Format; Regional Settings Control Panel; Taskbar; Time Format; Time Zone Default Settings*

Defragmenting a Disk

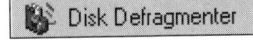

As files on your computer grow, they may become fragmented. Fragmented files are too large to fit in one location, so Windows 95 spreads the file over several disk locations, slowing the time it takes for the hard disk to find and retrieve the file as a whole. You can speed up the hard disk response time by running the Disk Defragmenter program. This program rearranges the files so that all segments of a file are stored together in one section of the hard disk. Larger sections of free space are also stored together.

Follow these steps to use the Disk Defragmentor:

1. Select Start ➤ Programs ➤ Accessories ➤ System Tools ➤ Disk Defragmenter.

2. Select the disk to be defragmented and click on OK. A dialog box will show the percent of fragmented files you have. Select one of these options:

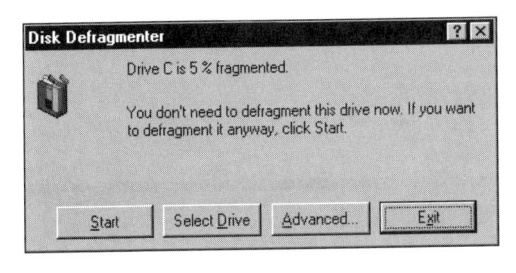

Start will start the defragmenting program.

Select Drive will allow you to change the disk to be defragmented.

Advanced allows you to specify the defragmentation method: Full defragmentation (which includes both files and free space),

COMMAND AND FEATURE REFERENCE

Defragment files only, or Consolidate free space only. You can also specify whether you want to check the drive for errors, and whether the Defragmentation method selected should be the default, or to use it this time only.

Exit will allow you to leave the Disk Defragmenter without running it.

3. If you choose Start, the Disk Defragmenter will begin. You can choose to Stop it, Pause it, or Show Details of how Disk Defragmenter is proceeding.

You can perform other work on the computer while Disk Defragmenter is running, but the response time will be slower.

TIP: *If you need to do other work, you can pause Disk Defragmenter temporarily by clicking Pause, and then continue the program.*

WARNING: *If, while you are performing other work, you save data on the disk while it is being defragmented, Disk Defragmenter will be forced to restart.*

NOTE: *If your disk contains errors, Disk Defragmenter will not be able to proceed until they are corrected. You will be told if this is the case. Run ScanDisk and then retry the Disk Defragmenter.*

SEE ALSO: *ScanDisk*

Deleting Files or Folders

To delete a file or folder, you can use one of four techniques after first selecting the file or folder you want in My Computer or Explorer.

DESKTOP

- Select File ➤ Delete. Verify that you want to delete the file. The selected file or folder will be placed in the Recycle Bin.

- Press Del and verify that you want to delete the selected file or folder, sending it to the Recycle Bin.

- Place the mouse on the file or folder and click on the right mouse button to open the popup menu. Select Delete and then verify that you want to delete the selected file or folder. It will be placed in the Recycle Bin.

- Place the My Computer or Explorer window so that you can also see the Recycle Bin on the Desktop. Drag the selected file or folder to the Recycle Bin and release the mouse button. The file will be placed in the Recycle Bin. You won't be asked to confirm your deletion to the Recycle Bin, although you can always retrieve it later.

NOTE: *If you find that you deleted the wrong file or folder by accident, you can select Edit ➤ Undo, press Ctrl+Z, or retrieve the file from the Recycle Bin. You cannot retrieve a deleted file or folder if the Recycle Bin has been emptied.*

TIP: *To delete a file without placing it in the Recycle Bin, select the file and then press Shift+Delete. Be warned that the file cannot be recovered if you do this. You will be asked to confirm the deletion.*

SEE ALSO: *Recycle Bin*

Desktop

The Desktop is what you see on the screen when you first bring up Windows 95. Initially, after the welcoming tips, it contains only a few icons on the

COMMAND AND FEATURE REFERENCE

left, plus the Taskbar with the Start button on the bottom. As you load programs, windows and other objects, such as dialog boxes and messages boxes, are placed on the desktop.

When you load Windows 95, you may want to place the programs you use most frequently on the desktop, so you can get to them easily.

You can also change the appearance of the desktop by clicking on the right mouse button and selecting Properties. This allows you to change display properties for the Desktop background and screen savers. You can also change the monitor type, as well as font types, sizes, and colors for objects on the screen.

SEE ALSO: *Arranging Windows; Display Control Panel*

Device Drivers

SEE: *Printers Folder; System Control Panel (Device Manager Tab)*

Device Profiles

SEE: *System Control Panel (Hardware Profiles Tab)*

Dial-Up Networking

Dial–Up Networking allows you to connect to remote computers. You can share information with other computers and potentially become part of a network to which a remote computer is connected.

When you bring up Dial–Up Networking, you can immediately dial up a remote computer. You can also save telephone numbers and other dialing specifications in a special Dial–Up folder to be used again.

NOTE: *If you do not have a modem, you will not be able to use Dial-Up Networking. If you have a modem, but have not yet installed it, Dial-Up Networking will guide you through the process.*

First Time Through Dial-Up Networking

The first time you bring up Dial–Up Networking, you will be shown a different sequence of screens and dialog boxes from what you will see after you have installed your modem. If you have not installed your modem, you will be given a chance to do so. The Install New Modem Wizard will guide you through the process. You can follow the Wizard here, or install the modem using the instructions in Add New Hardware.

Creating A New Connection

Once your modem has been installed, you can follow these steps to create a new record of a dial–up connection:

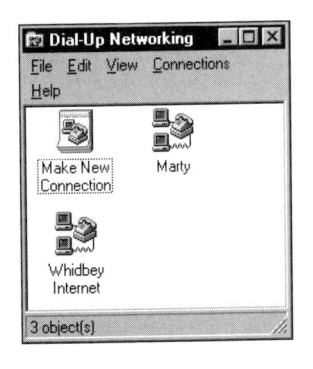

1. Select Start ➤ Programs ➤ Accessories ➤ Dial–Up Networking. The Dial–Up Networking folder will be displayed with any connections you have already made, as well as a folder for Make New Connection.

2. Double-click on Make New Connection.

3. After your modem is installed, the Make New Connection dialog

COMMAND AND FEATURE REFERENCE

box will be displayed, allowing you to create a record of a computer you want to call. Type a name to represent the connection you are creating. If you need to change a modem, click on the Select a modem drop-down list box, or click on the Configure button if you need to change the modem configuration. (If you have not installed your modem, you'll also have an Install button.) Click on Next.

4. Now enter the area code, telephone number, and country code. Click on Next.

5. You will be told that your new connection has been successfully entered. Click on Finish to continue to the Dial-Up Networking window. To dial-up, double-click on the icon representing your new connection.

6. You will be returned to the Dial-Up Networking folder, which now contains a folder for the new connection you have just created.

Dialing an Established Connection

Once you have set up the connection to another computer, follow these steps:

1. Select Start ➤ Programs ➤ Accessories ➤ Dial-Up Networking. The Dial-Up Networking folder will be displayed.

2. Double-click on the icon for the connection you want to dial. The Connect To dialog box will be displayed.

3. If you must change any of the settings displayed, or the dialing properties accessed from the Dial Properties button, do it before proceeding.

4. Click on Connect.

DIRECT CABLE CONNECTION

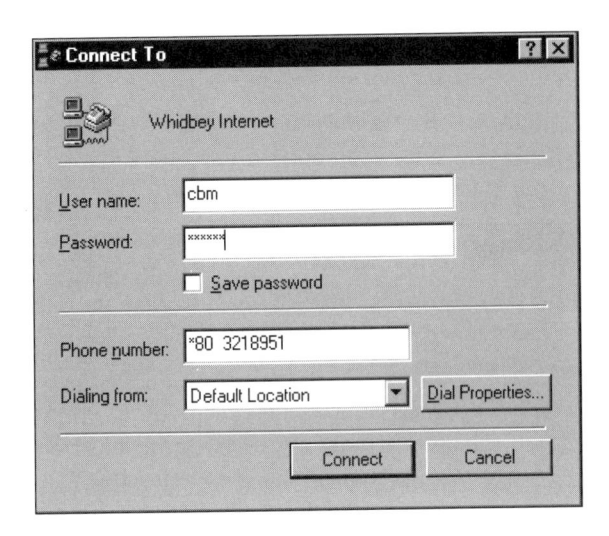

NOTE: *Both computers must have modems in order to use Dial-Up Networking.*

Dialer

SEE: *Phone Dialer*

Direct Cable Connection

A direct cable connection allows you to transfer files between two computers using a cable connecting either the serial or parallel ports on the computers. If one of the computers is connected to a network, then the direct cable–connected computer can also use it. An example of a direct cable connection is using a portable computer to access data from a desktop computer.

COMMAND AND FEATURE REFERENCE

Follow these steps to establish a direct cable connection:

1. Connect a cable to the serial or parallel ports of two computers between which you want to transfer files.

2. Select Start ➤ Programs ➤ Accessories ➤ Direct Cable Connection. The Direct Cable Connection dialog box will be displayed.

3. Determine whether you are using a host or guest computer. If you are using a host computer, other computers will seek the information or services your computer contains. If you are using a guest computer, you will be accessing another computer for the services or information you need. Click on either Host or Guest and then click on Next.

4. Select the port you are using to connect the computers, or click on Install New Ports to add a new port. Both computers must use the same type of port (serial or parallel). Click Next. A final screen will inform you that you have successfully set up the computer. If you are a host computer and want guests to use passwords, click on Use Password Protection. Click Finish.

NOTE: *You'll want to set the host computer first.*

5. Repeat Steps 2 through 4 on the second computer.

Once you have completed the direct cable connection, the guest computer will be able to access any shared resources on the host computer. Shared resources can include hard disks, CD-ROMs, printers, and faxes, as well as any shared resources on the network to which the host computer is attached.

Directories (Folders)

In previous versions of Windows, directories were groups of files or other directories organized according to the user's needs. In Windows 95, directories are now referred to as folders.

SEE ALSO: *Folders (Directories)*

Disabilities

SEE: *Accessibility Options*

Disassociating File Types

SEE: *Associating Files*

Disk Space

To determine the disk space required by one or more files and/or folders, click on them (hold down Ctrl to select more than one) in My Computer or Explorer. If the window's status bar is turned on in the View menu, you will see the number of objects selected and the amount of disk space they utilize. Alternately, you can select File ➤ Properties, and the General tab will display the size of the file(s), or if it is a folder, the size plus the number of files or other folders within it.

COMMAND AND FEATURE REFERENCE

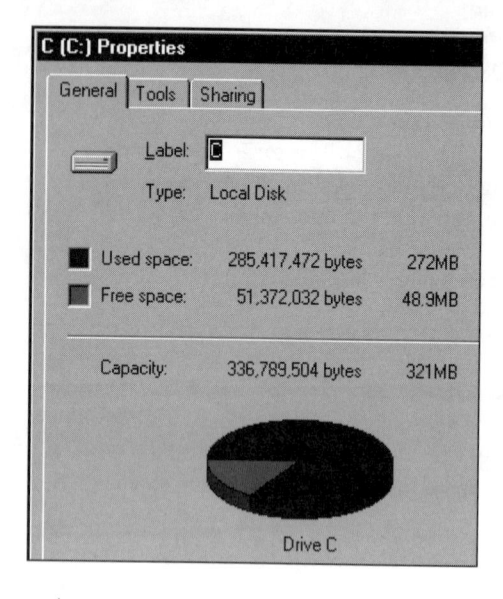

To see how much disk space remains on the entire disk, select the disk name in My computer or Explorer and then select File ► Properties. Both Used and Free space will be displayed in the Properties dialog box. The status bar of My Computer will also display the free space and capacity of a disk drive.

TIP: *Another way to find disk space parameters is to click on a disk, folder, or file with the right mouse button and then select Properties. The Properties dialog box will be displayed.*

Disk Tools

Many tools for managing your disks are found in My Computer and Explorer. With these programs you can copy, move, delete, and rename files and folders as well as copy, rename, and format disks. You can also find out the size of files and folders and how much space is available on your disks with the Properties option in the File menu.

SEE ALSO: *Backing Up Files and Folders; Comparing Files; Defragmenting a Disk; DriveSpace; Restoring Files; ScanDisk*

Display Control Panel

The Display control panel allows you to control how the objects on your screen look by presenting choices of patterns, colors, fonts, sizes, and other display elements. To access it, select Start ➤ Settings ➤ Control Panel and then double-click on Display. The Display Properties dialog box will open, containing four tabs: Background, Screen Saver, Appearance, and Settings.

TIP: *You can also open the Display Properties dialog box by moving the mouse pointer to the desktop, clicking the right mouse button, and selecting Properties.*

Background Properties

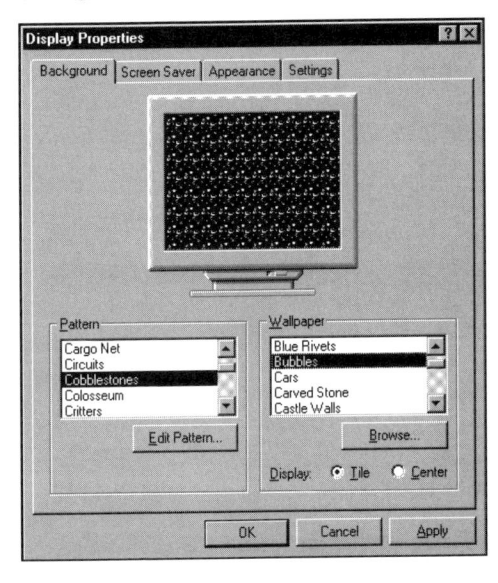

The pattern and wallpaper used for the Desktop background is controlled from the Background tab. Clicking on an option will cause it to be displayed in the preview box.

Pattern lists a variety of patterns for the background. Click on one to see it previewed in the display box.

Edit Pattern allows you to change the pattern.

Wallpaper lists several picture patterns.

COMMAND AND FEATURE REFERENCE

Browse allows you to search for patterns and wallpaper not available on the displayed list.

Tile displays the wallpaper pictures in patterns.

Center displays the wallpaper picture in the center of the screen.

Screen Saver Properties

A screen saver provides a constantly changing image on the screen to prevent a fixed image from being burned into the screen. A screen saver automatically appears after the computer is unused for a period of time. You can turn on, preview, and select a screen saver from the Screen Saver tab, which contains the following options:

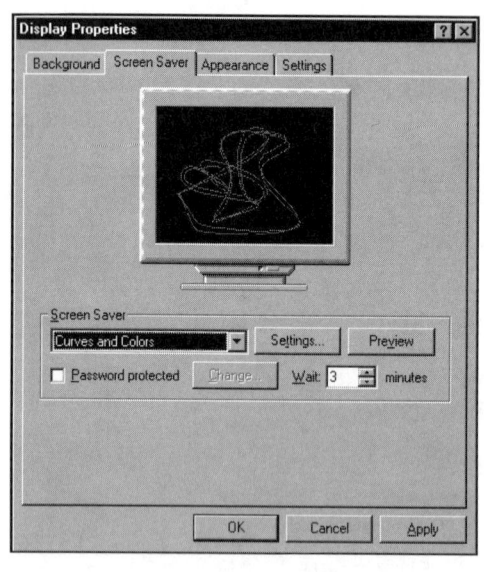

Screen Saver lists the available screen savers. Click on the one you want to see previewed in the display box.

Settings allows you to set the speed and density of the pattern of the screen saver.

Preview will display the screen saver in full screen mode. To return to the dialog box, move the mouse or press any key.

Password Protected allows you to require a password before allowing access beyond the screen saver. Windows will not clear the screen saver until the correct password is given.

Change allows you to change the password. It is only available when Password Protected is enabled. You must be able to confirm the old password to change to a new password.

Wait sets the amount of time before the screen saver is activated.

Appearance Properties

The Appearance tab shows how the screen currently looks. It can be changed with these options:

Scheme lists the schemes that change the appearance of windows, dialog boxes, and message boxes. You can select a scheme from the list or create your own. For example, the Evergreen 256 scheme displays borders of windows and boxes in green with a contrasting background.

Item allows you to select an item and customize its appearance. Based on the item selected, the next options become available.

- **Size** sets the size of the selected item, when appropriate.

- **Color** sets the color of the selected item, when appropriate.

Font sets the font for the selected item, when appropriate. The following options are available:

- **Size** sets the size of the font in the selected item.

- **Color** sets the color of the text in the selected item.

- **B** makes the text in the selected item boldface.

- **/** makes the text in the selected item italic.

TIP: *You can select an item on the screen whose appearance you want to change by clicking on that item in the upper part of the dialog box.*

COMMAND AND FEATURE REFERENCE

Settings Properties

The Settings tab allows you to vary the resolution and color palette used by your monitor and display adapter card. The following options are available:

Color palette establishes the color palettes that your monitor and display adapter supports—either 16-color or 256-color for lower resolution monitors and High Color (16 bit) and True Color (24 bit) for higher resolutions.

Desktop area sets the resolution or amount of information, in terms of pixels, that can be seen on your monitor.

Font size sets the text size that can be displayed. Do not use Large Fonts on lower resolution or smaller monitors, or some parts of dialog boxes will not be visible to you. To make this option available, you must move the Desktop area slider from Less towards More.

Custom allows you to create another size font for text. This will be available when Font size is available.

Change Display Type allows you to install another adapter or monitor type.

Documents, Starting

You can find and start a document from within an application, or you can use either of the following two methods:

- Select Start ➤ Documents, and click on a document name. The originating program will start and open the selected document. The documents displayed in the Documents list are the last 15 you have opened by double-clicking on them.

- From Explorer or My Computer, find the document file you want and double-click on it. The originating program will start and open the selected document.

SEE ALSO: *Arranging Applications; Associating Files; Shortcuts; Start Button*

DOS, Getting to

SEE: *MS-DOS Prompt*

Drag and Drop

Drag and Drop is a technique by which you can move, copy, activate, or dispose of files and folders. You do this by placing the pointer on a file, pressing the left mouse button, and dragging the file or folder to another disk or folder, and then releasing the mouse. The result depends on the file or folder being dragged and the destination. For example:

- Dragging a file or folder to another folder on the same disk moves it (press Ctrl to copy only).

- Dragging a file or folder to another disk copies it.

- Dragging a file to a shortcut printer icon on the Desktop prints the document.

- Dragging a file or folder to the Recycle Bin disposes of it.

COMMAND AND FEATURE REFERENCE

Drawing

SEE: *Paint*

DriveSpace

DriveSpace is used to compress the information stored on disks in order to provide more storage space and to manage or configure disks currently compressed with either DoubleSpace or DriveSpace.

Windows compresses the data on a disk by creating a sometimes hidden "host" drive that contains the compressed data, called a Compressed Volume File (CVF). DriveSpace software then manipulates this compressed drive to present to you and all the application software that uses it, a disk drive that looks exactly like the original uncompressed drive except that it has roughly twice the amount of total storage space. All disk operations are handled exactly as they were before compression. Windows, when compressing a drive, first renames the disk drive with another letter, such as H for Host. The original disk drive letter is then assigned to a file on the disk which contains the compressed data. Consequently, when you are looking for a disk drive letter, such as C, you will actually be looking at a file on disk drive H. This allows H to contain the compressed data (in the CVF called C, for instance) as well as free space now available on the disk.

You can also create a new compressed drive out of the free space on an uncompressed disk drive. In that case, a host drive, perhaps J, is created in the empty space containing an empty CVF for storing compressed data. You now have two or more disk drives in one.

The DriveSpace Window

To start DriveSpace, select Start ➤ Programs ➤ Accessories ➤ System Tools ➤ DriveSpace. The drives on your computer will be shown beneath the Menu bar.

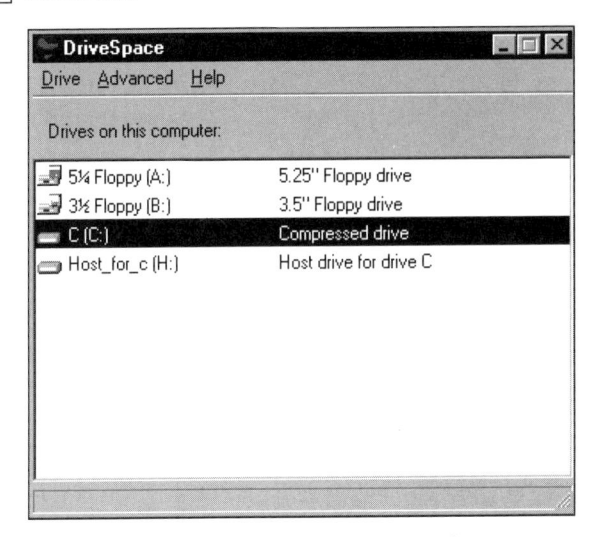

In addition to Help, the DriveSpace window contains two other menus. The tasks you can perform in DriveSpace are available from the Drive menu and the Advanced menu.

Drive menu

The Drive menu contains these options:

Compress leads you through the steps to compress the selected drive.

Uncompress leads you through the steps to uncompress a drive.

Adjust Free Space allows you to change the distribution of free space between the compressed drive and the host drive.

COMMAND AND FEATURE REFERENCE

Properties shows the distribution of free and used space for the selected drive, its label, and the type of drive (compressed or not).

Format formats a compressed drive.

Advanced menu

Mount allows you to connect a compressed-volume file to a selected drive. This is used with floppy disks that contain a compressed-volume file.

Unmount allows you to remove a compressed drive from its volume file.

Create Empty creates a new, empty compressed drive from the free space on an uncompressed disk. The drive must be a hard drive, not a floppy.

Delete deletes a compressed drive.

Change Ratio changes the estimated compression ratio that Windows 95 uses to estimate how much free space is available on a compressed drive. This ratio may be more or less than the actual compression ratio, depending on the type of data being compressed.

Change Letter changes the mapped host drive letter assignments.

Settings allows you to choose whether to automatically mount new compressed devices. You need this when you have a compressed disk that wasn't mounted when the computer was booted–a floppy disk, for example. With this option, the disk will be automatically mounted when it is inserted.

Refresh updates the DriveSpace window.

To Compress or Uncompress a Disk Drive

To compress or uncompress the data on a disk drive, follow these steps:

1. Select Start ➤ Programs ➤ Accessories ➤ System Tools ➤ DriveSpace. The DriveSpace window will be displayed.

2. Select the drive you want to compress, or uncompress, by selecting its name from the Drives on this computer list.

3. Select Drive ➤ Compress (or Uncompress). The Compress a Drive dialog box will be displayed.

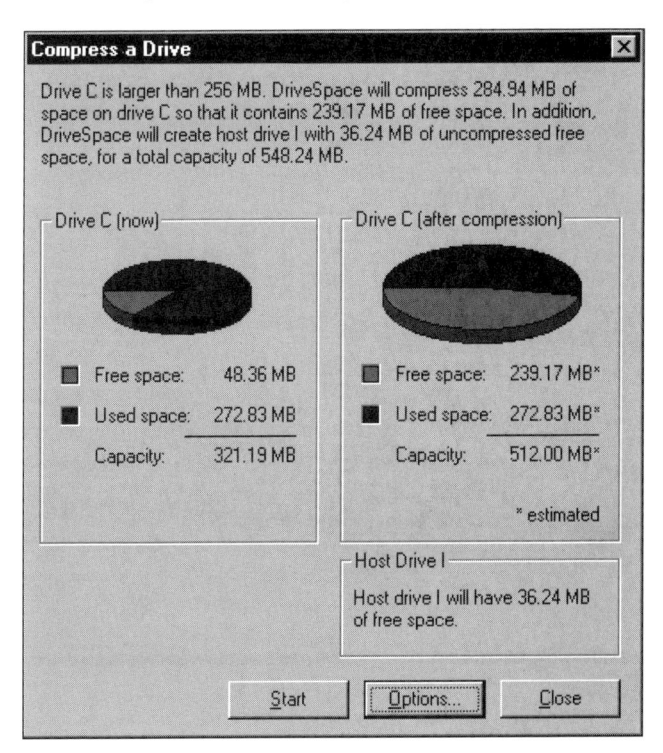

Compress a Drive

Drive C is larger than 256 MB. DriveSpace will compress 284.94 MB of space on drive C so that it contains 239.17 MB of free space. In addition, DriveSpace will create host drive I with 36.24 MB of uncompressed free space, for a total capacity of 548.24 MB.

Drive C (now)
- Free space: 48.36 MB
- Used space: 272.83 MB
- Capacity: 321.19 MB

Drive C (after compression)
- Free space: 239.17 MB*
- Used space: 272.83 MB*
- Capacity: 512.00 MB*

* estimated

Host Drive I
Host drive I will have 36.24 MB of free space.

[Start] [Options...] [Close]

COMMAND AND FEATURE REFERENCE

4. Click on Options to set these specifications:

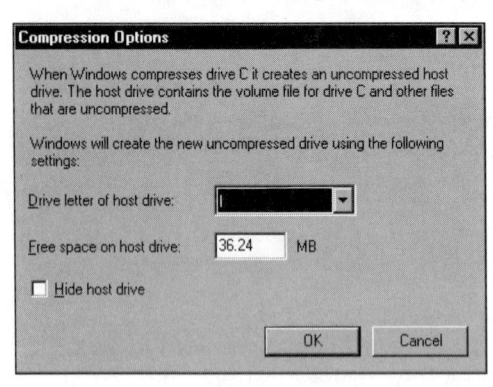

Drive letter of host drive displays a selection of possible letters for the host drive.

Free Space on host drive allows you to specify the amount of free space to set aside.

Hide host drive if checked, will prevent the host drive from being displayed in the system, such as in My Computer or Explorer.

5. Click on Start to begin the compression or uncompression.

6. Click on Back Up Files if you have not already done so, and follow the directions as you are prompted.

7. Click Compress Now (or Uncompress Now). You will be shown the percent of compression as it proceeds.

NOTE: *If a compressed disk drive is more than fifty percent full, it is very likely that you will not be able to uncompress it.*

Editors

SEE: *NotePad*

Electronic Mail (E-Mail)

Electronic mail enables you to send and receive messages to and from other computers on your local network, or by using a modem to remote computers. Windows 95 provides electronic mail services through the Inbox icon on the Desktop, which is part of the Microsoft Exchange. The e-mail recipient can also use Microsoft Exchange or another mail system on your network, such as Microsoft Mail, or be connected to you via the Internet or an information service such as Microsoft Network, Compuserve, or America Online.

To send or receive e-mail, you must do the following:

- Physically connect to other computers either through a network or through a modem and phone lines.

- Install Microsoft Exchange on your computer.

- Set up a Microsoft Exchange profile on your computer and have yourself established on the network post office and/or on the Internet or an information service.

- Place the addresses of e-mail recipients in the Personal Address Book; if an address is not in the address book, it can still be added at the time the message is created, but this is more complicated.

SEE ALSO: *Address Book; Mail and Fax*

COMMAND AND FEATURE REFERENCE

To Send E-Mail

Once you have set up the preliminary steps above, follow the next steps to send e-mail:

1. Double-click on the Inbox icon on the desktop, or select Start ➤ Programs ➤ Microsoft Exhange. The Inbox-Microsoft Exchange dialog box will be displayed.

2. Either select Compose ➤ New Message, or click on the New Message icon in the toolbar. A text entry screen will be displayed where you can address and enter the text of a message.

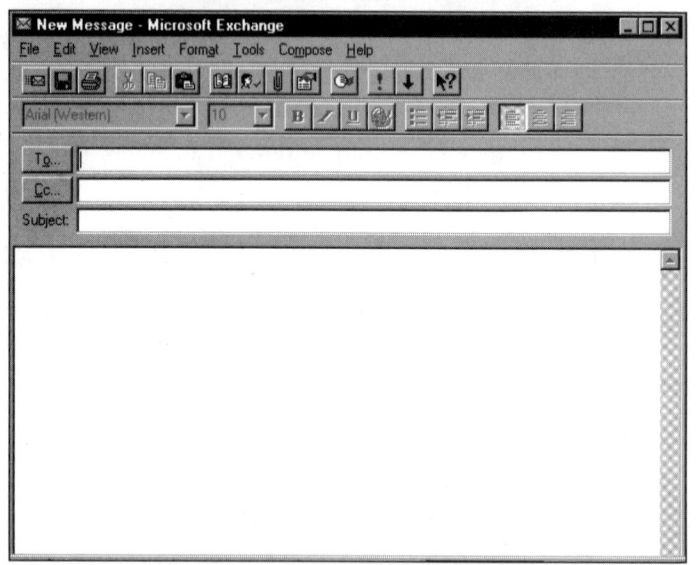

3. Type in the name of the person to whom the e-mail will be sent in the To box, and the names of any other recipients in the Cc box. If you have entered names in the Personal Address Book, you can click on the Address Book icon or the To or Cc buttonsto see a list of people. The names you click on will be automatically added to the message.

ELECTRONIC MAIL (E-MAIL)

4. Type the subject of the message in its box and then either press Tab or click in the text area and type the actual message.

TIP: *When the cursor appears in the text area, you will have access to the features in the formatting toolbar, such as fonts, font size, boldface, etc.*

5. You may find the following toolbar icons useful:

Insert File To attach a file to the message, click on the Insert File tool in the toolbar or select Insert ➤ File. A dialog box will open from which you can select the file you want to attach.

TIP: *You can also attach a message or object by using the Insert menu. Click on Message to attach an e-mail message from your Inbox. Click on Object to attach an object from an existing file or one that you want to create.*

Importance: High, Importance: Low To assign an importance level to the document, click on either the Importance: High or Importance: Low icon.

Read Receipt To receive notification when the message is read, click on the Read Receipt icon.

Properties To view and change the properties of the message, click on the Properties icon. You can set defaults for a standard message by selecting the options you want for Importance, Read Receipt, Delivery Receipt, and whether to save a copy in the Sent folder.

Check Names To check the spelling of a name, or have Windows fill in a name for you, enter a few letters of the name and click

COMMAND AND FEATURE REFERENCE

on the Check Names icon. If the name is close to one in the active Address Book, it will be corrected or completed. If not, you will have a chance to change the spelling yourself, insert a new name into the Address Book, or change the Address Book being searched (from the Show More Names button).

> **TIP:** *You can save e-mail by clicking on the Save icon or selecting File ➤ Save.*

6. When you are finished with the message, select File ➤ Send or click on the Send icon. You will be returned to the Microsoft Exchange dialog box.

> **NOTE:** *When the message is sent, a small envelope will appear—eventually—in the recipient's Taskbar, and the message will appear in their Inbox. They will be able to double-click on the icon and see the message the next time they open Microsoft Exchange.*

If the name as you have typed it is not in the Personal Address Book, the Check Names dialog box will be displayed for you to correct, add, or search for the name.

SEE ALSO: Address Book

To Reply to E-Mail

To reply to e-mail sent to you, select the message to which you want to respond, and then click on the Reply to Sender icon. A text entry box with To, Cc, and Subject filled in will be displayed. Add your own reply to the bottom of the message or change the message to be your reply, and then click on the Send icon.

EMBEDDING INFORMATION

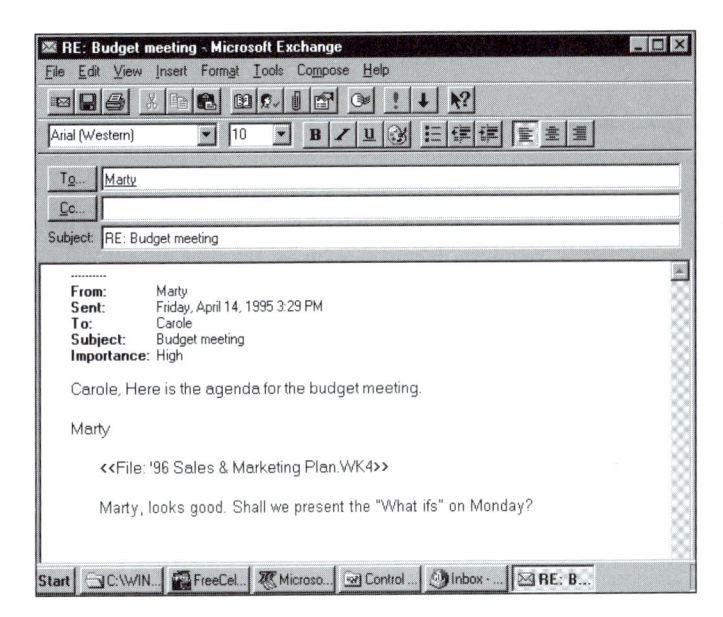

> **NOTE:** To send a reply to the Cc names also, click on the Reply to All icon. To forward a message from one person to another not mentioned in the original e-mail, click on the Forward icon.

SEE ALSO: *Communications on a Network; Mail and Fax; Microsoft Exchange*

E-Mail

SEE: *Electronic Mail*

Embedding Information

SEE: *Linking and Embedding Information*

COMMAND AND FEATURE REFERENCE

Event

An event is an action that your computer can sense, and which occurs as a result of either some action performed by you or by a program. Examples of events are typing an alphabetic key in a numeric field, trying to drag a file some place it can't be moved or copied, sensing your printer has run out of paper, and receiving e-mail. You may want to be alerted about some events. If you have a sound card in your computer, you can attach sounds to events and have the sounds played when the event occurs. The Sounds Control Panel controls the assignment of sounds to events.

SEE ALSO: *Sounds Control Panel; Sound Recorder*

Exchange

SEE: *Microsoft Exchange*

Exiting

SEE: *Closing Files or Windows*

Explorer

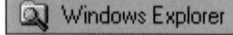

Windows Explorer

Explorer has replaced the File Manager in Windows 95. With it, you can "explore" your disks, folders, and files, performing such tasks as copying, moving, renaming, deleting, formatting, and so on. To access Explorer, select Start ➤ Programs ➤ Windows Explorer. You may want to create a shortcut for it on the Desktop, or in the Start menu itself, since it is used so often.

TIP: *To create a shortcut for Explorer, open either Explorer or My Computer, locate the \Windows folder, and then locate the Explorer.exe file. To create a shortcut on the Start menu itself, or on the Desktop, drag the Explorer.exe file to the Start button or to the Desktop. In either case, a shortcut will be created while leaving the file in its original place.*

The Explorer Window

If you place the pointer on any button in the toolbar (Select View ➤ Toolbar), a small popup label will tell you what it is. The following icons as described in *Folder Window* are available in Explorer:

TIP: *In the Detail view, the column sizes can be changed by dragging the column break. You can also sort the Detail view by clicking on a column heading. It acts as a toggle switch: the first time you click, you'll see an ascending sort; the second time, a descending sort will be displayed.*

NOTE: *The Status Bar is available from the View menu. It explains the menu items when the pointer is placed on an option, or an icon when the pointer presses on one. It also displays status messages about your actions and lists data related to disk storage space, such as the number of items in a folder, and the occupied and free disk space.*

SEE ALSO: *Folder Window; Mapping Network Drives*

COMMAND AND FEATURE REFERENCE

Finding a File or Folder with Explorer

When you open Explorer, the Exploring window is displayed. On the left, you can see all the disks and folders available on your computer. On the right, you can see the contents of the disk or folder you selected on the left. Follow these steps to find the file or folder you want:

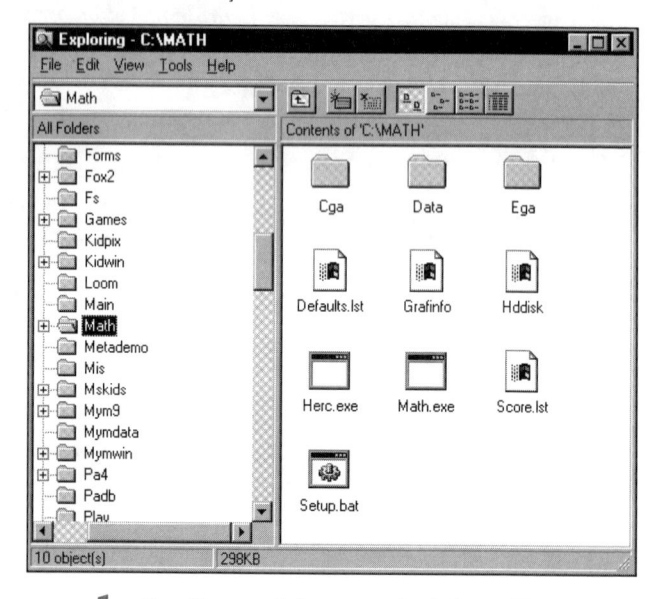

1. Scroll up and down on the left scrollbar. On the left, you can see all the disks on your computer plus those that are shared on your network, and all the folders within each disk. On the right, you will see all the folders and files within the selected disk or folder.

2. Click on a disk or folder on the left to see its contents displayed on the right.

TIP: A plus sign next to a disk or folder indicates that more folders are contained within it. Click on the plus sign to see the additional folders displayed on the left. If you click on the minus sign, the folders contained within will be removed from the screen display.

3. Once you have found the file or folder, double-click on it to open it.

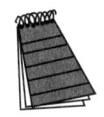

NOTE: *One of the beauties of Explorer is the ability to drag a file or a folder from the right pane to any object in the left pane. If you do this within the same disk drive, you will* move *the object you are dragging to the new location. If you press Ctrl while dragging or you drag to an object outside the current disk, you will* copy *the object you are dragging.*

TIP: *If you click the right mouse button on a file, a popup menu that duplicates many functions in the File and Edit menus will open. This popup menu gives you the ability to open the file, send a copy to a fax or another disk, cut or copy it, create a shortcut for it, delete or rename it, or display the Properties dialog box for it. Clicking the right mouse button on a folder will give the same options plus Explore (which displays its contents on the right), Find (which opens the Find dialog box), and Sharing (which sets parameters for allowing the folder to be shared). Clicking on a disk icon with the right mouse button will also allow you to format a disk.*

Extensions on File Names

SEE: *Files; Naming Files and Folders*

Faxing

Microsoft Fax is used to send and receive faxes to and from other computers or fax machines. You can send a fax in two ways: by "printing" a document to

COMMAND AND FEATURE REFERENCE

the fax instead of a printer, or by using the fax feature in Microsoft Exchange to send a message there.

NOTE: *In order to use the fax feature, you must have a fax modem on one of the computers on your network, and recipients of any messages must also be listed in your Microsoft Exchange or in another mail system connected to your workgroup network. They must, of course, have either a fax machine or a computer with Windows 95.*

Setting Up Your Fax

To set the default settings for your fax from the Inbox–Microsoft Exchange dialog box, follow these steps:

1. Double-click on the Inbox icon, or select Start ➤ Programs ➤ Microsoft Exchange.

2. Next select Tools ➤ Microsoft Fax Tools. A submenu will present four options. Select Options. The Microsoft Fax Properties dialog box will be displayed with four tabs: the Message tab, the Dialing tab, the Modem tab, and the User tab. When you have set the information in the font tabs as you want them, click OK.

Message Tab

The message tab sets defaults for all fax messages. It contains these options:

Time to send determines when the fax will be sent. It can be As soon as possible, Discount rates (click on Set to set the times when discount rates begin and end), or a Specific time (which you set by clicking the up and down arrows).

Message format determines if the message being sent to another person is able to be edited. You can send a message that is Editable (this is only possible for recipients who also have Microsoft Fax), Editable

FAXING

only (this would send only a message that can be edited—if the recipient does not have Microsoft Fax, they will not receive the message), or Not Editable (only a noneditable bitmap image will be sent).

Paper allows you to set the paper specifications: Paper size, Portrait or Landscape Orientation, and Image quality—you can choose between Fine (200dpi), Draft (200x100dpi), 300dpi, and Best Available.

Default Cover Page determines whether a cover page is sent at all, and if so, what kind it is. Some cover pages available include: Confidential, For your information, General purpose, Generic, or Urgent! If you prefer to create your own cover page, click on New. If you want to view or change a cover page listed, click on Open. If you want to search for one, click on Browse.

Let me change the subject line of new faxes I receive allows you to change the subject line so that you may remember it better.

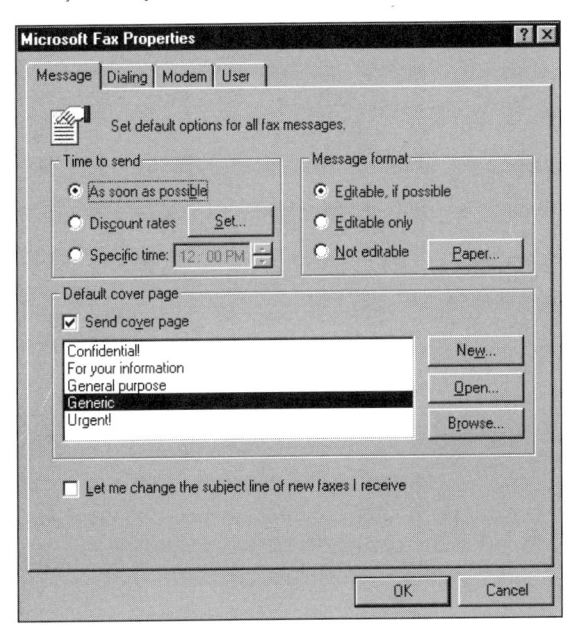

COMMAND AND FEATURE REFERENCE

TIP: *To create your own cover page, select Start ➤ Programs ➤ Accessories ➤ Fax ➤ Cover Page Editor. The Cover Page Editor window will be displayed. You can enter text, graphics, and even database fields to create your own cover page.*

Dialing Tab

The Dialing tab specifies how fax numbers are dialed. It contains these options:

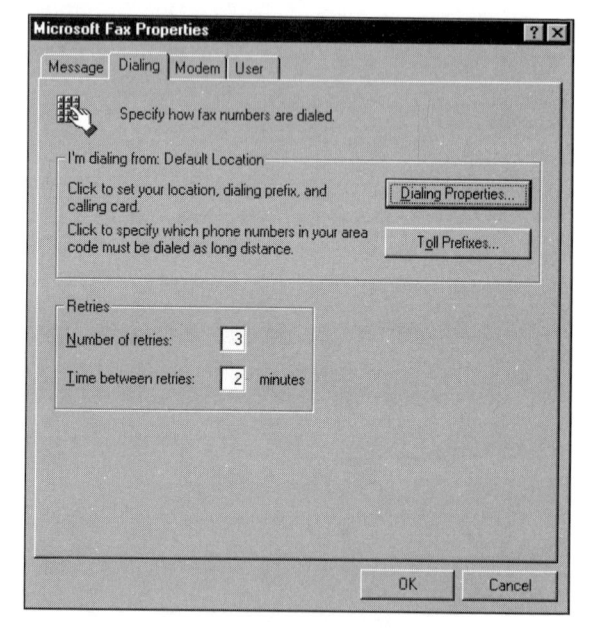

Dialing Properties sets the default location, area code, country, and specific dialing instructions. It specifies whether to dial another number to get an outside line or to dial long distance, whether to use a calling card, when to first disable call waiting, and whether the phone uses Tone or Pulse dialing.

Toll Prefixes identifies phone number prefixes that are inside the default area code, but which must have the area code dialed first.

Retries specifies how many times a number is to be retried and how long to wait between retries before redialing.

TIP: *Common codes for disabling call waiting are *70 and *80.*

Modem Tab

The Modem tab lets you select or install the modem for sending faxes.

User Tab

The User tab records information about you. It identifies your full name, country, fax number, company name and address, title, department, office location, and home and office telephone numbers. Any information filled in will be used in the cover pages of the fax.

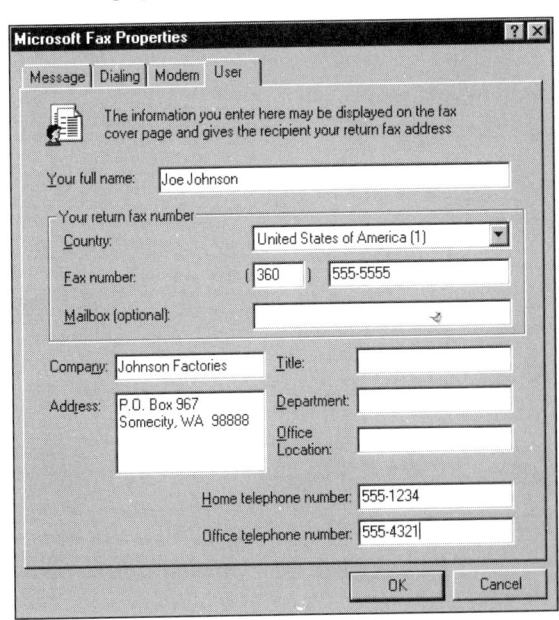

COMMAND AND FEATURE REFERENCE

> **SEE ALSO:** Modems

Retrieving a Remote Fax

You can call a remote computer or fax machine to retrieve a specific document or all the documents available. When the documents are retrieved, they will be placed in your Inbox.

Follow these steps:

1. From the Inbox–Microsoft Exchange dialog box, select Tools ➤ Microsoft Fax Tool ➤ Request a Fax. (You can also select Start ➤ Programs ➤ Accessories ➤ Fax ➤ Request a Fax. The Request a Fax dialog box will be displayed.)

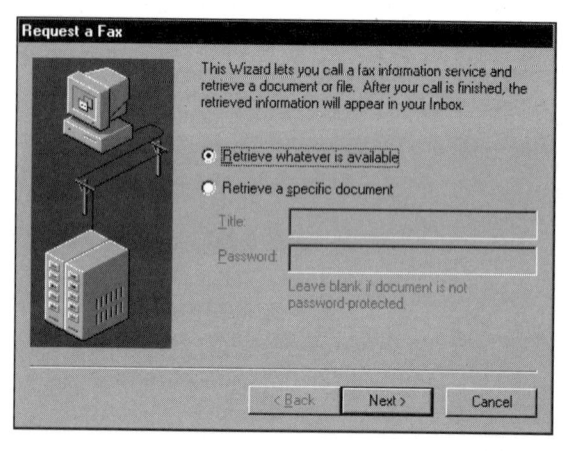

2. To retrieve all faxes stored at the remote site, click on Retrieve whatever is available. To retrieve a specific document, click on Retrieve a specific document, and then type the title of the document and its password, if there is one. Click on Next.

3. Type in the name to whom the retrieved fax will be routed in the To box. Click on Add to place the name in the Send request to box. You may place more than one name there. If you need to retrieve a name from the Address Book, click on that button, select a name, and then click on Add.

Verify the country, and type in the fax number. Click on Next.

4. To specify when you want to call, select from As soon as possible, When phone rates are discounted, or A specific time. Click on Next.

5. Click on Finish to complete the request.

Composing a New Fax

There are three ways to create a fax:

- Select Start ➤ Programs ➤ Accessories ➤ Fax ➤ Compose New Fax. The Compose New Fax wizard will guide you through creating and sending a fax.

- Click on the Inbox icon on the Desktop and when the Inbox–Microsoft Exchange dialog box is displayed, select Compose ➤ New Fax. The Compose New Fax Wizard will be displayed again.

- Click on a file with the right mouse button, and from the popup menu, select Send To ➤ Fax Recipient. You'll see the Compose New Fax Wizard again.

Follow these steps to compose a new fax message:

1. Bring up the Compose New Fax dialog box using one of the techniques discussed above.

2. Verify or change the dialing properties by clicking on Dialing Properties. If you are not using a portable computer, you can click on I'm not using a portable computer, so don't show this to me again. Click on Next.

3. Complete the information on the person to whom you want to send the fax. Type in a name, country, fax number, and a recipient list, if applicable. Since you can't type into the Recipient list

COMMAND AND FEATURE REFERENCE

directly, place the name in the To field and click on Add to List, or select a name from the Address Book. Click on Dial area code if necessary. Click on Next.

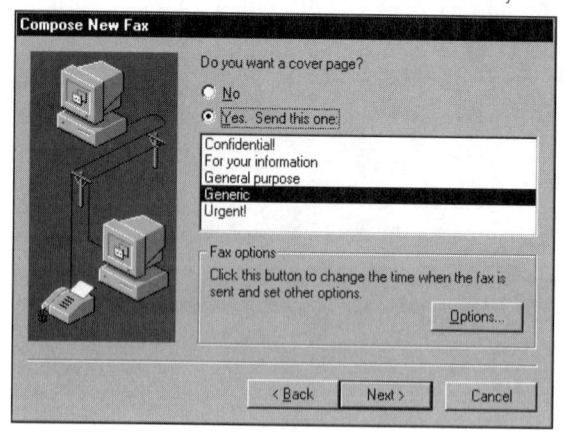

4. Select whether to send a cover page, and what type. Click on Options to specify when to send the fax, whether it is to be editable, and the cover page type. Also, if you want your fax to be secured, click on Security and select the appropriate options. Click OK to return to the Compose New Fax dialog box. Click on Next.

5. Type the subject of the fax, and under Note, type the contents. Place a check mark in the check box if you want the Note contents to be part of the cover page. Click on Next.

6. If you want to send a file with the fax, click on Add File, and with the Open a File to Attach dialog box, search for the file you want to attach and click on Open. The name will appear in the Files to send text box. Click on Next.

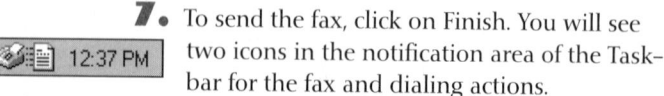

7. To send the fax, click on Finish. You will see two icons in the notification area of the Taskbar for the fax and dialing actions.

TIP: *To list the faxes that are scheduled to be sent, select Tools ➤ Microsoft Fax Tools ➤ Show Outgoing Faxes. The Outgoing Faxes dialog box will be displayed, showing the Sender, Subject, Size, Recipients, and Time to Send.*

NOTE: *From the Inbox-Microsoft Exchange dialog box, you can request and set up security precautions to protect faxes by selecting Tools ➤ Microsoft Fax Tools ➤ Advanced Security. This enables you to establish a key set for sending and receiving key-encrypted faxes.*

SEE ALSO: Electronic Mail; Microsoft Exchange

Files

SEE: Accessing Disks, Folders, and Files; Associating Files; Defragmenting a Disk; Explorer; Folders (Directories); Naming Files and Folders; Printing; Sharing Files

File Manager

SEE: Explorer

File Names

SEE: Naming Files and Folders

File Types

File types are determined by their extensions, which identify the program that created them. For example, a .doc file may be a Word file type; an .xls, an Excel file type; .zip, a pkzip file type, and so on.

SEE ALSO: Associating Files

COMMAND AND FEATURE REFERENCE

Finding Computers

To find a computer on your network, Use Network Neighborhood or the Find command in either the Start menu or Explorer.

Using Find to Locate a Computer

To locate a computer on your network using the Find command in either the Start menu or Explorer, follow these steps:

1. Either select Start ➤ Find ➤ Computer, or in Explorer, select Tools ➤ Find ➤ Computer. The Find Computer dialog box will be displayed.

2. Enter the computer name or select it from a list of previous searches by clicking on the Named down-arrow.

3. Select Find Now to activate the search. Stop will terminate the search, and New Search will allow you to enter the criteria for a new computer search.

SEE ALSO: *Explorer; Network Neighborhood*

Finding Files and Folders

To find a file or folder, you can either use My Computer or Explorer to scan the disks yourself, or you can use the Find command to have Windows 95 conduct the search for you.

To use the Find command, follow these steps:

1. Select Start ➤ Find ➤ Files or Folders, or in Explorer, select Tools ➤ Find ➤ Files or Folders.

FINDING FILES AND FOLDERS

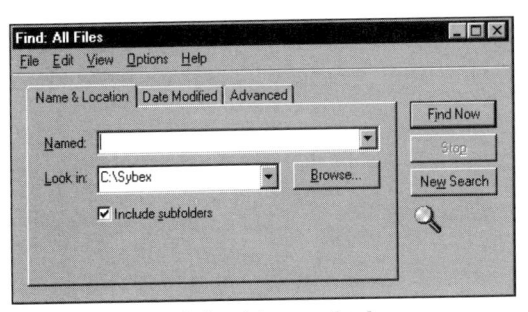

2. In the Find: All Files dialog box, you will see three tabs: the Name and Location tab, the Date Modified tab, and the Advanced tab.

Name & Location Tab

The Name & Location tab contains the following options:

Named shows the name of the file or folder you're searching for. If you click on the down arrow, you will see the most recent searches you have performed.

Look in directs Windows 95 to search a specific path for the file or folder. If you click on the down arrow, you will see a list of the disks and folders on your computer.

Browse lets you look through the available disks and folders to find the one you want to search.

Include subfolders searches sublevels of folders as well as the level you specified.

Date Modified Tab

The Date Modified tab contains the following options:

All files searches all files in the specified path for the desired file or folder.

Find all files created or modified restricts the search to a given date between two specified dates during the previous number of months, or during the previous number of days (the default is about the last 3 months).

COMMAND AND FEATURE REFERENCE

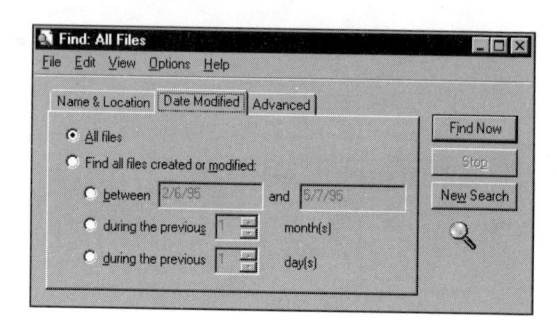

Advanced Tab

The Advanced Tab contains the following options:

Of type searches for a specific type of file. If you click the down arrow, you will see a list of registered types.

Containing text specifies a string of text contained in a file or folder.

Size is retricts the search for files to At Least or At Most (selected by the first down arrow) the number of kilobytes specified (typed or entered using the arrow keys).

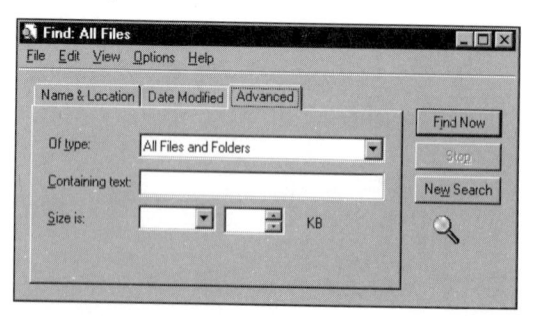

3. Enter the Find specifications you want, and then select one of the following commands:

- **Find Now** activates the search.
- **Stop** terminates the search.
- **New Search** allows you to enter new search criteria.

FOLDERS (DIRECTORIES)

You can save a particular search, including its parameters, by choosing File ➤ Save Search. You can also save the results of a search by selecting Options ➤ Save Results. To make a search case-sensitive, select Options ➤ Case Sensitive.

Folders (Directories)

In Windows 95, folders are used to store files and other folders, just as directories did in previous versions of Windows. You can identify a folder by its unique icon. Folders can be handled much like files with the exception that they cannot be associated with an application.

Most of the functions you will need to perform with folders can be done with either Explorer, My Computer, or the right mouse button. The following table shows you your options.

	Explorer	My Computer	Right Mouse Button
Close	x	x	
Copy, Cut, Paste	x	x	x
Create a new folder	x	x	
Create a shortcut	x	x	x
Delete	x	x	x
Find	x	x	x
Open	x	x	x
Properties	x	x	x
Rename	x	x	x
Send to another computer, disk, or fax	x	x	x
Share	x	x	x
Undo previous folder action	x	x	

COMMAND AND FEATURE REFERENCE

> **NOTE:** A menu option may be unavailable depending on the specific folder selected and which Windows 95 program you are using.

Folder Window

The folder window is the primary window used in Windows 95. Since most Windows 95 functions—such as Explorer, MyBriefcase, Exchange, and Recycle Bin—can be thought of as operating out of a folder, they use the folder window with a similar set of menus and tools.

Folder Menus

Generally, the File, Edit, and View menus for folders contain the same options, regardless of which program they are in. There may be other menus for serving a specific program, such as Tools in Explorer, but the three will contain common options with these exceptions:

- For some options, an object must be selected before the options are available.

- The type of object selected can cause different options to be presented.

For these reasons, you may not see all of these options on a given menu, and there may be options not listed here. However, the standard folder menus and their most likely options are as follows:

File Menu

The File menu displays basic file management options. It allows you to **Open** a folder or file; **Explore** the contents of a selected computer, disk, or folder; **Find** a file or folder; **Print** a file or get

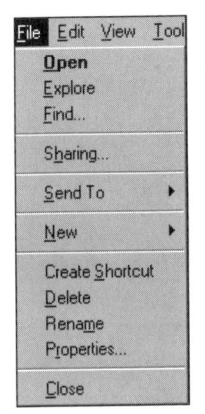

FOLDER WINDOW

a **Quick View** of the contents of a file (not shown on the menu unless it is available); set parameters for **Sharing** the folder with other users; use **Send To** to move the file to a floppy disk, the Microsoft Exchange, My Briefcase, or another destination; create a **New** folder or shortcut; use **Create Shortcut** to make a shortcut of the file or folder; **Delete** or **Rename** the file or folder; display the file's **Properties**; or **Close** it.

Edit Menu

The Edit menu allows you to work with the contents of a folder or file. You can **Undo** the previous actions; **Cut, Copy,** and **Paste** folders or files (essentially copy or move one); **Paste Shortcut** within a folder, **Select All** files and folders; or use **Invert Selection** to select all files except those already selected, which become deselected.

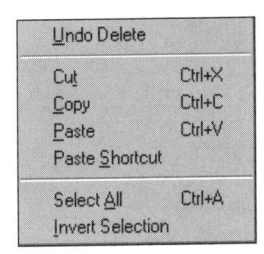

View Menu

The View menu allows you to change the window to include, or not include, a **Toolbar** and/or a **Status Bar**. You can choose how the files and folders are displayed: with **Large Icons** or **Small Icons**, in a **List**, or with **Details** describing the size and type of a file, and the date modified. You can use **Arrange Icons** to sort the icons by name, type of file or folder, size, or date created or last modified. You can also **Line Up Icons** into neatly arranged columns and rows. **Refresh** causes your screen to be redisplayed. **Options** displays a dialog box with two tabs that allow

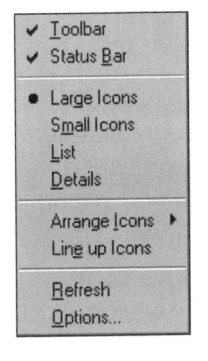

COMMAND AND FEATURE REFERENCE

you to set defaults on which file types are to be displayed (you can hide types of files; display certain other information, including which file types are registered; and add, edit, or delete file types from the list.

Help Menu

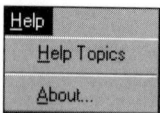

The Help menu provides the Help files and windows for the specific Windows 95 program you are in.

SEE ALSO: *Folders (Directories); Help System; Registry*

Folder Toolbar

A typical folder toolbar contains these buttons:

Go to a different folder drop-down list box lists the disks and top-level folders on your computer. When you select from this list box, the contents of the folder or disk will be shown in the right pane. If you don't have this drop-down list box, select View ➤ Toolbar.

Up One Level redisplays the right side of the Explorer up one level from where it was.

Map Network Drive enables you to map (or identify) a disk on another computer on your network to a drive on your computer. For example, drive C on another computer on your network is mapped to (becomes) drive E on your computer (you already have drives C and D in this case). This allows an application to directly access the remote drive by accessing drive E.

Disconnect Net Drive removes the mapped identification of a network drive on your computer, although the physical network connection remains.

FOLDER WINDOW

Cut enables you to move the contents of a file or folder. It places the contents in the Clipboard until you Paste them into another file.

Copy duplicates a file or folder, placing its contents in the Clipboard so they can be pasted into another file or folder.

Paste copies the contents of the clipboard into a new file, labeled Copy of *file name*. A destination folder must already be created and selected in order for a copy of a folder to be pasted.

Undo causes the previous action to be cancelled. The label changes depending on what you did last—for example, Undo Delete or Undo Copy.

Delete deletes the selected file or folder, placing it in the Recycle Bin.

Properties displays the Properties dialog box for the selected disk, file, or folder.

Large Icons causes the right-hand side of Explorer to display larger-sized icons representing the contents of the selected folder or disk.

Small Icons causes the right-hand side of Explorer to display smaller-sized icons in a horizontal, columnar list representing the contents of the selected folder or disk.

List causes the right-hand side of Explorer to display the contents as seen in Small Icons, except in a vertical rather than horizontal orientation.

Details causes the right-hand side of Explorer to display the contents in a detailed list with additional information about the file size, file type, and modification date.

SEE ALSO: *Mapping Network Drives*

COMMAND AND FEATURE REFERENCE

Fonts

Fonts are the different styles of type used in displaying and printing text. Windows 95 maintains a library of fonts that is used by all the applications that run under it. You can access this library by double-clicking on the Fonts folder in My Computer or Explorer.

Fonts Folder

The Fonts folder, opened by selecting Start ➤ Settings ➤ Control Panel and double-clicking on the Fonts icon, displays all of the fonts you have installed on your computer. There are two types of fonts predominately used with windows applications: TrueType fonts (represented by the pair of "T"s in the icon) and Adobe fonts (represented by the "A" in the icon). If you have acquired some new fonts, you can add them to those that come with Windows 95 by choosing File ➤ Install New Font. In the Add Fonts dialog box, you can find out which fonts are available, and choose those you want to install.

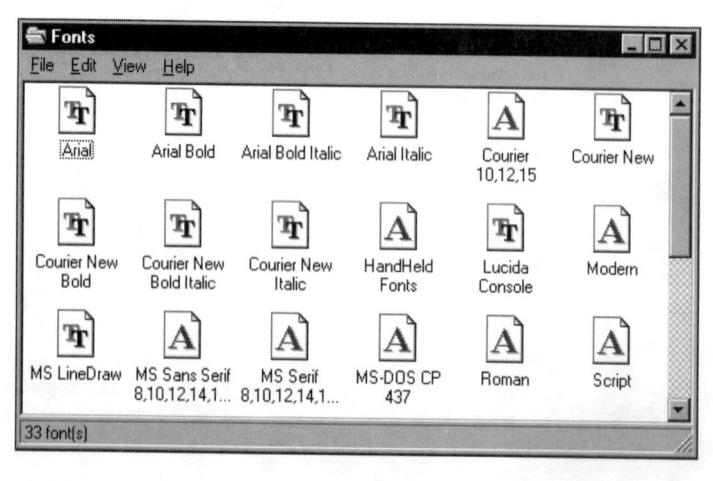

In addition to the standard Large Icons, List, and Details views found in the View menu of the Fonts window, there is a unique and quite useful view for fonts called List Fonts by Similarity. This shows the fonts that are reasonably alike, which can be very handy if you know approximately how the the font should look and want to look at variations. Another useful and unique option in the View menu is Hide Variations. If you have a lot of fonts, this option helps reduce the selection to just the main fonts by hiding bold, italics, and so on.

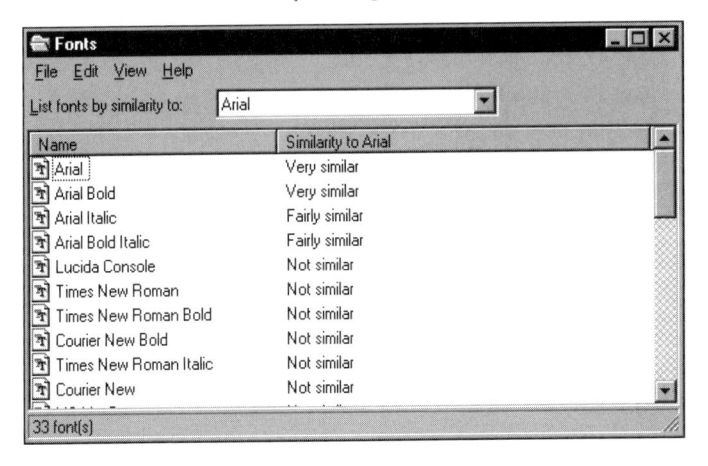

Name	Similarity to Arial
Arial	Very similar
Arial Bold	Very similar
Arial Italic	Fairly similar
Arial Bold Italic	Fairly similar
Lucida Console	Not similar
Times New Roman	Not similar
Times New Roman Bold	Not similar
Courier New Bold	Not similar
Times New Roman Italic	Not similar
Courier New	Not similar

33 font(s)

Fonts Used in Windows 95

The defaults for the size and type of fonts used in the Windows 95 windows and dialog boxes are set in the Display Properties dialog box. You can vary the font and size for text objects, and in menus, message boxes, and title bars. To get this dialog box, right-click on the Desktop and choose Properties from the popup menu, or select Start ➤ Settings ➤ Control Panel, and then double-click on Display. Two tabs, Appearance and Settings, allow you to control two types of fonts: the size of fonts on the screen and the size and typeface of fonts for selected objects on the screen.

COMMAND AND FEATURE REFERENCE

To control the size of fonts on the screen, select the Settings tab.

To change the fonts displayed on the screen for selected items, choose the Appearance tab.

SEE ALSO: *Display Control Panel*

Formatting Disks

Disks must be formatted before they can be used the first time. Formatting a *used* disk erases all the information on it, so it must be used with extreme care.

To format a disk, follow these steps:

1. From My Computer, select the disk drive containing the disk you want to format and then select File ➤ Format. You can also click the right mouse button on the disk drive in My Computer or Explorer.

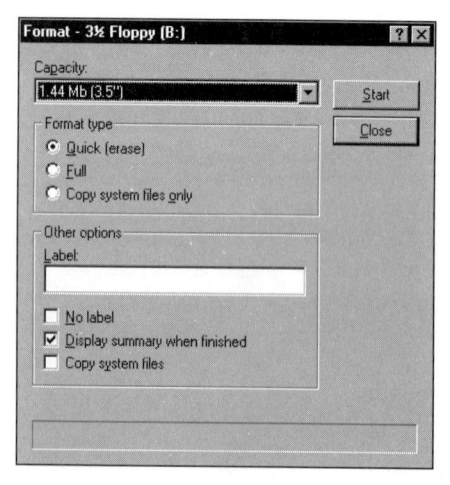

2. Enter the following specifications:

- **Capacity** specifies the maximum data held on the disk.

- **Format Type** controls the type of formatting that will be done. Choose Quick (erase) if the disk to be formatted contains no bad sectors. Choose Full to have Windows check for bad sectors and attempt to repair them. Choose Copy system files only to produce a bootable disk which you can use to boot the system using the specified drive (the disk will not be formatted; only system files will be copied to the disk).

- **Label** allows you to place a name on a disk so it can be more easily identified.

- **No Label** places no name on the disk and removes any that was previously there.

- **Display summary when finished** causes a report to be displayed on the screen disclosing the space available on the disk and any bad sectors.

- **Copy system files** copies system files to the disk after formatting so that it can be used for booting.

3. Click on Start to begin the formatting. Clicking on Close will close the dialog box without saving the specifications you have made.

Games

Four games are provided with Windows 95: FreeCell, Hearts, Minesweeper, and Solitaire. They are provided both on the Windows 95 CD-ROM and floppy disk, but you must specifically install them. Hearts can be played over the network with other players. To get to the games, select Start ➤ Programs ➤ Accessories ➤ Games, and then click on the game you want.

Click on Help for instructions on how to play.

Hardware

SEE: *Add New Hardware; Profiles*

COMMAND AND FEATURE REFERENCE

Help System

Windows 95 has an extensive Help system to provide you with online assistance at any time.

The Help Window

To Use Help, select Start ➤ Help. The Help Topics dialog box will be displayed.

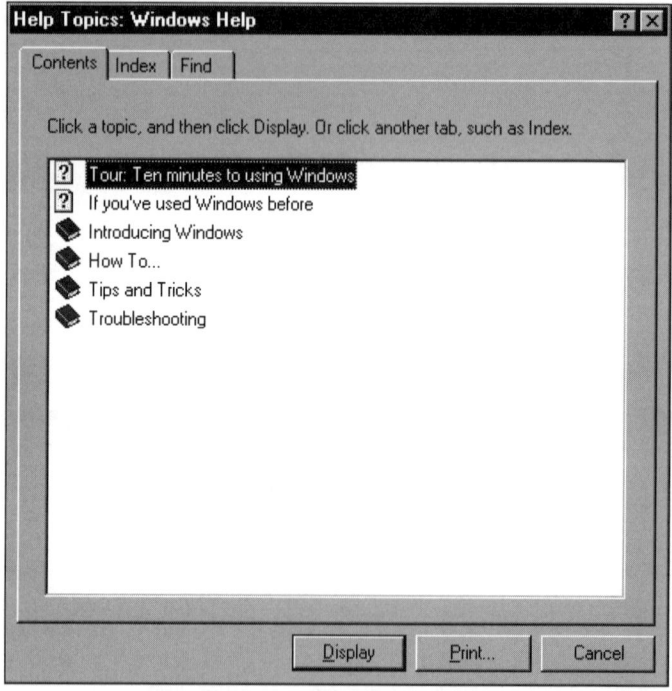

The Help Topics: Windows Help dialog box contains three tabs:

Contents lists the categories that are available in Help for the Help system itself and a general overview of Windows 95. Each category is a folder containing subjects or other categories. If you double-click on a folder, you will see the subjects contained within the one category. If you double-click on a subject, you will see the Help information for that subject.

Index lists all the subjects in the Help system. When you click on the Index tab, you will see a dialog box containing a text box and a display box. Click on the first and type the first few letters of the word you're looking for. The list display box will automatically scroll to the subject closest in spelling to what you have typed. Or you can scroll to it yourself by using the vertical scroll bars on the right of the display box. When you get to the subject you want, double-click on it or select it and click on Display.

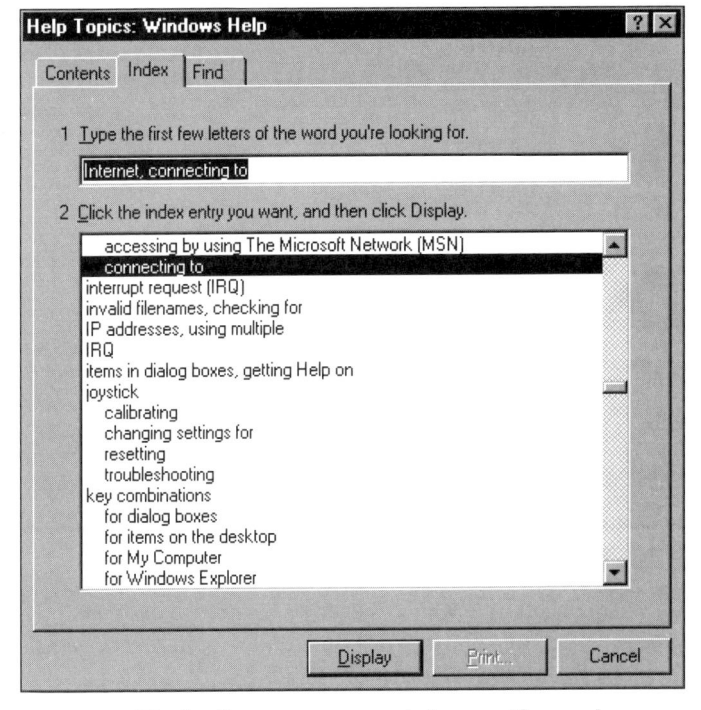

Find allows you to search for specific words or phrases contained within a Help topic. To do this,

COMMAND AND FEATURE REFERENCE

Windows 95 must create a database containing words used throughout the Help system. When you click on the Find tab, the Find Setup Wizard will be displayed. You can choose between Minimize database size, Maximize search capabilities, or Customize search capabilities. The minimum database choice will be faster, although the custom choice will be smaller in size. The Maximize search capability will take the longest to perform. When the database is created, you can then use the Find tab to search for the specific word or phrase you want.

NOTE: *Context-sensitive help is also available within certain dialog boxes. When it is available, you will see a special Help icon. Click on the Help icon and then click on another object in the dialog box to get an explanation of it.*

TIP: *Help menus within applications provide help on the specific application. Select the Help menu to see what help is available.*

TIP: *When a Help topic is displayed, you may see a shortcut icon which, when clicked, allows you to quickly see the specific dialog box or window being discussed in Help. The Help window will remain on top, and can be closed when you want to see the window or dialog box beneath it.*

> 1 Click here to display Accessibility properties.

HyperTerminal

HyperTerminal is used to connect to another computer, perhaps with a different operating system such as UNIX, or to an information service such CompuServe or bulletin boards. You can use this type of connection to download or transfer files.

Creating a New HyperTerminal Connection

To create the phone numbers and specifics for initiating a HyperTerminal connection, follow these steps:

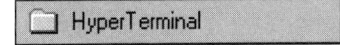

1. Select Start ➤ Programs ➤ Accessories ➤ HyperTerminal. The HyperTerminal folder will be opened.

2. Double-click on Hypertrm.exe to load the program. The Connection Description dialog box will be displayed.

3. Enter a name for the connection, and then choose an icon. Click OK.

4. In the Phone Number dialog box, verify the Country code and Area code, type in the telephone number, and verify the modem type. Click OK. The Connect dialog box will be displayed.

5. Verify the phone number. If it is incorrect, click Modify to change it. To verify the dialing properties, click on Dialing Properties. When you are ready to dial, click on Dial. You will be connected to the computer and a named window for the connection will be displayed. If you do not want to dial right now, click Cancel and the named window for the connection will be displayed.

HyperTerminal Window

The HyperTeminal window can be used to perform a number of functions, such as calling a remote computer, creating a new connection, downloading or transferring files, and changing modem settings or file transfer protocols. These tasks can be done through the menus or with the toolbar.

The toolbar contains the following icons:

New creates a new connection.

COMMAND AND FEATURE REFERENCE

Open opens an existing HyperTerminal Connection folder.

Connect displays the Connect dialog box so that the number can be dialed. Click on Dial to proceed with the connection.

Disconnect terminates the connection.

Send sends a file to a remote computer. You can select or change the protocol used during the transmission of a file using the drop-down list.

Receive allows you to specify the name of a folder where a file is to be received from a remote computer. You select the protocol of the sending computer from a list.

Properties presents two tabs where you can modify information about this HyperTerminal connection. These tabs present options for modifying phone number and terminal settings information. The options will differ depending on the connection.

The menus and their unique options are as follows (common options are explained in *Folder Window*):

File provides a **New Connection** option which opens the Connection Description dialog box so that you can create a new connection.

Edit provides two unique options. **Copy** copies the selected contents of the terminal window to the Clipboard. **Paste to Host** sends the contents of the Clipboard to the remote computer's terminal window.

Call allows you to **Connect** to or **Disconnect** from a remote computer.

Transfer provides the means to **Send** or **Receive** a file, set up a file name to **Capture Text**, **Send**

Text to Printer, or **Capture** to send a text file directly to the printer.

Inbox

Inbox is both the name of a folder that contains your incoming files and messages from other computers and a shortcut for Microsoft Exchange. Double-clicking on the Inbox icon is the primary way to enter Microsoft Exchange.

NOTE: *If you do not have an Inbox icon on your Desktop, you have not yet installed Microsoft Exchange on your computer.*

SEE ALSO: *Add/Remove Programs; Electronic Mail; Faxing; Microsoft Exchange.*

Installing Applications

Applications from floppy disks and CD-ROMs can be installed from the Add/Remove Programs control panel. You can also select Start ➤ Run to directly begin the Install or Setup program.

SEE ALSO: *Add/Remove Programs; Run Option*

Installing Printers

SEE: *Printers Folder (Adding a New Printer)*

COMMAND AND FEATURE REFERENCE

International Characters (Regional Settings)

International characters are set in the Regional Settings control panel. You can set defaults for language; and formatting for numbers, currency, time and date. If you only need one or two international characters, you may find them in one of the fonts available in the Character Map. In this case, you would select the individual characters to insert into your own documents.

SEE ALSO: *Character Map; Currency Format; Date/Time Settings; Regional Settings Control Panel*

Internet

The Internet is a network made up of information services and communications channels from hundreds of business firms, universities, governments, and other organizations around the world. You can use it to access databases, bulletin boards, and discussion groups, and to send electronic mail or transfer files.

There are two ways you can access the Internet using Windows 95 features:

- Through the Microsoft Network
- Through Dial-Up Networking

Before you can access the Internet you must have a modem or network adapter card. You must also have an account with an Internet access provider or with Microsoft Network, for example. This will provide you with a telephone number to call, a password, an account type (it must be a Point-to-Point

INTERNET

Protocol account, or PPP), certain protocol information, and perhaps some instructions on what to do once you're there!

SEE ALSO: *Network Control Panel*

Accessing the Internet Through Microsoft Network (MSN)

Using Microsoft Network is the simplest way to connect to the Internet, because it requires less setting up and provides more guidance once you are there. You can use the Internet either to send and receive e-mail or to explore a wealth of information and services. Follow these steps to reach the Internet through Microsoft Network.

The Microsoft Network

1. Sign on to Microsoft Network by clicking on the Microsoft Network icon on the desktop.

2. The Microsoft Network screen will be displayed. Click on either E-mail or Categories.

- If you choose Categories, a Categories window containing many topics will be displayed. Choose Internet Center, and then double-click on the choices you want as they are presented to you.

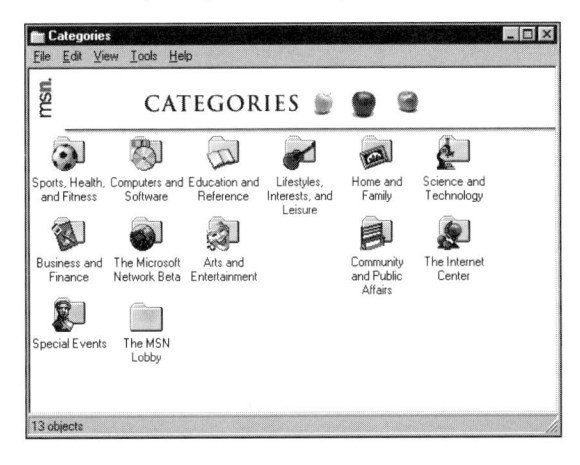

COMMAND AND FEATURE REFERENCE

- If you choose E-mail, Microsoft Exchange will be loaded, and you can proceed as you normally would.

3. Disconnect by selecting File ➤ Sign Off or by clicking on the Close button.

TIP: *If you want to receive Internet mail on MSN, give your correspondents your Internet address, in the format UserID@msn.com.*

NOTE: *You may not be able to write to some of the Internet Newsgroups (bulletin boards). The title bar will contain READ ONLY if you are restricted to reading the information only.*

SEE ALSO: *Electronic Mail*

Accessing the Internet Through Dial-Up Networking

Accessing the Internet through Dial-Up Networking requires substantial setup and manipulation of profiles and properties. However, Microsoft Plus! contains many tools for setting up connections to the Internet and navigating through it. You will find:

Internet Setup Wizard to guide you through setting up and configuring the Microsoft Exchange profiles and network protocols

Internet Control Panel where you can manage and change the Internet properties

Internet Explorer to navigate, browse, and transfer files through the Internet once it is installed and activated

To set up and use the Internet with Dial-Up Networking, follow the instructions that come with Microsoft Plus!

SEE ALSO: *Dial-Up Networking; Microsoft Exchange; Microsoft Network; Networks and Networking*

Interrupting Printing

You may find that you want to interrupt the printing of a document, perhaps to change the type of paper or to print a different set of pages. Follow these steps to stop a print job:

1. Double-click on the Print icon in the TaskBar to display the printer's print queue.

2. After selecting the document, choose Document ➤ Cancel Printing to stop Printing permanently, or Pause Printing to temporarily interrupt printing.

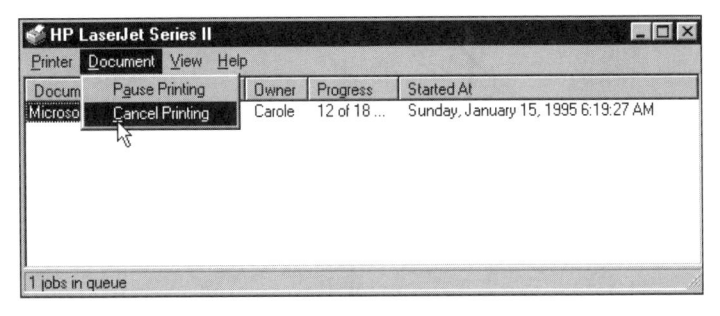

Keyboard Control Panel

The Keyboard control panel allows you to set the defaults for keyboard properties, such as the language displayed and at what speed a key must be pressed to be recognized as a repeat key. Follow these steps to set the keyboard properties:

1. Select Start ➤ Settings ➤ Control Panel, and then double-click on Keyboard. The Keyboard Properties dialog box will be displayed, showing

COMMAND AND FEATURE REFERENCE

three tabs: the Speed tab, the Language tab, and the General tab.

2. Select the options you want from the three tabs and then click OK.

The **Speed** tab contains the following options:

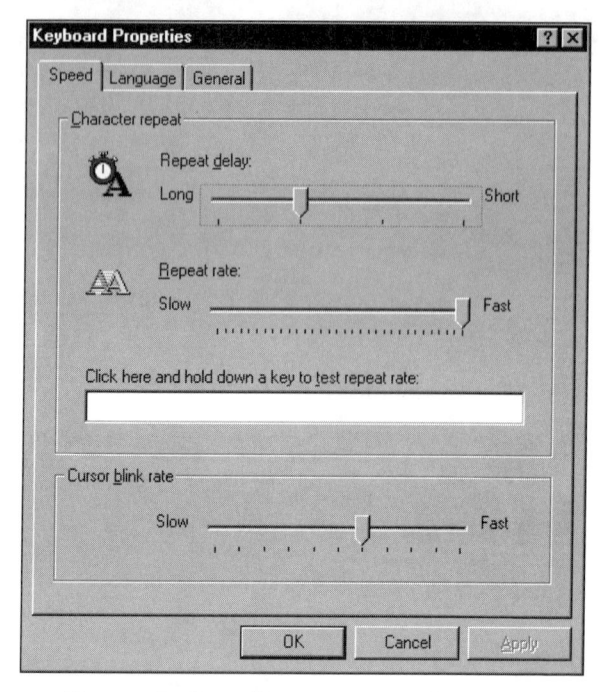

- **Repeat Delay** allows you to set the length of time you must hold down a key before the repeat feature kicks in. Drag the slider between Long and Short to get the time you want.

- **Repeat Rate** sets the characters per second that a character is repeated while a key is held down. Adjust the slider between Slow and Fast to get the repeat rate you want.

- **Click here and hold down a key to test repeat rate** tests the repeat delay and repeat rate speeds that you have chosen.

KEYBOARD CONTROL PANEL

- **Cursor Blink Rate** sets the rate at which the cursor blinks, making the cursor easier to spot in some instances.

The **Language** tab contains the following options:

- **Language and Layout** displays the language and keyboard layout that is loaded into memory when the computer is booted. These are the defaults used in Windows 95. If you double-click on the layout displayed for language or keyboard, the Language Properties dialog box will be displayed where you can select another language layout.

- **Add** allows you to add a language or keyboard layout to the ones loaded into memory when the computer is booted.

- **Properties** allows you to change the keyboard layout default. (For example, for the United States, there are at least three keyboard layouts possible.) This will display the Language Properties dialog box as shown above.

- **Remove** allows you to delete the language or layout default that is currently selected from the list. It will no longer be loaded into memory when you boot the computer.

- **Set as Default with more than one language installed** makes the currently selected language and keyboard layout the default to be used when the computer is started.

- **Switch Languages** allows you to switch between two or more language and layout settings, as listed above. Click on the key combination you want to use to switch the default.

- **Enable indicator on taskbar** allows you to display a language on the right of the taskbar.

When you click on this indicator, you can quickly get a dialog box that allows you to switch language defaults.

The **General** tab contains the following options:

- **Keyboard type** displays the type of physical keyboard you currently have attached to the computer.

- **Change** displays a Select Device dialog box where you can change the keyboard you are using. Select Show compatible devices to list keyboard models that are compatible with your hardware. Select Show all devices to list all keyboard models if yours is not on the list of compatible models. You may also install the keyboard from a disk by clicking on Have Disk.

Language

SEE: *Keyboard Control Panel;Regional Settings Control Panel*

Linking and Embedding Information

Linking and embedding are two ways to insert information or objects from one document or source into another. You can link or embed text, graphics, sound, and video objects. Linked and embedded copies can be inserted in documents created by other programs.

When you link an object, any updates to the original object will be reflected in the linked object. Windows does not make a copy of the original object in the new document—only a link-address, or reference, to it. When you want to make changes to a linked object, you must make the changes to

LINKING AND EMBEDDING INFORMATION

the original; those changes will then be reflected in the linked copy. Windows enables you to do this easily by displaying the menus and toolbars of the program that created it.

When you embed an object, a copy is inserted into the new document, along with all the information it needs to be maintained—for instance, a reference to the program that created it. The embedded copy will be totally separate from the original object. Updates to the original will not be reflected in the embedded copy. When you begin to edit an embedded object, the menus and toolbars of the program that created it will be loaded and made available for you. Again, Windows facilitates this process by allowing you to easily transfer in and out of the editing window.

To Insert Linked or Embedded Information

To link or embed one document into another, follow these steps:

1. Select the information to be embedded or linked into another document.

2. Select Edit ➤ Copy.

3. Bring up the document into which the linked or embedded information will be placed. Click on the location in the document where you want the data to be placed.

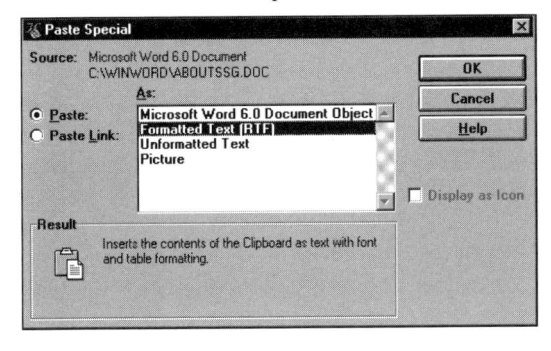

4. Select Edit ➤ Paste Special, and then click on the format that you want to use. If you want to embed the document,

COMMAND AND FEATURE REFERENCE

select Paste from the Paste Special dialog box. The document will be embedded. If you want to link the document, select Paste Link.

To Modify a Linked File

To edit a linked file, you must edit the source, since there is no copy. To do this, double-click on the linked image. This will cause the original object to appear in a special editing window with the toolbars and menus of the original program that created it. When you want to return to the linked file, click outside the linked object. Follow these steps to edit a linked file.

1. Double-click on the linked copy. An editing window will be displayed, and the original object with the toolbars and menus of the program that created it will be loaded.

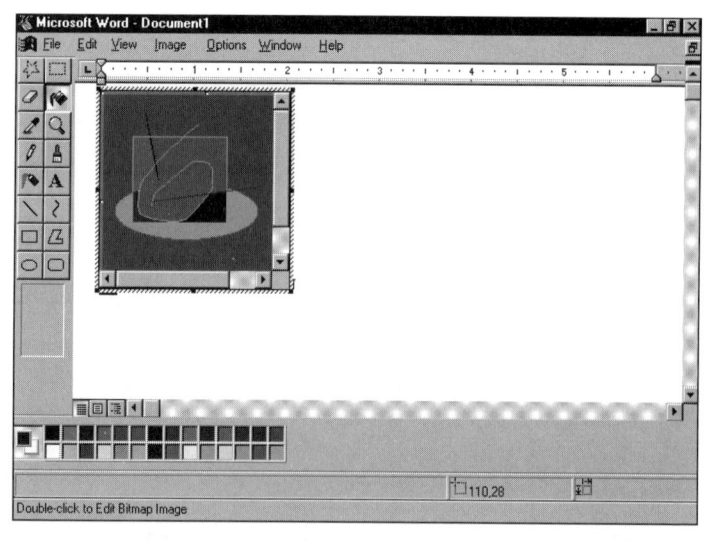

2. Make your changes to the original copy.

3. When you are finished modifying the original, click outside the linked object. You will be returned to the original window with the linked copy, where all the changes will be reflected.

To Modify an Embedded Object

To edit an embedded object, you will use the program that created the object. When you first begin to edit the object, a special editing window will surround it, and the program's menus and tools will be displayed. Follow these steps:

1. Double-click on the embedded object. If it has been produced by another program, that program's menus and toolbars will be displayed.

2. Make the changes you want.

3. When you are finished, click outside the embedded object to close the program that created the object, and return to the original window.

TIP: *Linking and embedding is not supported by all programs. If it is not supported, the Paste Special command will not appear on the Edit menu.*

SEE ALSO: *OLE*

Links to Files (Shortcuts)

SEE: *Shortcuts*

Logging On and Off

SEE: *Profiles; Shut Down*

COMMAND AND FEATURE REFERENCE

Lost File Fragments

SEE: ScanDisk

Mail and Fax

To use Mail and Fax, you must have a modem, network adapter card, or other communications hardware. When you run Windows 95 Setup, you will be asked to indicate whether you intend to use Microsoft Mail, Microsoft Fax, or The Microsoft Network. You can, at that time, install the components and specify hardware, fax phone number, and other characteristics. If you install hardware later with Add Hardware rather than in the Windows 95 Setup, then when you first bring up Mail and Fax, you will get another chance to specify the characteristics.

In addition, to use Mail and Fax features within Microsoft Exchange, you must establish profiles. A profile defines a messaging session–what types of services (such as Microsoft mail for networks, Internet mail, or fax) are available, where your Inbox, Outbox, and address lists are located, what folders are used to store messages, and so on.

When you first set up Microsoft Exchange, usually during Windows 95 Setup, you establish a profile, by default called MS Exchange Settings. The Mail and Fax control panel allows you to set up additional profiles, if needed. You have a choice of setting up one profile to handle all your information services (such as fax, e-mail, Internet, The Microsoft Network, or Compuserve), or a separate one for each service. Multiple Profiles can also be used to enable multiple persons to use a computer with their own unique settings.

To Set Up a Mail or Fax Profile

You will want to add a profile for each user on your computer and possibly for each different service you use. Before you start, you will need to know the path to your computer postoffice (see *Microsoft Mail Postoffice* for a description), your password for the postoffice, your computer name, and where your personal addresses and information folders are stored (usually mailbox.pab and mailbox.pst, which are automatically created for you). Follow these steps to add a profile:

1. Select Start ➤ Settings ➤ Control Panel and then double-click on Mail and Fax. The MS Exchange Settings Properties dialog box will be displayed.

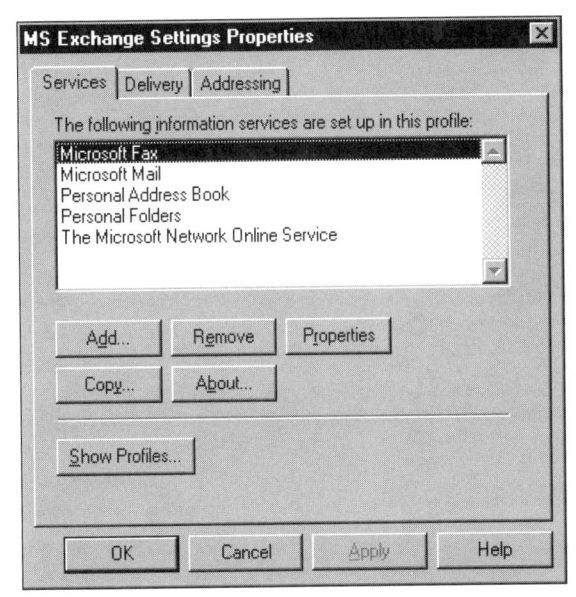

2. Click on the Services tab, if it is not selected. This tab shows the information services contained in the current profile.

COMMAND AND FEATURE REFERENCE

3. Click on Show Profiles. You will see the current profiles listed.

4. To create another profile, click on Add. The Inbox Setup Wizard will be displayed.

5. Place a check mark next to the information services that you want included in the profile. Or click on Manually configure information services to select and set up the properties manually. Click Next.

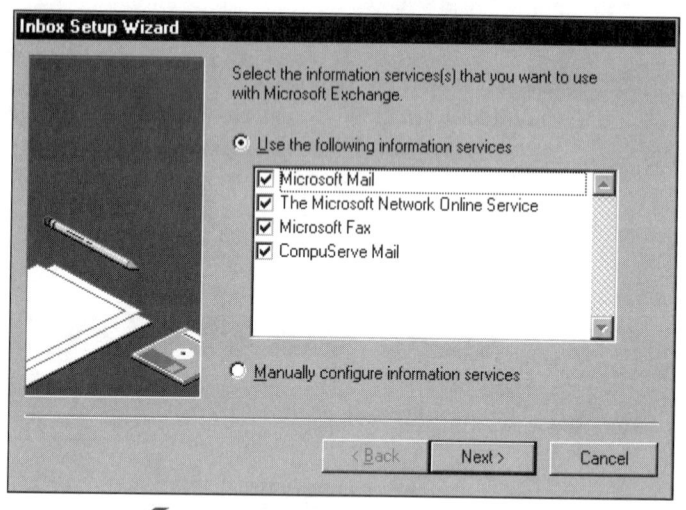

6. Type a name that you will recognize for this profile. Click Next.

7. You will be asked for specific information related to the information services you have chosen, such as the fax modem and phone number, path to the post office or the folder that will store information service files, your password, your computer name, and the paths to your Personal Address Book (*mailbox.pab*) and to your personal folder (*mailbox.pst*). If you don't have some of the services installed, you will be able to install them now. Enter the information as requested.

8. At the end, select whether the Inbox is to become part of your Startup folder so that when Windows 95 is loaded, Microsoft Exchange will be active. Click Next.

9. Click Finish to complete the profile, and Close to close the Microsoft Exchange Profiles dialog box.

To Change the Properties of a Mail or Fax Profile

To change the properties of a profile, or of an information service included in a profile, follow these steps:

1. Select Start ➤ Settings ➤ Control Panel, and then double-click on Mail and Fax. The Microsoft Exchange Settings Properties dialog box will be displayed.

2. Select the Service tab to add, remove, copy, or change the properties of any of the information services included in a profile.

TIP: *Copy can be used, for example, to create a duplicate of an existing profile and then change it slightly, quickly creating a new profile.*

3. Select the Delivery tab to alter the folder ("postoffice") where the mail for this profile will be stored. When receiving mail, you can vary the order in which address lists are searched by clicking on an arrow to change the order of the services listed.

4. Select the Addressing tab to add, delete, or change the address list's order of search, and where personal addresses are to be kept. When sending mail, you can vary the order that address lists will be searched by clicking on an arrow to change the order of the displayed list.

COMMAND AND FEATURE REFERENCE

5. When you are finished modifying the profile properties, click on OK.

SEE ALSO: *Electronic Mail (E-mail); Faxing; Microsoft Exchange; Internet; Microsoft Mail Postoffice; Microsoft Network*

Mapping Network Drives

Mapping network drives gives a unique name on your computer to a shared drive on another computer, and enables you to access its data. For example, to avoid duplicating the name Drive C, you might map another computer's Drive C to be Drive E on your computer. Mapping a drive letter allows you to access its data from within an application. The tools to map network drives are available in Explorer, My Computer, or Network Neighborhood.

NOTE: *You do not have to map a network drive to be able to access its data. If it is a shared drive, you'll be able to access it through Network Neighborhood.*

Mapping a Network Drive

Follow these steps to map a drive to your computer:

1. Bring up Explorer, My Computer, or Network Neighborhood. If the toolbar is not available, select View ➤ Toolbar.

2. Click on the Map Network Drive icon. The Map Network Drive dialog box will be displayed. The Drive list box contains the suggested name of the drive.

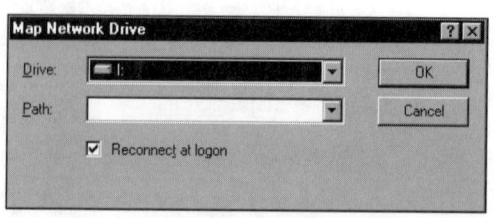

3. Click on the arrow to open the list box, and then select the name of the drive, or type a new name. The list will be displayed containing the names already assigned to other drives.

4. Click on the Path box and type two back-slashes followed by the path to the disk you are mapping, such as \\computer\drive.

TIP: *If you have already mapped the drive, click on the arrow on the right of the list box and select the name you want.*

Next time the My Computer, Explorer, or Network Neighborhood screen is displayed, the mapped drive will be displayed as a drive on your computer. You will see the folders available within the selected drive.

Unmapping or Disconnecting a Network Drive

When you disconnect or unmap a mapped resource, you remove it from the list of resources available and free up its drive letter. Follow these steps to unmap or disconnect a network drive:

1. Bring up My Computer, Explorer, or Network Neighborhood. If the toolbar is not available, select View ➤ Toolbar.

2. Click on the Disconnect Network Drive icon. The Disconnect Network Drive dialog box will be displayed, listing all mapped drives on your computer.

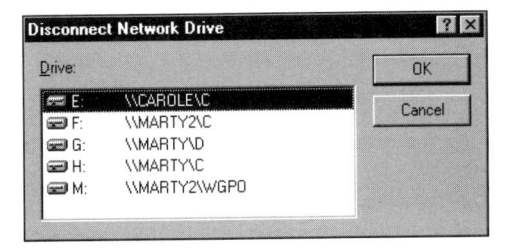

Disconnect Network Drive	
Drive:	
E: \\CAROLE\C	OK
F: \\MARTY2\C	Cancel
G: \\MARTY\D	
H: \\MARTY\C	
M: \\MARTY2\WGPO	

COMMAND AND FEATURE REFERENCE

3. Select the network drive you want to disconnect and click on OK. The mapped resource will be removed from those available to you.

NOTE: *The Map Network Drive and Disconnect Network Drive commands are also available on the Tools menu.*

Maximize/Minimize Windows

If you need to reduce the size of the window, you may place the pointer on the border, and when the two-headed arrow appears, drag the border in the direction in which you want to increase or decrease its size.

The Maximize and Minimize buttons in the upper-right of a window are other ways to change the size of windows. Click the Maximize icon to increase the window to full-screen size or the Minimize icon to place the window's icon in the Taskbar. The Maximize button changes to Restore once the window is maximized.

SEE ALSO: *Arranging Windows*

Media Player

The Media Player allows you to play multimedia files, such as video, animation, and sound clips. What you can play depends on the hardware you have available. From the Media Player you can also change certain settings for the file currently in use.

The Media Player Window

To access the Media Player, select Start ➤ Programs ➤ Accessories ➤ Multimedia and then click on Media Player. When you bring up Media Player, you will see a series of icons that allow you to control the start, stop, and incremental play of the clip:

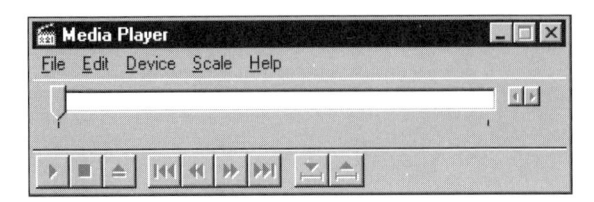

Play starts the clip.

Stop immediately interrupts the play.

Eject forces a disk in the CD-ROM drive to be ejected.

Previous Mark repositions the clip to the previous marked position.

Rewind repositions the clip at the beginning.

Fast Forward accelerates the forward motion in the clip.

Next Mark positions the clip at the next marked position.

Start Selection marks the beginning of a section of the clip. This is often used along with End Selection to copy a specific part of the clip.

End Selection marks the end of a section of the clip.

COMMAND AND FEATURE REFERENCE

Slider is used to position you in the clip. When a clip is loaded, the slider will have a scale displayed beneath it. As you drag the slider to the right, the clip advances accordingly. In addition to dragging the slider, you can also click on the backward and forward arrows on the right. The arrows advance the clip in very small increments while the slider is used to quickly move to a general area of the clip. The slider is often used with the Start and End Selection commands to select an area of the clip to copy or to play.

Media Player Menus

The Media Player menus contain options for controlling certain settings for the clip being played. The options will vary depending on what kind of media it is. In general, these are the options that are available from the specific menus:

File contains the **Open** and **Close** options.

Edit allows you to **Copy** an object. If you have used the **Start** and **End Selection** options, only the selected part will be copied. Otherwise, the whole clip will be copied onto the Clipboard, where it can be inserted into another document. Another option in Edit is **Options**, which contains certain settings pertinent to the multimedia file being played. **Selection** allows you to precisely select a section of the media file.

Device lists files available for a type of media device.

MEDIA PLAYER

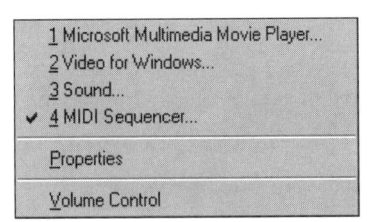

> 1 Microsoft Multimedia Movie Player...
> 2 Video for Windows...
> 3 Sound...
> ✓ 4 MIDI Sequencer...
>
> Properties
> Volume Control

- **Properties** allows you to set certain playback options, depending on the device.

- **Volume Control** offers a way to control the audio volumes and balance for the types of multimedia devices you have, such as CD Audio Balance, Microphone Balance, Synthesizer Balance, Wave Balance, Line-In Balance, and Volume Control Balance.

Scale allows you to set whether the scale of the clip is to be viewed in Time, Frames, or Tracks. Scale is automatically set for you according to the device type being used. You can change it for devices having more than one applicable scale.

Using the Media Player

Media Player contains several command icons and menu items which are only available when a file is open. To see the options and understand their functions, you might want to open a sample file included with the Windows 95 CD-ROM. Follow these steps to get started.

1. Select Start ➤ Programs ➤ Accessories ➤ Multimedia, and then click on Media Player. The Media Player window will be displayed.

2. Open a file by selecting File ➤ Open, select the CD-ROM drive, and then select \Funstuff\Videos \Goodtime.avi. (If you are searching for files on another drive, you may need to change the Files of type to be Video for Windows [*.avi]) The Media Player dialog box and the video clip will both be displayed. Many of the menu and icon options will now be available.

3. Using the toolbar and menu descriptions above, "play" with the video clip.

COMMAND AND FEATURE REFERENCE

4. When you are finished, click on the Close icon.

TIP: *You can also open a file by selecting a device type from the Device menu. When you click on Device, the types of files your computer can play will be listed. When you click on a type of device, the available files of that type will be displayed.*

Microsoft Exchange

Microsoft Exchange is the messaging center for Windows 95. It consolidates all the messaging functions under one program. Whether you are sending e-mail or a fax to a local or remote computer, or tapping into the Internet or an information service such as CompuServe or The Microsoft Network, you can use Microsoft Exchange.

MICROSOFT EXCHANGE

The advantages of Microsoft Exchange are that it:

- Is a common place to perform all messaging functions

- Has a common address book that contains all calling or addressing information needed for messaging functions (e.g. telephone numbers, e-mail addresses, and mailing addresses)

- Collects all incoming messages into one consolidated folder, regardless of the source

- Forwards one type of message to another (i.e. you can take incoming e-mail and fax it to someone else, and vice versa)

Before You Use Microsoft Exchange

Before you can use Microsoft Exchange, you must perform some preliminary tasks:

- Physically connect to other computers through a network or modem and phone lines.

- Set up a Microsoft Exchange Profile (See *Mail and Fax*).

- Establish yourself on the network postoffice, Mail and Fax, on the Internet, or on another information service, such as CompuServe.

- Place the addresses of e-mail recipients in your Personal Address Book. (This can be done at the time you send messages, but it is more awkward.)

When you install Windows 95 using Setup, you will indicate which of Microsoft Exchange's components —Microsoft Mail, Microsoft Fax, and The Microsoft Network—you will be using. If you select one or all of them, you will have an opportunity to define their initial settings, including hardware, your fax phone number, the mail postoffice address, and more. If you do not install the components then, you will have another opportunity when you first bring up the control panels for Microsoft Exchange,

COMMAND AND FEATURE REFERENCE

The Microsoft Network, Mail and Fax, or Microsoft Mail Postoffice.

Microsoft Exchange Window

To access Microsoft Exchange, double-click on the Inbox icon. When Microsoft Exchange is loaded this way, you will see the contents of the Inbox, which contains all of your incoming messages, regardless of the source. To read a message, double-click on it or select it, and then select File ➤ Open.

NOTE: *What you see displayed when you first bring up Microsoft Exchange depends on how you activate the program. If you bring up Microsoft Exchange by double-clicking on the Inbox icon, you will see the Inbox contents. If you bring it up by selecting Start ➤ Programs ➤ Microsoft Exchange, you will see a two-pane view with the folders on the left and the contents of the selected folder on the right. Once you bring up and then leave Microsoft Exchange, the view you see the next time you open it will be the one you previously left.*

The mail in the Inbox is listed with several columns of information that help determine the type of mail:

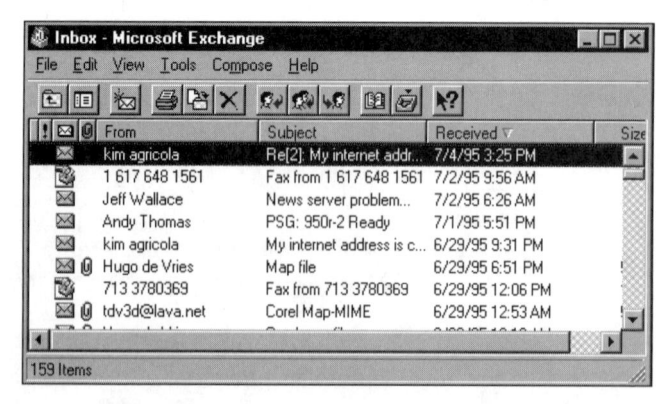

!	From	Subject	Received	Size
	kim agricola	Re[2]: My internet addr...	7/4/95 3:25 PM	
	1 617 648 1561	Fax from 1 617 648 1561	7/2/95 9:56 AM	
	Jeff Wallace	News server problem...	7/2/95 6:26 AM	
	Andy Thomas	PSG: 950r-2 Ready	7/1/95 5:51 PM	
	kim agricola	My internet address is c...	6/29/95 9:31 PM	
	Hugo de Vries	Map file	6/29/95 6:51 PM	
	713 3780369	Fax from 713 3780369	6/29/95 12:06 PM	
	tdv3d@lava.net	Corel Map-MIME	6/29/95 12:53 AM	

159 Items

Importance is a code to help you determine whether an item is important or not. There are three levels of importance: high, low, and normal. An exclamation mark indicates high importance;

MICROSOFT EXCHANGE

a downward pointing arrow, low importance; a blank, normal importance. These are set when you create a new message by clicking on icons in the toolbar. They can also be set by right-clicking on a message, selecting Properties from the popup menu, and then clicking on the Importance options.

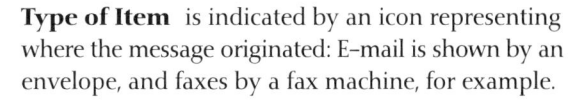

Type of Item is indicated by an icon representing where the message originated: E-mail is shown by an envelope, and faxes by a fax machine, for example.

Attached indicates with a paperclip if the file is attached to the message, or remains blank if no file is attached.

From lists the computer from which the mail originated.

Subject lists the description of the message.

Received displays the date and time received.

Size displays the size of the file.

If you bring up Microsoft Exchange from Start ➤ Programs, or select View ➤ Folders, you will see a different view—the Folder View. This view shows all the folders currently in Personal Folders in the left pane. It contains an Inbox for all incoming messages, Outbox for all messages ready to be sent, Sent Items for messages already transmitted, and Deleted Items, for messages removed from other folders. The selected folder's contents are shown in the right pane.

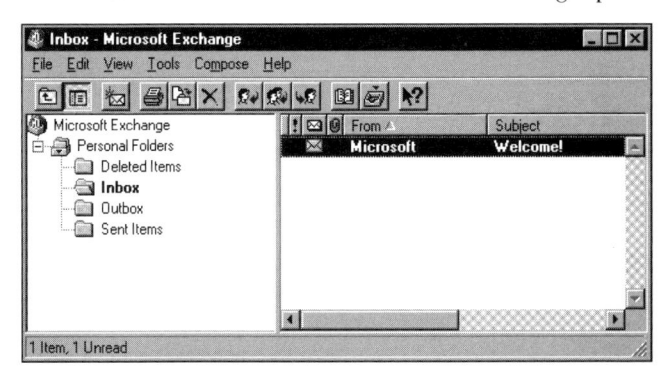

COMMAND AND FEATURE REFERENCE

The Microsoft Exchange Toolbar

The toolbar contains several tools that duplicate functions in the menus. Use the toolbar icons to speed up familiar tasks:

Up One Level goes "up" the hierarchy of folders and subfolders by displaying the folders one level up from those being displayed

Show/Hide Folder List switches between displaying the folder view and the current selected folder, usually Inbox.

New Message allows you to create a message.

Print prints the selected message.

Move Item moves the selected folder or file from one location to another.

Delete sends the selected message to the Deleted Items folder.

Reply to Sender allows you to reply to a received message.

Reply To All replies to everyone listed in the copy (Cc) list box.

Forward allows you to send a message you receive from one person to another.

Address Book displays the address book.

Inbox opens the inbox and displays its contents.

Help when clicked, turns into a special pointer, which you use to click on an object to get context-sensitive help.

MICROSOFT EXCHANGE

The Microsoft Exchange Menus

The Microsoft Exchange menu contains the usual File, Edit, and View menus, with some new commands on each.

File Menu

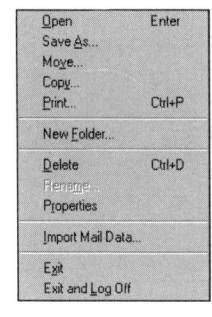

The File menu contains the following unique options:

Import Mail Data allows you to import a message from another source.

Exit leaves Microsoft Exchange.

Exit and Logoff leaves Microsoft Exchange and also makes a notation in the event log.

Edit Menu

The Edit menu contains these unique options:

Mark as Read Marks one item or all items of mail in a folder as read. If a message is marked as Read, it will be displayed in normal typeface.

Mark as Unread Marks one item or all items of mail in a folder as unread. If a message is marked as Unread, it will be displayed in boldface.

View Menu

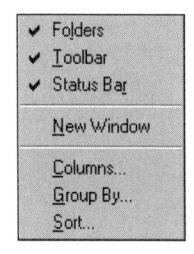

The View menu contains the following unique options:

Folders switches the view between Folder View, where you can see in the left pane the names of the Inbox, Outbox, Sent Items, and Deleted Items folders, and in the right pane, the contents of the selected folder, and viewing just the selected folder's contents.

COMMAND AND FEATURE REFERENCE

New Window opens a window so that you can see more than one view at one time.

Column allows you to customize which columns of data will be displayed in the list of mail items.

Sort allows you to sort mail by one of the columns of information, such as Importance, Type of Mail, Attachment, etc.

Tools Menu

The Tools menu provides several features for working with Microsoft Exchange messaging, including the following:

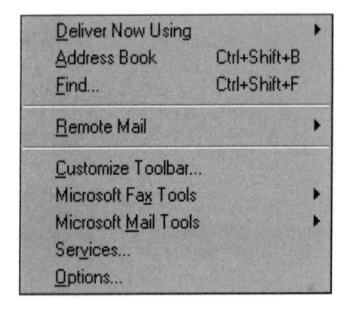

Deliver Now Using	▶
Address Book	Ctrl+Shift+B
Find...	Ctrl+Shift+F
Remote Mail	▶
Customize Toolbar...	
Microsoft Fax Tools	▶
Microsoft Mail Tools	▶
Services...	
Options...	

Deliver Now causes messages in your Outbox to be sent. If you have multiple services defined in the current profile, you will see **Deliver Now Using** with a submenu. For example, the submenu might have All Services, Microsoft Mail, The Microsoft Network, Microsoft Fax, and Compuserve Mail listed.

TIP: *This is also a way to initiate a search for incoming messages.*

Address Book loads the Address Book in Microsoft Exchange. It has several address options, including Postoffice Address List, which contains all computers on your network, and Personal Address Book, which contains all persons with whom you might want to exchange messages. When you double-click on a name, you'll be able to change their address, phone number, and other information. You may have an address book for each service you have defined in the current profile, such as The

Microsoft Network or Compuserve, or just one common address book for all. (See *Address Book*.)

Find opens a dialog box that allows you to find a specific message or item in a folder, such as the Inbox.

Remote Mail displays a dialog box where you can send and retrieve messages from a remote computer. Using the mail headers (which consists of the sender, subject, date received, etc.) you can select which messages to retrieve, delete, copy, or move to your own Inbox.

Customize Toolbar allows you to add to or remove icons or buttons from the toolbar. When you add buttons, you move them from the left list to the right list. When you remove a button, you move it to the left list. The buttons on the right are currently displayed on the toolbar along with empty slots that can be used. Double-click on an Available button on the left to add it to the toolbar. Double-click on a button on the right to remove it from the toolbar. Clicking on Reset returns the toolbar to its default state.

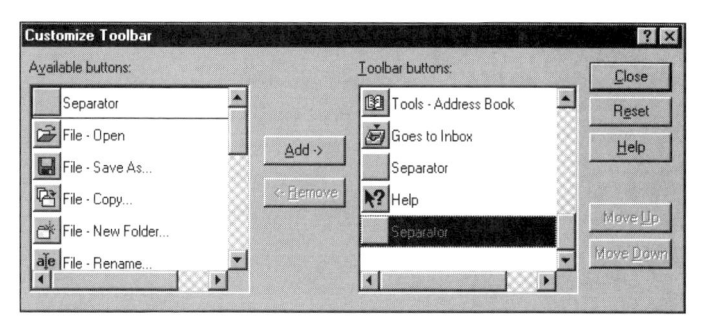

Microsoft Fax Tools offers advanced options for dealing with Faxes. (See *Faxing*.) This option is only available if you have a fax service installed.

Microsoft Mail Tools allows you to Change the Mailbox Password and Download Address Lists if

COMMAND AND FEATURE REFERENCE

you are the mail administrator, Schedule Remote Mail Delivery (perhaps at discounts rates), and View the Session Log.

Services displays the current profile, allowing you to add, delete, or change properties for the services you have included.

Options displays a dialog box with six tabs for setting defaults for Microsoft Exchange:

- The **General** tab contains options for setting overall defaults, such as what to do when mail arrives, when an item is deleted, and when Microsoft Exchange is started.

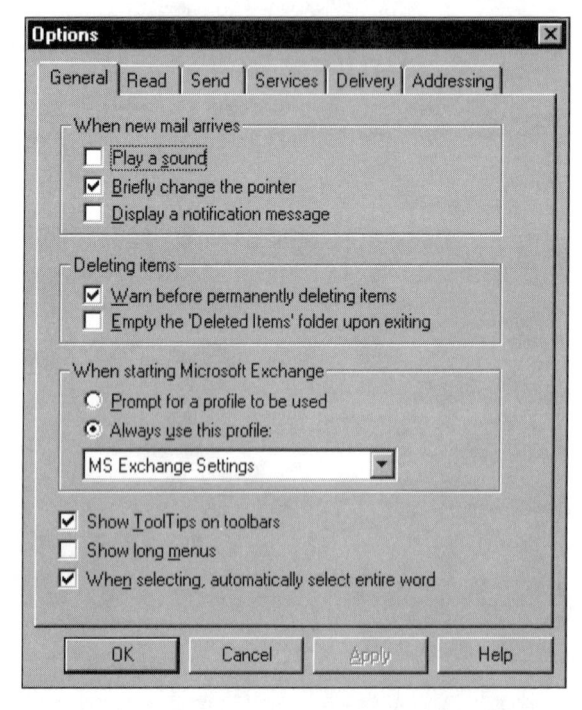

- The **Read** tab sets defaults for how to handle moved or deleted messages, and creating or forwarding replies.

MICROSOFT EXCHANGE

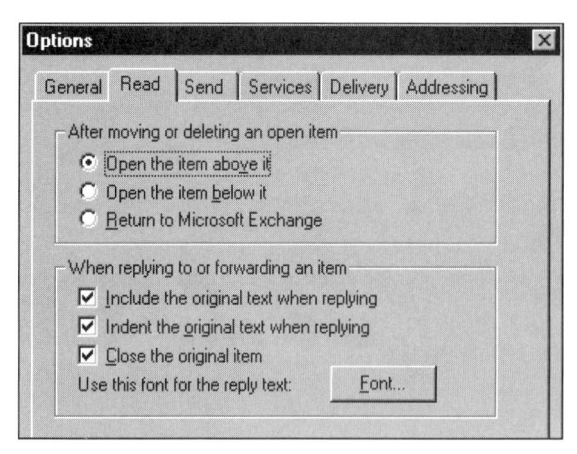

- The **Send** tab sets defaults for sending messages.

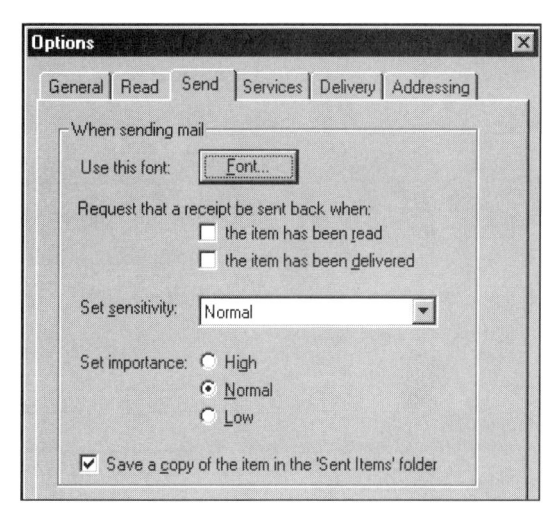

- The **Services** tab, duplicating the Services option on the Tools menu, enables you to add, remove, or edit the current Profile's information.

- The **Delivery** tab sets certain defaults for incoming mail, such as where to store it, and where to look for recipient addresses.

COMMAND AND FEATURE REFERENCE

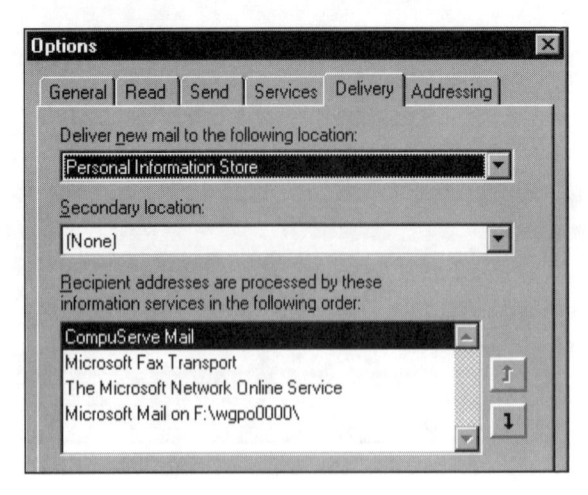

- The **Addressing** tab allows you to set defaults that relate to the addressing of messages, such as where to look first for addresses, and in which order address lists should be searched.

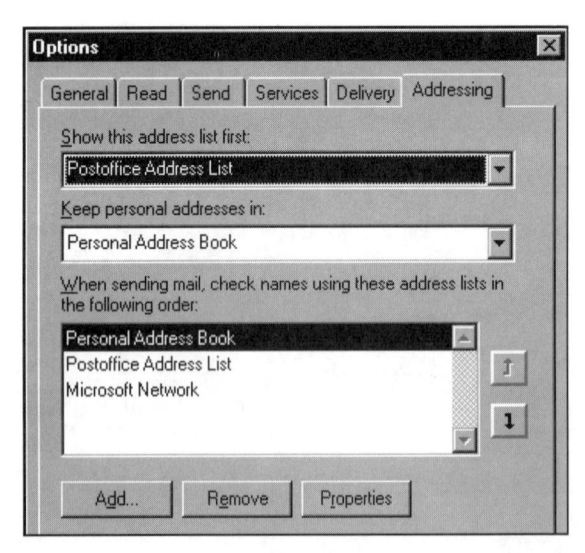

Compose Menu

The Compose menu provides several options for creating and replying to messages:

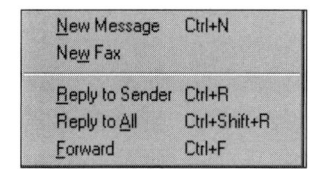

```
New Message     Ctrl+N
New Fax

Reply to Sender Ctrl+R
Reply to All    Ctrl+Shift+R
Forward         Ctrl+F
```

New Message provides a dialog box for creating a new message. You specify the recipient, create the text, and send the message with this single command.

New Fax allows you to create a new fax. It is available only if Fax is one of the services defined in your current profile.

Reply to Sender displays a dialog box containing the selected Inbox message, and enables you to reply quickly and efficiently.

Reply to All enables you to reply to the sender and all cc-recipients on the received message.

Forward allows you to pass on a message you have received to another address.

> **SEE ALSO:** *Address Book; Electronic Mail; Faxing; Mail and Fax*

Microsoft Fax

> **SEE:** *Faxing*

Microsoft Exchange Profiles

> **SEE:** *Mail and Fax*

COMMAND AND FEATURE REFERENCE

Microsoft Mail Postoffice

In order to use Microsoft Mail, your network requires a "postoffice." You can create a postoffice for a workgroup network with the following steps:

1. Bring up the Microsoft Mail Postoffice dialog box by selecting Start ➤ Settings ➤ Control Panel, and then double-clicking on Microsoft Mail Postoffice. The Microsoft Workgroup Postoffice Admin dialog box will be displayed. It will guide you through either administering an existing Workgroup Postoffice or allow you to Create a new Workgroup Postoffice.

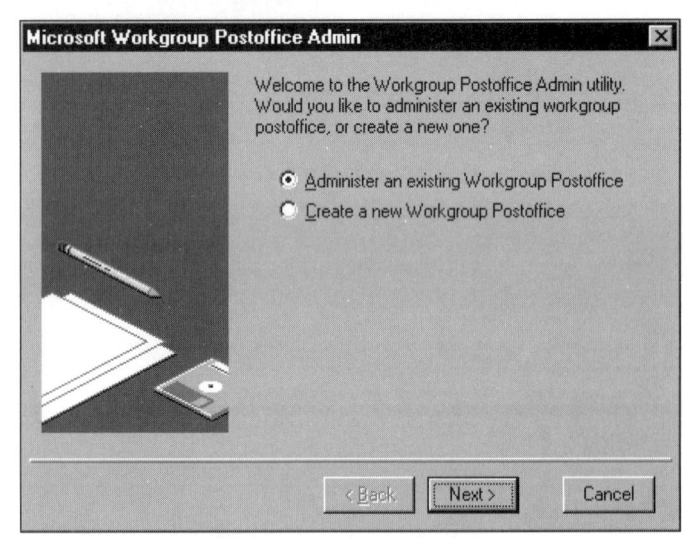

2. Place a check mark next to Create a new Workgroup Postoffice, and then click on Next. You'll be given an opportunity to enter the Postoffice Location. Microsoft Mail creates a folder named Wgpo0000 and places it in the root folder. Wgpo0000 is used to contain the post office programs and subfolders.

MICROSOFT MAIL POSTOFFICE

3. If you want Wpgo0000 contained in another folder (other than the root folder) enter the folder where the Workgroup Postoffice is to be located. The folder must already be created. Click on Next. The postoffice address will be displayed for you.

4. If you agree with the address assigned to the postoffice, click on Next. Otherwise, click Back and reenter the Postoffice Location.

5. Type in the Administrator Account Details: Name, Mailbox name, Password, Phone #1 and Phone #2 numbers, Office and Department identification, and any Notes. Click on OK.

6. A mail message will be displayed advising you to specify that your postoffice folder or directory must be shared in order for others to use it. Click on OK.

7. Bring up Explorer and find the folder you have just created.

8. Click on it with the right mouse button to open the popup menu. Select Sharing from the menu.

9. Click on Shared as, and fill in the rest of the specifications that apply. Specify the Access Type as Full to allow others to freely use your postoffice, or limit it to Read–Only or Depends on Password. Click on OK when you're finished.

> **TIP:** *You can specify one password for all users (available with the Depends on Password option), or specify one password for Read-Only users and another for Full access users.*

> **TIP:** *To add new users to the postoffice, bring up the Microsoft Mail Postoffice control panel. Select to*

COMMAND AND FEATURE REFERENCE

Administer an existing Workgroup Postoffice. Continue through the screens, entering information as you are prompted, until you come to the Postoffice Manager dialog box. Click on Add User, filling in the required parameters. Click OK and then click Close to complete the entry.

NOTE: *After the post office is set up for the network, each user will need to have an individual mailbox in order for mail to be sent and received. Once that is done, you must coordinate the post office address with the service being used in your user profile, such as faxing or e-mail.*

SEE ALSO: *Electronic Mail; Faxing; Microsoft Exchange; Microsoft Network*

The Microsoft Network (MSN)

The Microsoft Network is an online service offering services similar to Compuserve, America Online, or Prodigy. Using the Windows 95 user interface, MSN offers a familiar approach to getting around, which is an advantage for new online users. Among the services available to you on MSN are:

- *Bulletin Boards* to exchange messages and files on a subject

- *Chat forums* to converse online with others in a real-time mode

- *Electronic Mail* to send and receive e-mail messages.

THE MICROSOFT NETWORK (MSN)

- *Information services* for information on news, weather, stock market prices, and hundreds of other topics
- *Libraries* for access to databases of articles, programs, graphics, and research information
- *New product information* for Microsoft products
- *Access to the Internet and Compuserve*

Registering To Use MSN

In order to use The MSN, you must first register. Microsoft allows you to register online when you first bring up The Microsoft Network. To use it you must, of course, have a modem and phone line connected to your computer, and The Microsoft Network must be installed. When you register online, be prepared to supply your name, address, phone number, a credit card number and expiration date, a user name, and a password. Follow these steps:

1. From the Desktop, double-click on the Microsoft Network icon. The first MSN window will be displayed. Click OK for a free trial and more information, and to become a member of MSN. (If you are already a member, click on the applicable check box, and then click on OK.)

2. Enter your area code and the first three digits of your phone number. Click OK and then Connect. After a short wait, the initial MSN sign-up window will be displayed.

> **NOTE:** MSN uses an 800 number to allow you to sign up as a member. After that, you are required to use a different telephone number that is supplied to you when you register.

COMMAND AND FEATURE REFERENCE

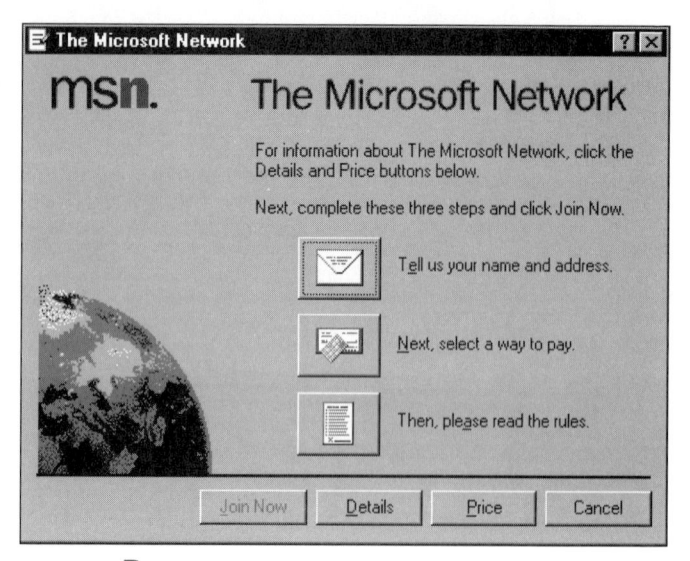

3. To read about the types of services that MSN offers, click on Details. For pricing information, click on Price.

4. Then click on Tell us your name and address. The name and address entry dialog box will be displayed.

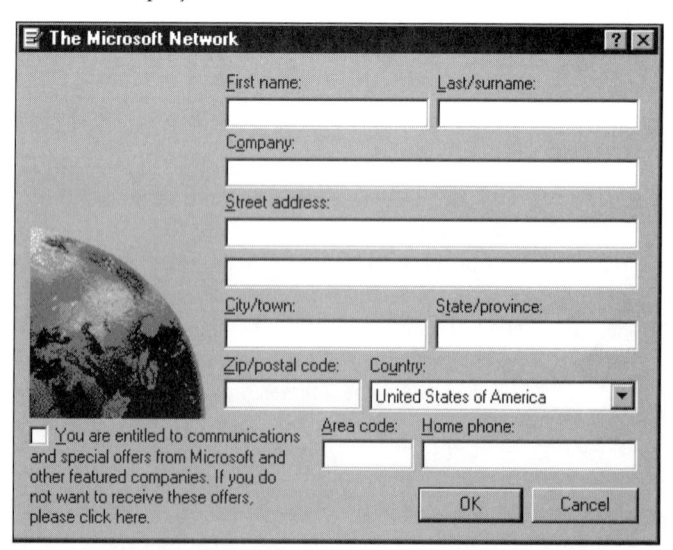

THE MICROSOFT NETWORK (MSN)

5. Enter the name and address information and click OK. You will be returned to the previous window.

6. Click on Next, select a way to pay. The payment method dialog box will open.

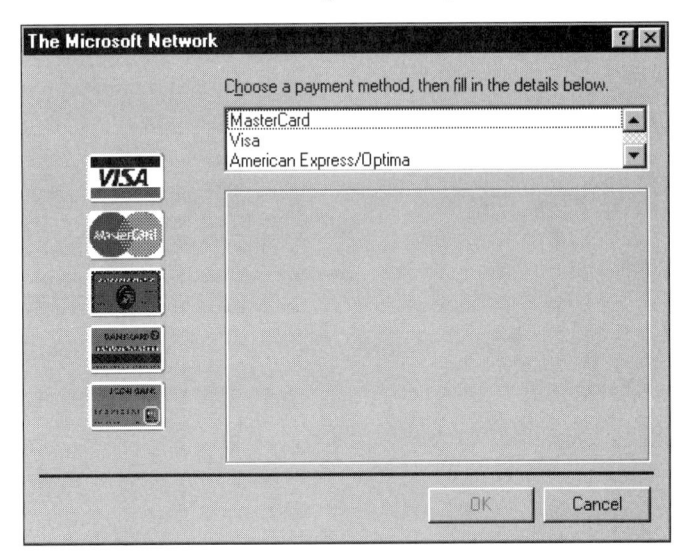

7. Click on the credit card you want to use, then fill in the details. Click OK.

8. From the previous window, click on Then, please read the rules to see the membership agreement.

9. After reading the rules, click on I Agree. To proceed, click on Join Now.

10. You will be asked to pick the access phone number that is best for you. Click on Change to get a list.

11. Select your country, state, and then select the phone number from the city that is closest to you. Click OK, and then repeat this for a secondary number. Click OK twice.

COMMAND AND FEATURE REFERENCE

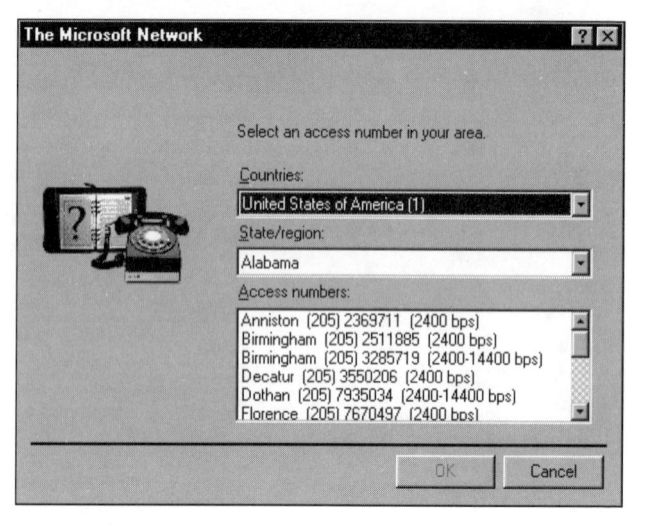

12. Click on Connect, and MSN will connect to the online service.

13. At this point, you must enter your user name and password. The user name can be any-thing you want, but it must be a unique name, and be at least six characters long. The Password can also be anything you want, but it must be between 8 and 16 characters long. Click OK.

14. You will now see a Congratulations screen and be disconnected. Click on Finish.

The Sign In dialog box will be displayed for you to connect to MSN as a member.

Signing On To MSN

Follow these steps to Sign On to Microsoft Network after you have become a member.

1. Double-click on the MSN icon on the Desktop. The Sign on screen will be displayed. Fill in your Member ID and password. If you want to avoid reentering your password, click on

THE MICROSOFT NETWORK (MSN)

Remember my password. Click on Connect to continue.

NOTE: *If your computer will be used by others who might use your access to MSN without your knowledge or permission, do not save your password. Reenter it each time you log in.*

2. If you have received new mail, you will be informed of it and asked if you want to review it. If you click Yes, Microsoft Exchange will be loaded, where you can read your messages. (If you click No, you can get your mail later.)

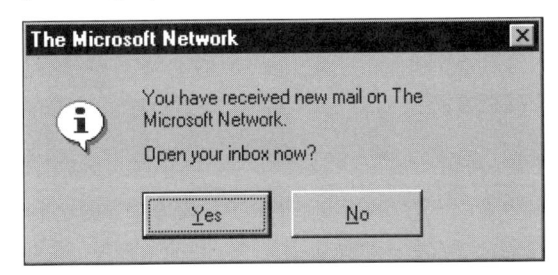

> **The Microsoft Network**
>
> ⓘ You have received new mail on The Microsoft Network.
> Open your inbox now?
>
> [Yes] [No]

3. The Microsoft Network base window, called MSN Central, is displayed. From here you can explore MSN. Select among the following options:

- **MSN Today** lists current topics and a calendar of events.

- **E-Mail** loads Microsoft Exchange and your Inbox.

- **Favorite Places** opens a folder where you can insert your most frequently used online services and information services.

- **Member Assistance** opens a folder containing folders for Microsoft members to help them with the network's operations, such as First-Time User Experience, Member Agreement (so you can get a printout of

COMMAND AND FEATURE REFERENCE

your agreement), Member Guidelines, Member Assistance Kiosk, and others.

- **Categories** opens a series of folders on topics and subtopics such as Arts & Entertainment, Business & Finance, Computers & Software, Home & Family, Internet Center, and more. Browse it for your own interests.

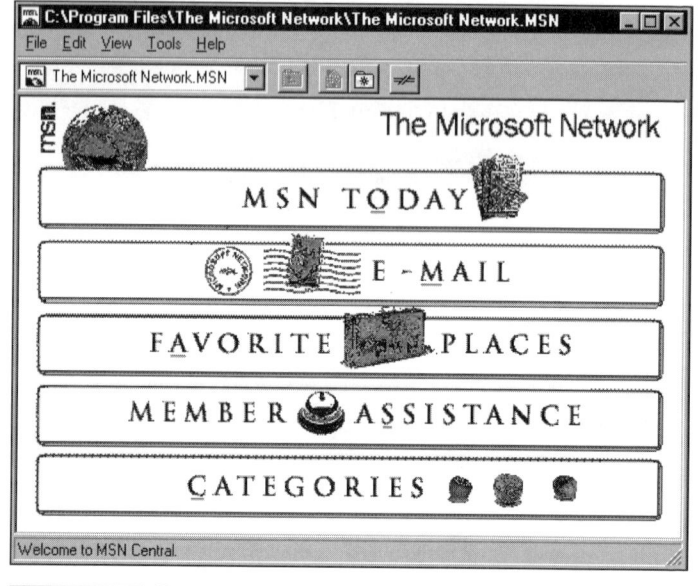

4. When you are finished with your MSN session, sign off by clicking on the Sign Off icon on the toolbar, or by right-clicking on the MSN icon in the notification area of the Taskbar. A submenu will be displayed. Select Sign Off to disconnect.

The MSN Window

When you sign on, the first screen you will see is MSN Central. MSN Central, the base from which you branch out and to which you return, provides menus and a toolbar containing many familiar

The MSN Standard Toolbar

The Toolbar, if not showing, can be displayed by selecting View ➤ Toolbar. Some of the toolbar buttons you will see are as follows:

Go to MSN Central returns you to the initial MSN screen.

Go to Favorite Place places you in the Favorite Places folder.

Sign Out allows you to disconnect from MSN.

Add to Favorite Place allows you to add a folder to your Favorite Places folder so that you can get to it easily in the future.

There are other icons unique to functions you may choose to bring up, such as Chat. Place the pointer on them to find out their function.

File Menu

The File menu contains only three new commands:

Add to Favorite Places adds the selected folder to the Favorite Places folder, which is available to you from MSN Central. In this way, you can immediately go to your Favorite Places without having to click through a number of intermediary folders.

Sign In, Sign Out commands allow you to sign in to MSN, and then sign out when you're finished. Sign In is unavailable unless you are working offline. Then it becomes available so that you can sign in again when you are ready.

COMMAND AND FEATURE REFERENCE

Edit Menu

The Edit menu offers a Go To option, which displays a submenu with the following commands:

Favorite Places brings up the Favorite Places folder.

Other location lets you specify your destination.

MSN Central brings you back to the beginning MSN Central menu.

View Menu

The View menu contains one special Option command in addition to the common Toolbar, Status Bar, and Refresh commands. The Options command displays a dialog box with four tabs:

- **View** identifies file types to hide from being displayed.

- **File Types** registers new file types found on the network.

- **General** sets the defaults for Disconnect after x minutes of inactivity, whether to Show MSN Today title on start up, which language to view material in, and whether to Include foreign language content.

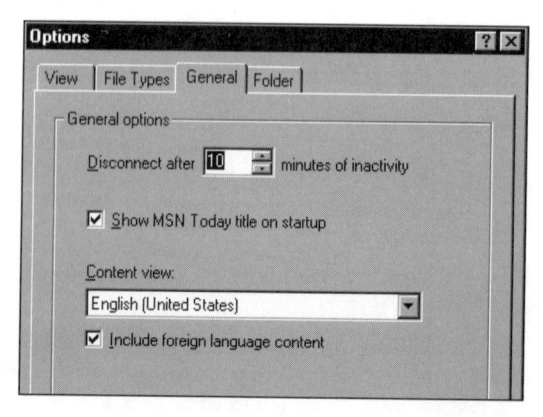

- **Folder** sets the Browsing options—whether to use a separate window for each folder or to use a single window that changes as each folder is opened (the default).

Tools Menu

The Tools menu contains several MSN-specific commands:

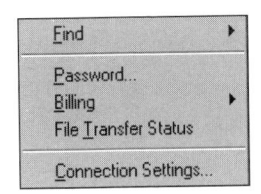

Find finds a file or folder on the network.

Password allows you to change your password.

Billing allows you to alter your Payment Method or name being billed, to see a summary of Charges, to get an online statement, and to enter changes to Subscriptions.

File Transfer Status lets you track how file transfer operations are proceeding.

Connection Settings lets you change Access Numbers, Dialing Properties, and Modem Settings.

Modems Control Panel

You need to have a modem in order to communicate with remote computers over phone lines. To install and edit settings for a modem, select Start ➤ Settings ➤ Control Panel, and then double-click on Modems. The Properties for Modems dialog box will be displayed, containing two tabs: General and Diagnostics.

COMMAND AND FEATURE REFERENCE

The General Tab

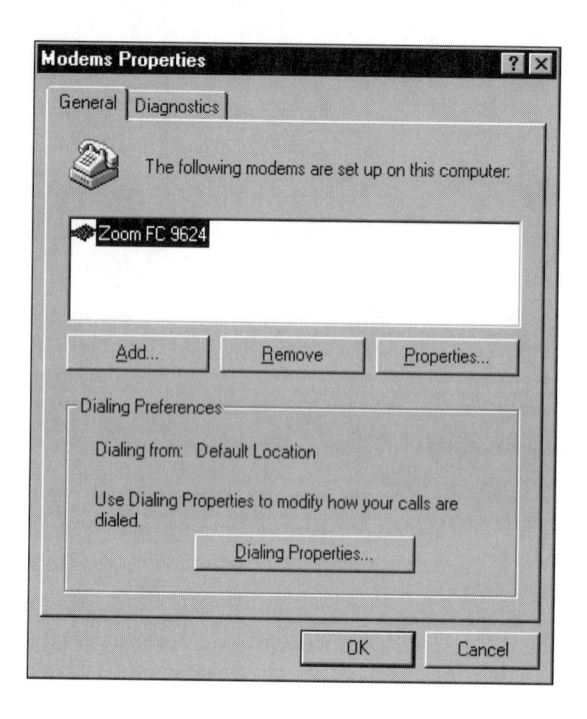

The General tab is where you add, remove, or edit the properties of a modem. When the tab is first displayed, it contains the names of the modems currently installed on your computer. You have the following options:

Add will guide you through the installation of your modem. Be sure to physically add the modem to your computer and turn it on so that Windows 95 can sense its presence. You can also specify that you will select the modem from a list, rather than having Windows 95 search for it.

Remove deletes the current modem settings from your computer.

Properties displays a separate dialog box with two tabs.

- **The General tab** allows you to specify the Port used for the modem, the Speaker volume, and the Maximum speed to be used, which is scaled according to your modem's capabilities.

- **The Connection tab** is used to set Data bits, Parity, and Stop bits settings, and to specify certain Call Preferences, such as Wait for dial tone before dialing, Cancel the call if not connected within *x* seconds, or Disconnect a call if idle for more than *x* minutes. On this dialog box is also an Advanced button, which sets error control, flow control, and other hardware settings.

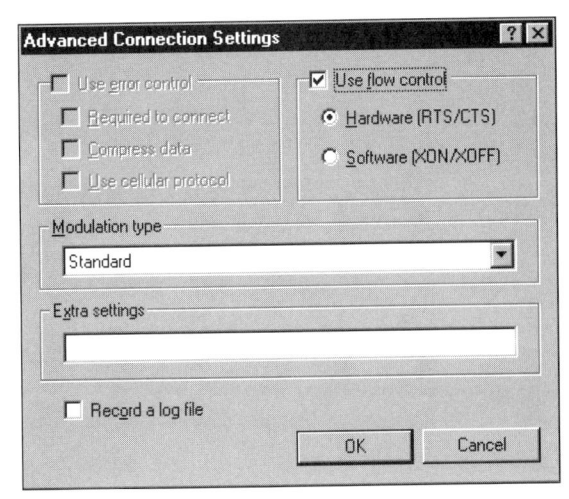

The Diagnostics Tab

The Diagnostics tab identifies which devices are assigned to specific ports, and allows you to seek more information on drivers and general items.

COMMAND AND FEATURE REFERENCE

This tab can help you when you want to install a new device but are not sure what ports are in use. There are two buttons:

Driver shows the selected device driver file name, size, and date the device was installed.

More Information shows the resource information on the selected device.

Mouse Control Panel

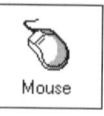

The mouse properties are controlled from the Mouse Control Panel. To access the control panel, select Start ➤ Settings ➤ Control Panel, and double-click on Mouse. The Mouse Properties will be displayed, containing four tabs.

The Buttons Tab

The Buttons tab sets the mouse button configuration and speed with these options:

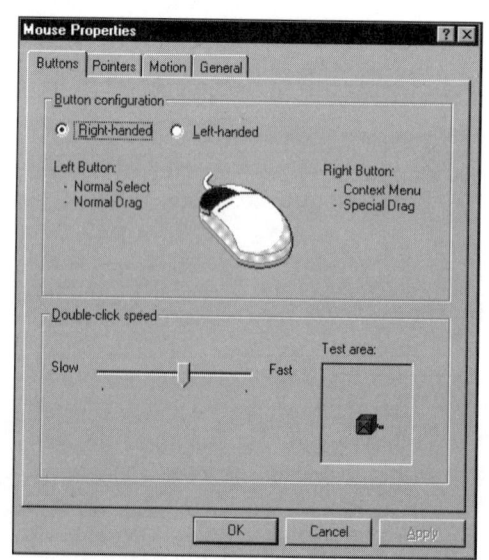

Button Configuration allows you to switch functions from the default right-handed use of the mouse buttons to left-handed. When you select Left-handed, the left button will then perform secondary functions, such as displaying the Context Menu, and performing Special Drag functions. The right button will perform the primary functions of selecting and dragging.

Double-click speed allows you to set and then test the speed at which a double-click is recognized. This allows you to slow or hasten the speed with which you must press the mouse button in order for it to be recognized as a double-click.

The Pointers Tab

The Pointers tab allows you to change the appearance of the pointer. For example, you can change the pointer when it's in wait state from an hourglass to a symbol or caricature of your choice.

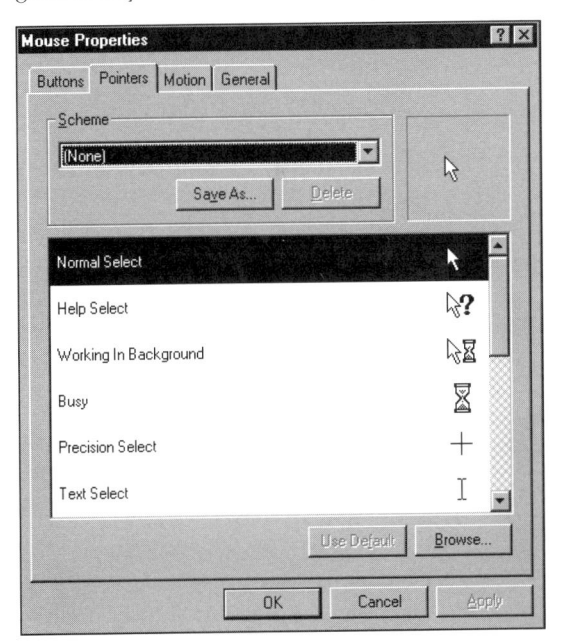

COMMAND AND FEATURE REFERENCE

Scheme contains the list of pointer schemes in Windows 95. By selecting one of the options, you'll see the set of pointers belonging to the Scheme's functions displayed below in the display box. You can create additional schemes by replacing the individual pointers in it. You do this by searching for additional pointers with Browse (selecting .ani or .cur files) and double–clicking on the files you want. Once you have assigned the new pointers to the Scheme's functions, you can save it by clicking on Save As. Clicking on Delete will remove a Scheme. Clicking on Use Default will restore the original default pointers.

The Motion Tab

The Motion tab controls the pointer speed and whether a pointer trail is present, making it easier to see on LCD screens. If the pointer trail is present, you can determine whether it is a long or short trail.

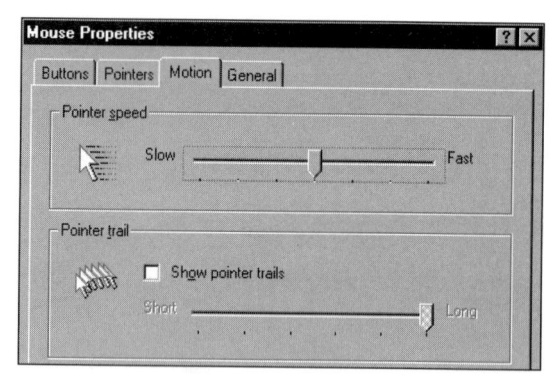

The General Tab

The General tab allows you to select the specific mouse or pointing device you are using. It has two buttons:

Change allows you to select a mouse model from a list. You can also install a new mouse not shown on the list by clicking Have Disk for your own mouse driver.

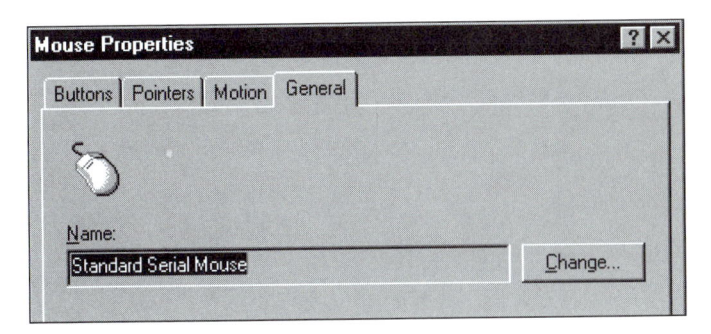

Mouse Properties

Buttons | Pointers | Motion | General

Name:
Standard Serial Mouse   Change...

Moving Files and Folders

Windows 95 offers three ways to move files and folders: you can use the drag and drop method, the Edit menu's Cut and Paste commands, or the right mouse button. Unlike copying, when you move a file or folder, you move the original to another location—there is no duplicate made.

To Move Using Drag and Drop

To use the drag and drop method, you must have both the source and the destination folders visible, say in Explorer, or on the Desktop. Hold down the left mouse button and drag the file or folder from one location to another. When the file or folder is in the correct destination folder, release the mouse button. The source and destination folders must be on the same drive to be moved; the file or folder will be copied if it is dragged to a different drive. To move to a different drive, drag the file or folder with the right mouse button.

NOTE: *If you hold down Ctrl, the file or folder will be copied rather than moved.*

COMMAND AND FEATURE REFERENCE

To Move Using the Edit Menu

The Edit menu in My Computer, Explorer, or any folder window provides a Cut and Paste feature.

1. Select the file or folder you want to move.

2. Select Edit ➤ Cut, or click on the Cut button in the toolbar.

3. Find the destination file or folder and open it.

4. Choose Edit ➤ Paste or click on the Paste button in the toolbar.

TIP: *You can select multiple files or folders to be moved by holding down Ctrl (or Shift to select contiguous files—click on the first and last file or folder of your selection) and clicking on the objects you want.*

To Move Using the Right Mouse Button

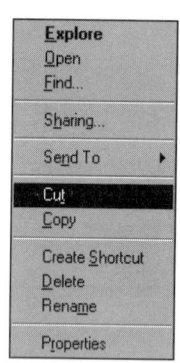

Clicking the right mouse button on a file or folder causes a popup menu to appear, which can be used to perform a number of functions, including moving. Follow these steps:

1. Locate the file or folder you want to move, and click the right mouse button on it. A menu will be displayed. Select Cut.

2. Open the destination folder, click the right mouse button, and select Paste (available only after you Cut or Copy).

TIP: *If you drag a folder or a file with the right mouse button, you will get a popup menu when you release the button. It will allow you to choose between copying or moving the object, or creating a shortcut.*

SEE ALSO: *Copying Files and Folders*

Moving Windows

SEE: Arranging Windows

Moving/Arranging Icons

Icons can be moved or arranged in several ways. When you are in My Computer, Explorer, or Network Neighborhood, you can move or arrange icons from the View menu. The same commands on the View menu are available in the toolbar as icons.

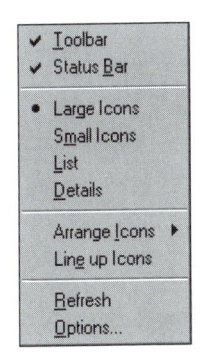

Large Icons displays the files and folders as larger-sized icons.

Small Icons displays the files and folders as smaller-sized icons.

List lists the icons and names of the files and folders.

Details displays the List style with added details: size of file, date last modified, and type of file.

Arrange Icons displays a submenu with choices. In Explorer, the choices are to sort the icons by Name, by Type of file, by Size of file, or by Date. Auto Arrange arranges the icons on an invisible grid. In My Computer, your choices are by Drive Letter and by Free Space. In Network Neighborhood, you can also arrange by Comment.

On the Desktop or in a folder, you can move icons simply by dragging them. Or, you can open the right mouse button popup menu and select Arrange Icons to sort them, or Line Up Icons to line them up in straight vertical and horizontal lines on the Desktop. In a folder, you also have a View option which allows you to display the icons with the Large Icons, Small Icons, List, and Detail options.

MS-DOS Environments

There are three DOS environments available with Windows 95:

MS-DOS Prompt allows you to run a program in a Windows 95 MS-DOS window or full screen. Windows 95 will be operating.

MS-DOS Mode allows you to run a program without Windows 95, but under Windows 95 MS-DOS.

Previous Versions of Windows allows you to run DOS programs under whatever previous version of DOS you may have. Windows will not be operating.

Each of the three environments represents decreasing influences of Windows 95. If you are trying to run a DOS program, first try running it under MS-DOS Prompt, then MS-DOS Mode, and lastly under previous versions of DOS.

SEE ALSO: MS-DOS Mode; MS-DOS Prompt; MS-DOS Startup Menu

MS-DOS Mode

MS-DOS mode, still Windows 95 DOS, is used for DOS programs that require many of the system resources, such as memory, or which require the use of real-mode drivers instead of Windows 95 protected-mode drivers (used since 386 processors).

MS-DOS MODE

When you run a program in MS–DOS Mode, it controls the whole system. Windows 95 and all active windows and programs are closed, the MS–DOS program is run, and when it is finished, Windows 95 is restarted. To place a program in MS–DOS Mode, follow these steps:

1. Using Explorer or My Computer, find the folder containing the MS–DOS–based program and click on it.

2. Select File ➤ Properties.

3. Next select the Program tab, and then click on the Advanced button.

4. Place a check mark in the check box next to MS–DOS Mode. More options will then become available for using MS–DOS mode, with the current or new configuration files (Autoexec.bat and Config.sys), and whether a warning will be displayed before all other programs are shut down.

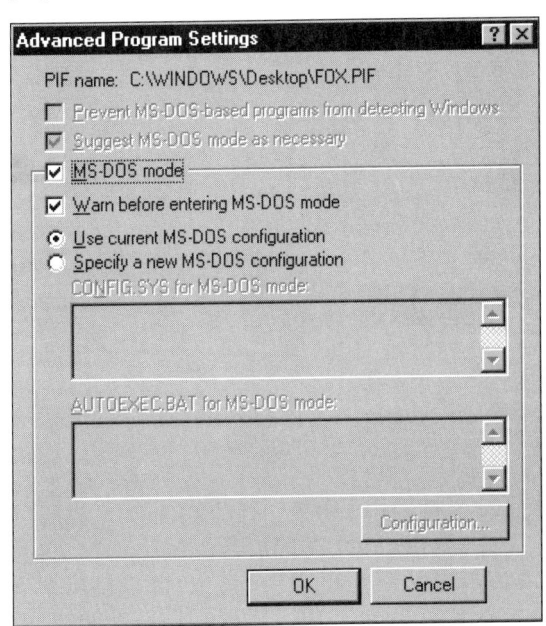

5. The current Config.sys and Autoexec.bat files will be used by default anytime MS–DOS Mode is not active. If you want to change them for MS–DOS Mode, click on Specify a new MS–DOS configuration and type in the Config.sys and Autoexec.bat parameters that you want. Click OK twice.

6. Then, when you are ready, select Start ➤ Shut down ➤ Restart the computer in MS–DOS mode, and click Yes. The computer will reboot in MS–DOS mode. You'll have to reboot to restart Windows or type win at the MS–DOS prompt. Or you can start the DOS program by double-clicking on it. Windows will be shut down, DOS started, and the DOS program will execute. When it finishes, Windows will automatically be restarted.

SEE ALSO: *MS-DOS Environments; MS-DOS Prompt; MS-DOS Startup Menu*

MS-DOS Prompt

The MS–DOS prompt opens an MS–DOS window, which can be used to load and run MS–DOS programs, although you can also load them directly from Windows 95. Whether the MS–DOS program begins in a full screen or a window is determined by the program's properties.

TIP: *To switch MS-DOS programs between a full screen and a window, press Alt+Enter (some MS-DOS programs cannot run in a window).*

To get to the MS–DOS prompt, select Start ➤ Programs ➤ MS-DOS Prompt. An MS-DOS window will be opened, and the prompt displayed. To leave the MS–DOS environment, type Exit.

TIP: *You can display the full pathnames of MS-DOS programs in the title bar and hide the MS-DOS file extensions by selecting View ➤ Options in Explorer or My Computer.*

TIP: *When you are at the MS-DOS Prompt, you can get help with MS-DOS commands by typing the command followed by /?.*

TIP: *To see a toolbar while you are in the MS-DOS window, click on the System Control icon, and select Toolbar.*

SEE ALSO: *MS-DOS Environments; MS-DOS Prompt; MS-DOS Startup Menu*

MS-DOS Startup Menu

In some cases, when you are attempting to diagnose a Windows problem, you might want to access the Microsoft Windows 95 Startup Menu. This menu presents several choices for loading parts of Windows so that you can attempt to segregate a problem. You can load previous versions of DOS (before Windows 95) using this menu. Follow these steps to get to this menu:

1. Restart the computer by selecting Start ➤ Shut Down ➤ Restart The Computer, and then click Yes.

2. When you see the message *Starting Windows*, press F8. A menu will be displayed for you containing the following options:

Normal starts Windows 95 with all the usual startup files.

Logged creates a system log while rebooting, documenting each step of the boot process.

COMMAND AND FEATURE REFERENCE

Safe Mode starts Windows by bypassing startup files (such as the Registry, Config.sys, Autoexec.bat and some sections of System.ini), loading only basic drivers (mouse, keyboard, and standard VGA device).

Safe Mode with Network Support starts Windows, bypassing startup files and loading basic drivers and basic networking.

Step–by–Step confirmation starts Windows by confirming each of the steps of the startup files, line by line.

Command Prompt Only starts MS–DOS with startup files and the Registry, and displays only the command prompt.

Safe–Mode Command Prompt Only bypasses the startup files, loading only Command.com and DoubleSpace or DriveSpace, starts MS–DOS, and displays only the command prompt.

Previous Version of MS–DOS starts the version of MS–DOS you had installed prior to installing Windows 95.

The contents of this menu can vary depending on the configuration of the computer and the contents of Msdos.sys. For additional information, refer to Microsoft documentation.

3. To leave the MS–DOS environment, you must reboot.

Multimedia Control Panel

The Multimedia Control Panel establishes the default settings for multimedia devices that are connected to your computer. Consequently, its contents will vary depending on the multimedia devices you have.

MULTIMEDIA CONTROL PANEL

To open the Multimedia Control Panel, select Start ➤ Settings ➤ Control Panel, and then double-click on Multimedia. The Multimedia Properties dialog box will be displayed, containing tabs that are appropriate for your computer. Some possibilities are: Audio for setting playback and recording controls (See *Audio*); MIDI for setting Musical Instruments Digital Interface controls and adding new instruments; CD Music for setting the drive letter and headphone volume defaults; and Advanced, which lists the multimedia devices on your computer and allows you to set or change properties for any of the listed devices you want to configure.

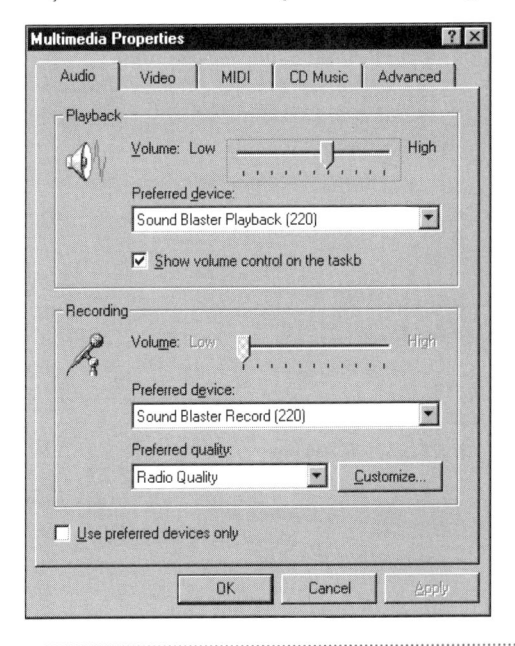

NOTE: *To add new multimedia devices, you must first install them with the Add New Hardware Control Panel.*

SEE ALSO: *Add New Hardware*

COMMAND AND FEATURE REFERENCE

My Briefcase

My Briefcase allows you to maintain current versions of a file by synchronizing the contents of two files. The feature is particularly useful for working with files off-site, perhaps on a portable computer. The Briefcase folder is identified by the My Briefcase icon. When you double-click on the icon, the My Briefcase dialog box is displayed, revealing the files contained within the Briefcase folder.

> **TIP:** *To use this feature, you must have installed My Briefcase with either the Portable or Custom options. If you do not see the icon on your Desktop, you will have to install it using the Add/Remove Programs.*

The files in My Briefcase show the location of the synchronized copy, whether it has been updated, the size of file, the file type, and the date on which it was last modified. You can see specific properties of any file by clicking on the file name and then selecting File ➤ Properties, or by right-clicking on the file name.

The My Briefcase Window

When you double-click on the My Briefcase icon and then click Finish on the Welcome to the Windows Briefcase screen (this welcome is only displayed once), you will see the My Briefcase window.

MY BRIEFCASE

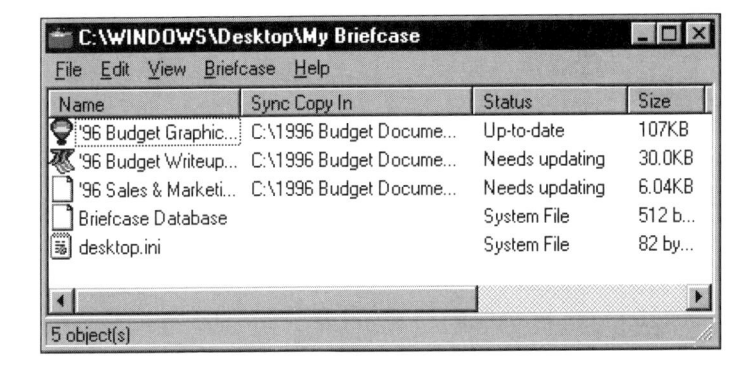

Name	Sync Copy In	Status	Size
'96 Budget Graphic...	C:\1996 Budget Docume...	Up-to-date	107KB
'96 Budget Writeup...	C:\1996 Budget Docume...	Needs updating	30.0KB
'96 Sales & Marketi...	C:\1996 Budget Docume...	Needs updating	6.04KB
Briefcase Database		System File	512 b...
desktop.ini		System File	82 by...

5 object(s)

The My Briefcase window contains five menus, four of which—File, Edit, View, and Help—are the standard folder window menus, and one of which—Briefcase—is unique to My Briefcase. It contains these options:

Update All updates all files in the Briefcase.

Update Selection updates only the files you select.

Split From Original "splits" a file from the Briefcase so that it is no longer updated when the original version changes.

Copying a File to the Briefcase

To use the Briefcase, you must first copy files to be synchronized to the briefcase. Follow these steps:

1. From the Explorer, or any other window displaying folders and files, find and select the file you want to keep synchronized.

2. Drag the selected file to the My Briefcase icon. It will appear as one of the files in the My Briefcase window.

COMMAND AND FEATURE REFERENCE

NOTE: *If you have split a file from one in My Briefcase it will be labeled an orphan. It will not be updated, since no link to the original file exists.*

3. In order to edit or work with the files on another computer, drag the My Briefcase icon to a floppy disk drive or another computer on your network.

TIP: *You should have only one Briefcase on a computer at a time for the synchronization to work.*

TIP: *You can use My Briefcase with a single computer—you may have different versions of a file maintained in different folders.*

Synchronizing Files in the Briefcase

To synchronize two or more versions of a file, follow these steps:

1. Insert the floppy disk or access the computer on your network containing the My Briefcase with the files to be synchronized. (My Briefcase may remain on the network or be copied onto your hard disk.)

2. Open My Briefcase by double-clicking on it, and from its window, select the files to be synchronized.

3. From the Briefcase menu, select Update All to update all files in My Briefcase, or Update Selection to update selected files.

The Update My Briefcase dialog box will be displayed showing the status of files in the Briefcase on the left verses the status of the source files on

MY BRIEFCASE

the right. An arrow between the two files shows the assumed direction of the update.

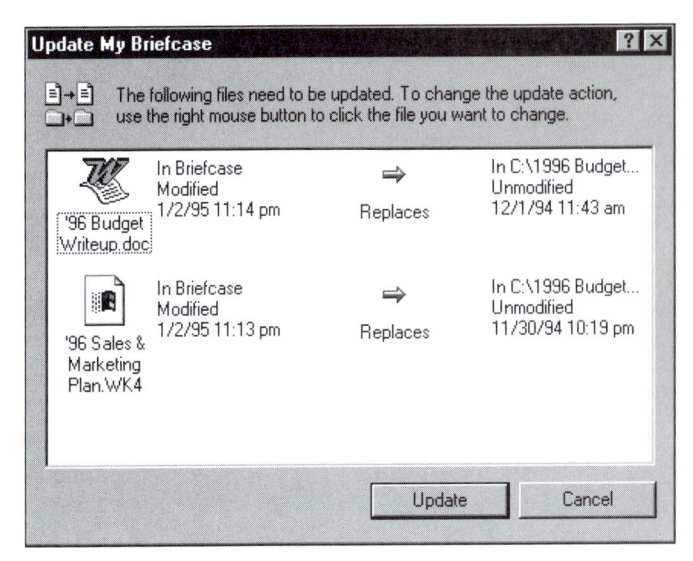

Update My Briefcase			
The following files need to be updated. To change the update action, use the right mouse button to click the file you want to change.			
'96 Budget Writeup.doc	In Briefcase Modified 1/2/95 11:14 pm	⇒ Replaces	In C:\1996 Budget... Unmodified 12/1/94 11:43 am
'96 Sales & Marketing Plan.WK4	In Briefcase Modified 1/2/95 11:13 pm	⇒ Replaces	In C:\1996 Budget... Unmodified 11/30/94 10:19 pm

[Update] [Cancel]

4. To change the update direction, click the right mouse button on the direction arrow and a popup menu will be displayed that allows you to choose the direction or to skip the update.

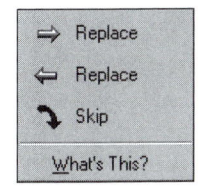

⇒ Replace
⇐ Replace
↘ Skip
What's This?

5. If you click on the What's This option, an explanation of the dialog box will be displayed. Click on the choice you want.

6. Click on Update to finish the file synchronization.

NOTE: *If the Briefcase detects that both copies have changed, the Skip option is displayed instead of the Replace option. If you click the right mouse button, you will be able to choose whether to skip the update, or to replace one of the files. If you choose to replace one file with another, you will lose the updates made in the replaced file.*

205

COMMAND AND FEATURE REFERENCE

My Computer

My Computer is one of the file management tools available with Windows 95. With it, you can locate folders, files, and disk or printer devices on your computer or on mapped drives on other computers on the network.

The My Computer Window

To start My Computer, double-click on the My Computer icon on the Desktop. The My Computer window will be displayed, showing an icon for each drive and drive-level folder on your computer. If you want to see the contents of one of the folders or drives on My Computer, double-click on the icon and its contents will be displayed in a separate window. To see other computers, select View ➤ Toolbar and click on the down arrow on the My Computer list box. You will then see other computer drives shared on your network.

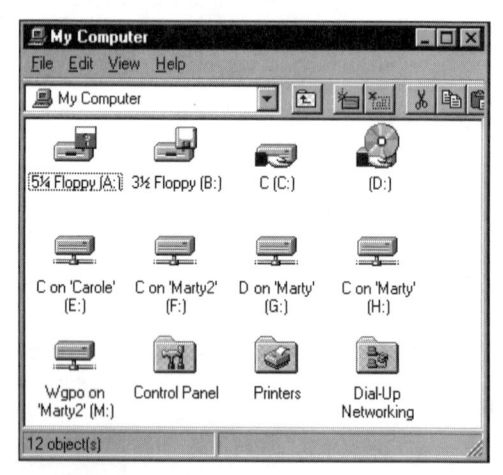

The Toolbar

In the toolbar, which you can turn on in the View menu, you will see the standard folder window icons. (See *Folder Window* for an explanation of what each icon does.)

Finding a File or Folder with My Computer

When you open My Computer, the My Computer window will be displayed, showing all the disks and folders available on your computer. Follow these steps to find the file or folder you want:

1. If the Toolbar is not showing, select View ➤ Toolbar. Click on the down arrow of the My Computer list box to find the device or folder you want. You will see all the shared disks on your network; important folders such as Control Panel, Printers, and Dial-Up Networking; and Windows 95 feature programs, such as Network Neighborhood, Recycle Bin, and My Briefcase. What you see will depend, of course, on what you have installed.

2. Double-click on a disk or folder to see its contents displayed in the window.

3. Once you have found the file or folder (it may be several levels down, requiring you to double-click several times), double-click on it to open it.

TIP: *If you click the right mouse button on a file, a popup menu duplicating many functions in the File and Edit menus will open. This menu gives you the ability to Open the file, Send a copy to a fax or another disk, Cut or Copy it, Create a shortcut for it, Delete or Rename it, or display the Properties dialog box for it. Depending on the file type, you may also see Print. Clicking the right mouse button on a folder will show the same options plus Explore (displays its contents on the right), Find (opens the Find dialog box), and Sharing (sets parameters for allowing the folder to be shared). Clicking on a disk icon with the right mouse button will allow you to Format a disk.*

COMMAND AND FEATURE REFERENCE

> **NOTE:** *You can access a remote computer by opening the Dial-Up Networking folder in My Computer. This allows you to establish connections to a remote computer over phone lines using a modem.*

> **SEE ALSO:** *Dial-Up Networking*

Naming Disks

To rename a disk, follow these steps:

1. Double-click on My Computer or Explorer.

2. Find the disk you want to rename, and click on it with the right mouse button.

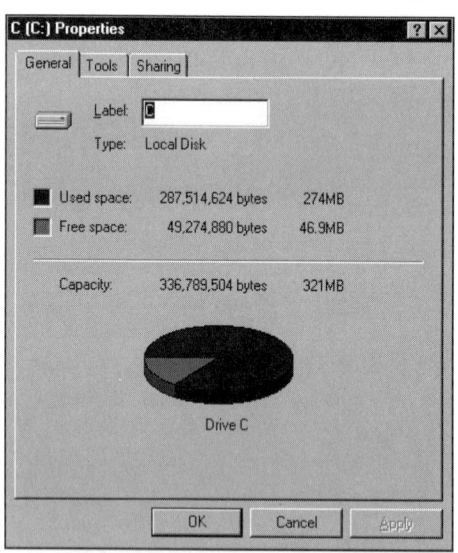

3. Select Properties for the disk Properties dialog box.

4. In the General tab, select the name in the Label text box, if it is not already selected, and type in the name you want. The name can contain up to 11 characters. Click OK.

Naming Files and Folders

The first time that you save a file using the Save or Save As command, you are required to name it. To name a folder, open Explorer or My Computer and select File ➤ New ➤ Folder. Names for files and folders can contain up to 255 characters, including spaces, but cannot contain these special characters:

/ \ ? : * " < > |

Renaming a File or Folder

File names can be changed by saving a file again under a different name. Both files and folders can be renamed in Explorer or My Computer. Follow these steps to rename a file or folder:

1. Open Explorer or My Computer and find the file or folder you wish to rename.

2. Click on the name once. Pause, and then click on it again. A box will enclose the name, and the name will be selected. If you move the mouse inside the box, the pointer will become an i-beam.

3. Type in the new name and press Enter.

NOTE: *You can see both file names either in the Properties dialog box for a file or folder (click the right mouse button on it and choose Properties), or in a DOS window (select Start ➤ Programs and click on the MS-DOS Prompt) where, if you type the dir command for a folder containing long file names, you will see the short name on the left and the long name on the right.*

Net Watcher

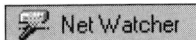

Net Watcher allows you to monitor who is currently using the shared resources on your network. It also allows you to add shared folders to those resources being monitored, and to disconnect users from using your

COMMAND AND FEATURE REFERENCE

computer resources. Net Watcher is available on CD-ROM and must be installed using the Custom installation procedure.

You must be using a network before you can use Net Watcher. Specifically, your computer must be set up to share files and printers in the Network control panel.

The Net Watcher Window

To access Net Watcher, select Start ➤ Programs ➤ Accessories ➤ System Tools ➤ Net Watcher.

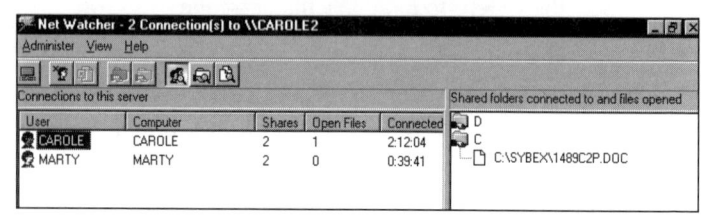

User	Computer	Shares	Open Files	Connected
CAROLE	CAROLE	2	1	2:12:04
MARTY	MARTY	2	0	0:39:41

Shared folders connected to and files opened:
- D
- C
  - C:\SYBEX\1489C2P.DOC

Net Watcher Toolbar

The Net Watcher toolbar contains the following buttons:

Select server allows you to select a computer so that you can monitor its shared resources.

Disconnect user disconnects a user from accessing your computer. Any files open and being shared may lose data if this is done without notification.

Close file closes a shared file.

Add share allows you to specify a folder to be added to the shared resources.

Stop sharing removes a folder from the shared status. If someone is using it and is unaware of the change, they could lose data.

Show users displays the users or computers connected to the network, and the resources currently being shared by them.

Show shared folders shows the devices and folders on the network currently available to be shared, and the names of any folders and files being shared by others.

Show files shows the files that are currently open and being shared by others on the network.

Net Watcher Menus

The Net Watcher menus duplicate some of the toolbar functions, and also contain some unique ones.

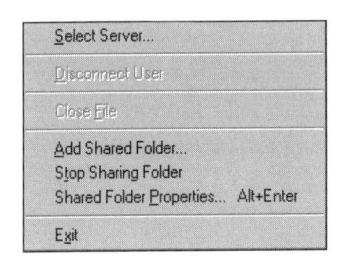

The **Administer** menu contains duplicate commands for the toolbar buttons: **Select Server**, **Disconnect User**, **Close File**, **Add Shared Folder** (same as Add share), and **Stop Sharing Folder** (same as Stop sharing). It also contains the **Shared Folder Properties** option, which displays the Properties dialog box for a selected shared device or folder.

WARNING: *Try to notify users before you disconnect them, close a file being shared, or stop sharing a folder. Unaware users could lose information if their operations are halted without warning.*

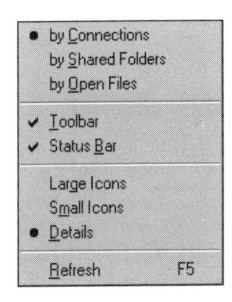

The **View** menu contains duplicates of these toolbar buttons: **by Connections** (same as Show users), **by Shared Folders** (same as Show shared folders), and **by Open Files** (same as Show files). It also contains the **Refresh** option, which renews the display of resources currently being shared.

COMMAND AND FEATURE REFERENCE

Network Control Panel

The Network control panel displays the properties of the network components and allows you to change the settings for the components in your configuration, including the names by which you are identified to others on the network, and how access to your resources is provided to others (i.e with or without passwords).

To open the Network control panel, select Start ➤ Settings ➤ Control Panel, and then double-click on the Network icon. When you bring up the Network control panel, you'll see a dialog box with three tabs.

Configuration Tab

The Configuration tab lists the four types of network components that Windows 95 needs in order to complete a network.

Client software handles accessing other computers to share their resources.

Service software handles sharing your computer resources with others.

Adapter cards or dial-up adaptors provide the interfaces between computers and cabling or modems and telephones.

Protocols define the method of communication between computers, so that they all speak the same "language."

The Configuration tab lists the components it has sensed during installation or which have been separately installed, and allows you to change, add, or delete components, and to designate a level of sharing. It contains the following features:

NETWORK CONTROL PANEL

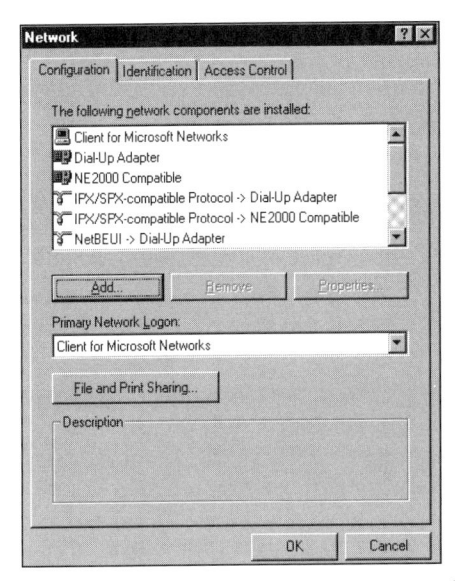

The following network components are installed lists the network components installed on your computer. If you are on a network, you will be able to see what Windows 95 has sensed or assumed from your installation.

Add allows you to add components to your network configuration. When you click on Add, you are shown the Select Network Component Type dialog box. Upon selecting one of the types of components (Client, Adapter, Protocol, or Service), other screens containing manufacturers and products will be displayed relating to the specific component you're adding.

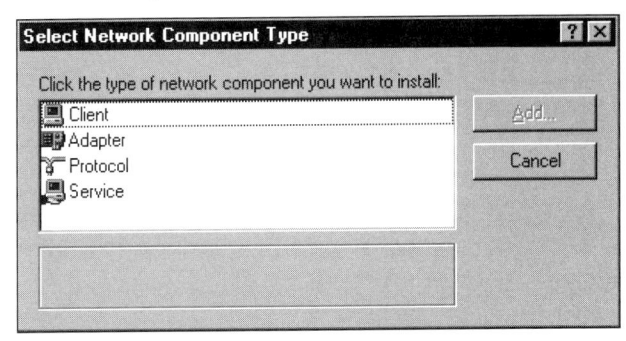

- **Client** software is used to connect your computer to other computers so you can access their disks, printer, and other resources. Examples available with

Windows are Artisoft LANtastic, Banyan VINES, Beame and Whiteside BW–NFS Network File Sytem, Microsoft Networks, NetWare Networks, Novell NetWare, and SunSelect. For a Windows 95 network, you would typically choose Client for Microsoft Networks. If you were a workstation on a Novell network, you would choose Client for NetWare Networks.

+ **Adapter** is a network adapter card that connects your computer to the cables that physically connect you to a network. Many common compatible adapter cards, such as NE2000, are listed under Novell/Anthem.

+ **Protocol** is the language of specialized codes and commands that enables your computer and another computer to recognize and communicate with each other. All computers on a network must use the same protocol. Examples are Banyan VINES, DEC PATHWORKS, Microsoft TCP/IP, NETBIOS, NetBEUI, IPX/SPX, Novell IPX ODI, and SunSelect PC–NFS. You must know the protocol for the network you are on before you can use it. For example, if you are on a Novell network, you would choose the IPX/SPX–compatible Protocol; whereas, if you are using a Microsoft Network, Windows NT, Windows for Workgroups, or Windows 95, you would use NetBEUI. TCP/IP is needed for the Internet.

+ **Service** software allows you to share the resources on your computer with other computers. Examples available with Windows are NetWare Networks, Microsoft Networks, ARCserve Agent, and Backup

Exec Agent. Microsoft's services pertain primarily to how files and printers are to be shared in Microsoft Networks and Novell's NetWare Networks.

Remove deletes the selected component from the list of components and from your computer. No message is displayed asking for confirmation. If you mistakenly remove an item, you will have to reinstall it.

Properties displays the properties for the highlighted component. Depending on the component, the screen may have more than one tab containing information on it. You can change the settings from these screens.

Primary Network Logon displays options for logging onto your computer. Select the Windows Logon option, for example, if you are not using the network, or select Client for Microsoft Networks or Client for NetWare Networks for using one of those networks. A description will be displayed under Description in the dialog box of the option selected.

File and Print Sharing displays a File and Print Sharing dialog box that allows you to select whether you want to give others access to your files and printer.

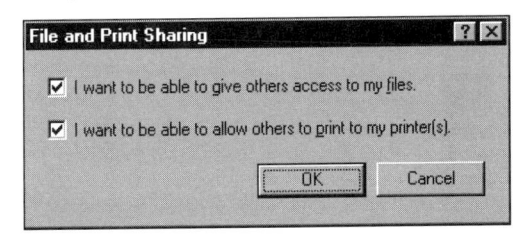

File and Print Sharing	? X
☑ I want to be able to give others access to my files.	
☑ I want to be able to allow others to print to my printer(s).	
	OK Cancel

Identification Tab

The Identification tab allows you to list and change the names by which you are known on the network.

COMMAND AND FEATURE REFERENCE

It contains the following options:

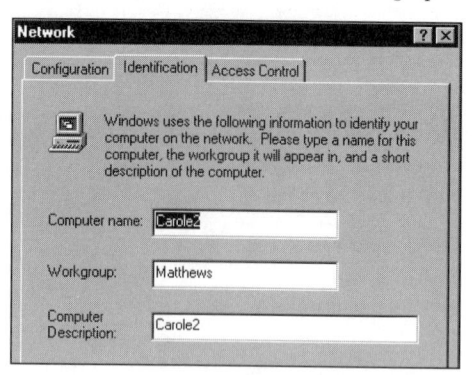

Computer Name identifies you to others on the network. Your name can be up to 15 characters, with no blanks.

Workgroup identifies the group of computers to which you belong. The name can be up to 15 characters and is usually set by the system administrator.

Computer Description is an optional comment which identifies you in more detail to others on the network. You can enter up to 48 characters.

Access Control Tab

The Access Control tab allows you to specify whether others will require a password to use your resources. It contains these options:

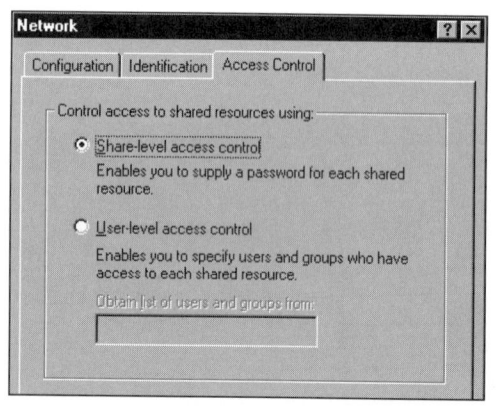

Share–level access control allows you to assign a password to shared resources. Others using the files or printer will need to know the password before they are allowed access.

User–level access control allows you to list specific persons who may have access to your files and printer without a password.

Obtain list of users and groups from (only available when User-level access control is selected) allows you to enter the network domain name or computer containing the list of users allowed to share resources.

Networks and Networking

Networks are groups of computers that are directly connected. There are two types of networks: local area networks (LANs), which are located in one facility, and wide area networks (WANs), which can be spread over a wide geography.

LANs are the most common network and are used in many organizations, including small and large businesses and schools. They provide access to shared information and computer resources, such as printers. There are two forms of networking on a LAN: peer-to-peer and client-server. In peer-to-peer networking, all computers on the network are equal and simply share each other's resources. In client-server networking, one (or occasionally more than one) computer on the network serves as a server and provides primary disk and other resources for the network. Windows 95 provides all the necessary software for peer-to-peer networking and for the client side of client-server networking. Common server software includes Microsoft's Windows NT or Novell's NetWare.

In a larger sense, networking loosely refers to communications between computers, regardless of the means of connection and the functions being performed. This would include the Internet, information services such as The Microsoft Network or CompuServe, and sharing information with a modem and phone lines.

COMMAND AND FEATURE REFERENCE

Some of the Windows 95 tools used for networking and other telecommunications tasks are as follows:

Microsoft Exchange is the primary messaging tool within Windows 95. It allows you to send and receive e-mail and faxes, either locally on a network or when connected remotely to computers, and to use information services such as Compuserve and the Internet.

Hyperterminal connects you to a remote computer for a variety of purposes, such as to download or transfer files, or to connect to a bulletin board.

The Microsoft Network is an online service, similar to CompuServe, that offers a variety of products and services. You can use it to find out information about such things as news or weather, and to download files, exchange messages, and connect to bulletin boards. You can also chat online with others on the network, buy products, connect to other services such as the Internet, and more.

Dial-Up Networking is an accessory used to connect to a remote computer or online service, such as the Internet. It must be installed using the Custom Installation.

Net Watcher is an accessory program used to monitor who is using the resources on your computer, and to change access to resources, if necessary. It is available on the CD-ROM version of Windows 95.

Setting Up Network Hardware

To have a network, your computer must be connected to others via a cable—whether a direct cable or telephone lines—or a wireless connection. You must install a network adapter card or other device that connects you to the network, and then use Add New Hardware to add the new device to

NETWORKS AND NETWORKING

your hardware configuration. Windows has the ability to recognize many manufacturers and models of network adapters. You will probably just have to select the one you are using from a list. If the model you have is not on the list, you may have to install it using the Have Disk option.

TIP: *If you have a generic NE1000 (8-bit), NE2000 (16-bit), or NE3200 (32-bit)-compatible adapter, you will find them under the adapter manufacturer Novell/Anthem.*

Setting Up Network Software

You must let Windows software know that you are on a network. Use the Network Control Panel to install the software you need. You may add four types of network components to those that come with Windows 95: Client, Adapter, Protocol, and Service. See *Network Control Panel (Configuration tab)* for a discussion of each of the types.

Follow these steps to install the software you need:

1. Select Start ➤ Settings ➤ Control Panel, and double-click on Network. The Network Properties dialog box will be displayed.

2. In the Configuration tab, click on Add. The Select Network Component Type dialog box will be displayed.

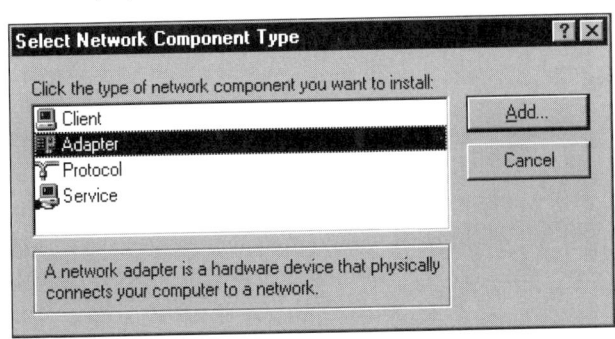

```
Select Network Component Type                    ? X

Click the type of network component you want to install:
  Client                                      Add...
  Adapter
  Protocol                                    Cancel
  Service

  A network adapter is a hardware device that physically
  connects your computer to a network.
```

COMMAND AND FEATURE REFERENCE

3. Select the type of network component to be installed. It can be Client, Adapter, Protocol, or Service.

4. Click on Add. The Select Network dialog box for the type of component you have selected will be displayed.

5. Click on the manufacturer and then on the model or version you need. If the software you need is not on the list, you will have to provide the information needed using an outside source. If you have a disk which has been prepared for use with Windows 95, click on Have Disk and follow the instructions.

6. Click on OK until the Network dialog box closes.

Sharing Resources

The sharing, or not sharing, of resources on a network can be done on two levels. One level sets the global sharing decision: to share or not to share. The second level determines sharing for individual resources.

Setting Global Sharing

If you are on a network and want to allow others to access your files, folders, printer, and other resources, you must specify this in the Network Control Panel by setting certain sharing options. You can also specify whether you want the sharing to be restricted by password, or to a list of persons.

Follow these steps:

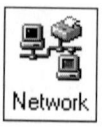

1. Select Start ➤ Settings ➤ Control Panel, and then double-click on Network. The Network Properties dialog box will be displayed.

2. Click on File and Print Sharing. A small dialog box will be displayed.

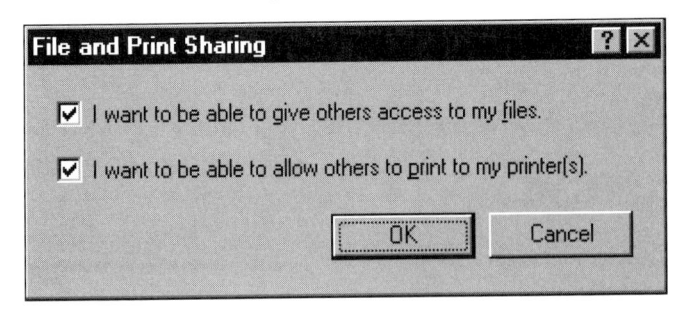

File and Print Sharing

☑ I want to be able to give others access to my files.

☑ I want to be able to allow others to print to my printer(s).

[OK]   [Cancel]

3. Click on the type of access you want to give others, and then click on OK.

TIP: You can limit access either by requiring a password to access your resources, or by creating a list of users that have permission to use the resources. Set these options on the Access Control tab in the Network Control Panel.

Setting Individual Sharing Properties

The second level of sharing is set with the individual resource. You can determine whether a particular disk, file, folder, printer, or other resource is to be shared, and if it is, what type of access it will have. Follow these steps:

1. Find and select the resource to be shared or not shared (for example, your hard disk, a file or folder, or the printer) in Explorer or My Computer.

2. Select File ➤ Properties, and then click on the Sharing tab.

3. Specify that the resource is Not Shared if it is to be made inaccessible to others on the network. Click on Shared As if you want to share the

COMMAND AND FEATURE REFERENCE

resource with others. Additional options will be made available if you choose to share the resource:

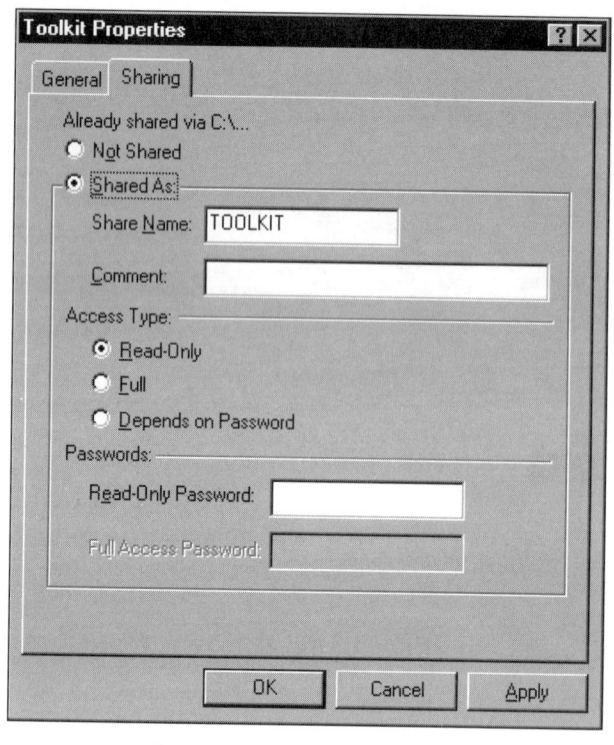

- **Share Name** specifies the name of the resource. Others will use this name to search for the resource.

- **Comment** contains notes about the resource, which will be available to others in the Details view of your computer.

- **Access Type** may be Read Only to restrict others to reading the file or folder only, Full to allow others to read and write to the resource, and Depends on Password to allow variations of accessibility.

NETWORKS AND NETWORKING

- **Passwords** may restrict users to Read Only Password or to Full Access Password.

5. Fill in the options you want and click on OK.

TIP: *To provide a quicker way to specify selective sharing, click on the folder, printer, or other resource with the right mouse button, and then click on Sharing. The Properties dialog box for the resource will be displayed, where you can specify the type of sharing you want.*

Troubleshooting Sharing Problems

If you find that you have setup your network and specified sharing but still cannot access others on your network, check out these possibilities:

- On the Configuration tab of the Network control panel (for the server computer), make sure File and Print Sharing are set correctly.

- On the Identification tab of the Network control panel, make sure the Computer Name and Workgroup are specified the same on both computers (for example, are the named hard drive and the mapped drive name the same?).

- On the Access tab of the Network control panel, make sure the access control is consistent between the computers.

- Is the resource to be shared (for example, the hard drive), designated as being Shared on the device Properties dialog box?

- Are the shared computer's resources adequately mapped to your own and vise versa? This is important when you are trying to access shared resources with a 16-bit program (one developed prior to Windows 95).

SEE ALSO: *Passwords; Properties*

COMMAND AND FEATURE REFERENCE

Network Neighborhood

Network Neighborhood, like My Computer and Explorer, is a file management system that presents system information from a network perspective. Like My Computer and Explorer, it allows you to access all computers on your network. However, the display of data in Network Neighborhood differs from Explorer in that you reach from one level of computer information to the next by first viewing the network components, then the computer contents, then the disk, then a folder, and finally files, rather than scrolling up and down a list of the network.

Network Neighborhood Window

If you are on a network, the Network Neighborhood icon will be present on your Desktop when you boot your computer. To bring up the Network Neighborhood window, double-click on the icon on the Desktop.

The Network Neighborhood window is very similar to My Computer and Explorer. For explanations of both the menus and toolbar, see *Folder Window*.

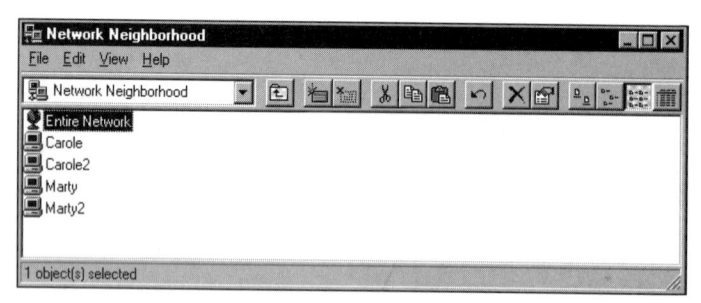

Here are some tips for making use of Network Neighborhood:

- After clicking on the Network Neighborhood icon, you will see the computers that are

NETWORK NEIGHBORHOOD

currently in your workgroup within your network. When double-clicked, the Entire Network icon displays the Workgroups on the network, and then the computers within the Workgroup.

- By double-clicking on one of the computer icons, you'll see another screen with the shared devices listed. (If you don't see a device, you may not have access rights.) If you double-click on a device, you'll see the shared files and folders. To open a device, file, or folder on your own computer, double-click on it.

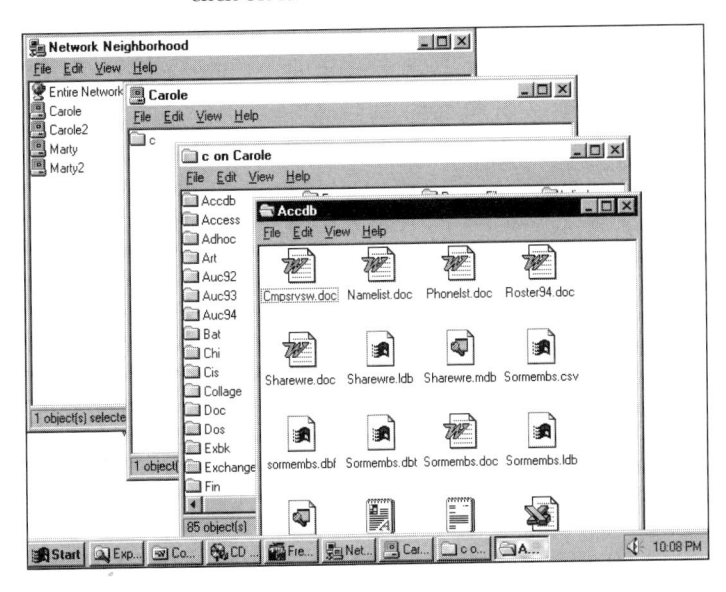

NOTE: *You can change the display of cascading windows by selecting View ➤ Options and then placing a check mark next to the option Browse folders by using a single window that changes as you open each folder.*

COMMAND AND FEATURE REFERENCE

Notepad

Notepad is an editor for small text files (less than 64K), that are not formatted. It can be used to look at the contents of the Clipboard, and to edit program listings. You can only open or save a file in ASCII format.

The Notepad Window

To access the Notepad, select Start ➤ Programs ➤ Accessories ➤ Notepad. The Notepad window will be displayed, containing the File, Edit, and Search menus.

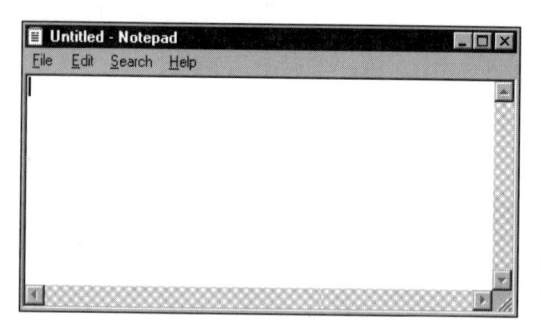

All of these menus contain standard options, which are described in *Folder Window*. Of note, though, is the File menu's Open command, which will strip the opened file of any formatting, making it into an ASCII file. In addition, the Edit menu contains a Word Wrap option, which is a switch for turning word wrap on and off.

Retrieving Text

To view text in Notepad, you have three options:

- You can type the text yourself.

- You can open a file from the File menu.

- After using the Copy or Cut commands to place data from another application in the Clipboard, you can Paste it into the Notepad text area from the Edit menu (Paste will not be available until something is in the Clipboard).

SEE ALSO: *Folder Window*

Number Format

To set the defaults for how negative and positive numbers are displayed, the number of decimal places included, the separator between groups of numbers, and so on, follow these steps:

1. Select Start ➤ Settings ➤ Control Panel, and then double-click on the Regional Settings icon. Select the Number tab.

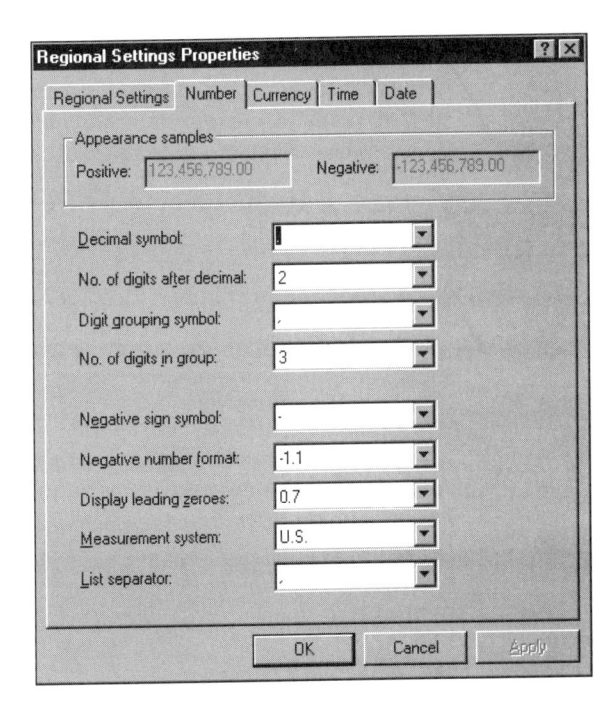

Positive	123,456,789.00
Negative	-123,456,789.00
Decimal symbol	.
No. of digits after decimal	2
Digit grouping symbol	,
No. of digits in group	3
Negative sign symbol	-
Negative number format	-1.1
Display leading zeroes	0.7
Measurement system	U.S.
List separator	,

2. Set the defaults for the following formatting possibilities:

- **Decimal symbol** establishes which symbol will be used as a decimal point. The default is a period.

- **No. of digits after decimal** specifies how many numbers will be placed to the right of the decimal point. The default is 2.

- **Digit Grouping symbol** defines the symbol that will group digits into a larger number, such as the comma in 999,999. The default is a comma.

- **No. of digits in group** sets how many numbers will be grouped together into larger numbers. The default is 3, as in 9,999,999.

- **Negative sign symbol** establishes which symbol is used to show a negative number. The default is a minus sign.

- **Negative number format** establishes how a negative number will be displayed. The default is to have the negative sign in front of the number, such as –24.5.

- **Display leading zeroes** determines whether a zero is shown in front of a decimal number. The default is yes, as in 0.952.

- **Measurement system** determines whether the system of measurment will be U.S. or metric.

- **List separator** determines which symbol will separate items in a list or series. The default is a comma.

3. After you have set the defaults, click on Apply and then OK.

OLE

OLE (Object Linking and Embedding) is a feature in Windows 95 that allows you to create documents containing linked or embedded objects that were created in a different program. For example, you might link or embed a graph created by Excel in a Microsoft Word document, along with a logo from Paint.

NOTE: *To use OLE, both the object-creating program and the "container" program must be OLE-compatible. Objects to be linked or embedded must have an extension that is recognized as an OLE-compatible application, such as Microsoft Word, Excel, and Paint.*

SEE ALSO: *Linking and Embedding Information*

Online Registration

In order to receive notices of product updates and access to customer support as well as other benefits, you can register as a user of Windows 95. The Online Registration feature is available on the welcome screen displayed when Windows 95 is brought up. To register, follow the online instructions.

Opening and Closing Windows

Opening and closing windows is the same as starting or closing an application. To open a window, find the program and double-click on its file name or on its icon. To close an application, select File ➤ Exit or click on the Close icon.

COMMAND AND FEATURE REFERENCE

SEE ALSO: *Finding Files and Folders*

Opening Files

Files can be opened in several ways. You can use menus, click on icons, or double-click directly on a file name:

- If you are already in a program and want to open a file, select File ➤ Open, specify the path and file name, and click OK. Some applications display an Open dialog box that gives you access to programs such as My Computer or Network Neighborhood, which you can use to find the file you want to open.

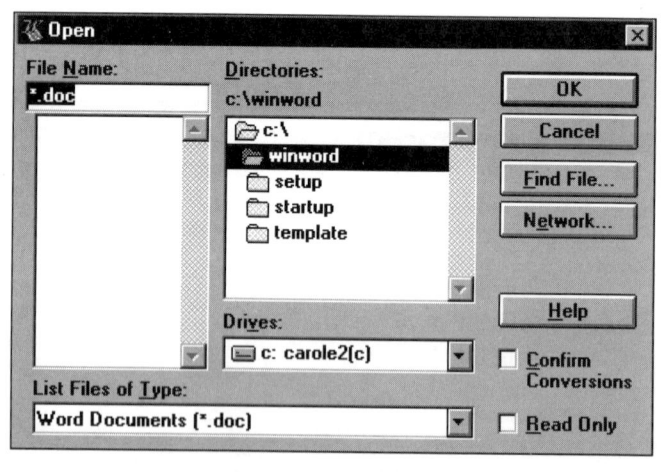

- Alternatively, if you are already in a program, you may click on the Open icon and follow the steps above.

- If you are opening a recently used document file, you can select Start ➤ Documents, and then click on the name of the document. You don't have to be concerned with loading the appropriate program, as Windows 95 will do this automatically.

- Using Explorer or My Computer, find the file you want to open and double-click on it.

SEE ALSO: *Explorer; My Computer*

Paint

Paint, a drawing program that comes with Windows 95, allows you to draw lines and shapes with or without color, and to place text within graphics. You can also use it to create backgrounds for the Desktop.

To access Paint, select Start ➤ Programs ➤ Accessories and click on Paint. The Paint window will be displayed.

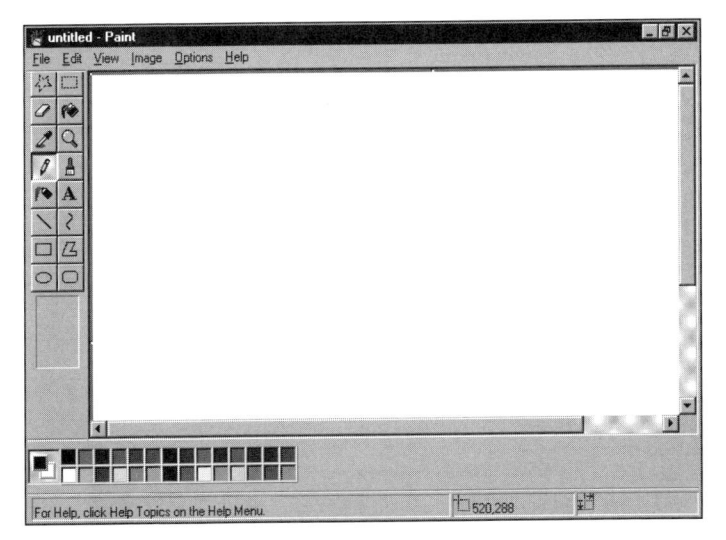

COMMAND AND FEATURE REFERENCE

The Paint Toolbox

The Paint toolbox provides the tools for drawing and working with color and text. When you place the pointer over a tool, its name is displayed in a popup label. The status bar, beneath the color palette, describes what the tool does.

Beneath the toolbox is an area containing optional choices for the type of tool chosen. For example, if you choose the Brush tool, a selection of brush edges will be displayed. If you choose Magnifier, a selection of magnifying strengths will be displayed.

The toolbox contains the following buttons for drawing lines and shapes, and for working with color:

Free–Form Select selects an irregularly shaped area.

Select selects a rectangular shaped area.

Eraser/Color Eraser erases an area as you move the eraser tool over it.

Fill With Color fills an enclosed area with color.

Pick Color selects a color when you click on an object that has that color. It is for use with the tool selected immediately before selecting Pick Color.

Magnifier enlarges the selected area. To return to the normal size, click on Magnifier again and then click on 1X in the area below the toolbox.

Pencil draws a line.

Brush draws lines of different shapes and widths.

PAINT

Airbrush places a pattern of dots on the drawing.

Text allows you to type text onto the drawing. Click on Text, click on the color you want for the text, and then drag a text box where you want the text to be inserted. In the font window that automatically appears, click on the font, size, and style (Bold, Italic, Underline) you want. Click within the text box, and begin typing.

Line draws a straight line. After dragging the tool to create a line segment, click once to anchor the line before continuing in another direction, or click twice to end the line.

Curve draws a curved line where one segment ends and another begins. After dragging the tool to create a line segment, click once to anchor the line before continuing. To create a curve, click anywhere on the line and then drag it. Click twice to end the line.

Rectangle draws a rectangular-shaped line. Select the shape characteristic from below the toolbar.

Polygon allows you to draw straight lines connecting at any angle. After dragging the first line segment, release the mouse, place the pointer where the second line segment is to end, click the mouse button, and repeat until the drawing is complete. Click twice to end the drawing.

Ellipse draws an elliptical shape. Click on Ellipse and select shape characteristic from below the toolbox.

Rounded creates a rectangle with curved corners. Select the shape characteristic from below the toolbar.

COMMAND AND FEATURE REFERENCE

Color Palette

To select a color, first select the tool, then the tool shape, if applicable, and then click on the color. The active color will be displayed in the top square on the left of the palette. To change the background color, click on Pick Color, and then click on the color you want. The next image created will use the new background color.

Paint Menus

The Paint menus contain many of the standard Windows folder options. The menus and their unique options are as follows:

File Menu

Set As Wallpaper (Tiled) places the Paint object (when saved) as the background wallpaper, with the design repeated in a tiled design.

Set As Wallpaper (Centered) places the Paint object (when saved) as the background wallpaper, with the design centered.

View Menu

Zoom displays a submenu with options for various ways to view the object:

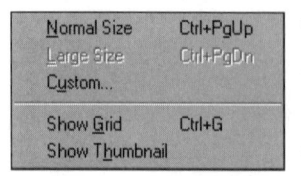

Normal Size	Ctrl+PgUp
Large Size	Ctrl+PgDn
Custom...	
Show Grid	Ctrl+G
Show Thumbnail	

- **Normal Size** image
- **Large Size** to see an enlarged object
- **Custom** to set specific zoom percentages
- **Show Grid** to display a grid against the object
- **Show Thumbnail** to show a small thumbnail display of the selected part of the object

View Bitmap displays a full screen-sized image; pressing any key returns you to the Paint window.

Image Menu

Flip/Rotate allows you to flip the image horizontally or vertically, and to Rotate the image by 90, 180, or 270 degrees.

Stretch/Skew allows you to stretch or skew the object in a horizontal or vertical direction by typing in precise percentages or degrees.

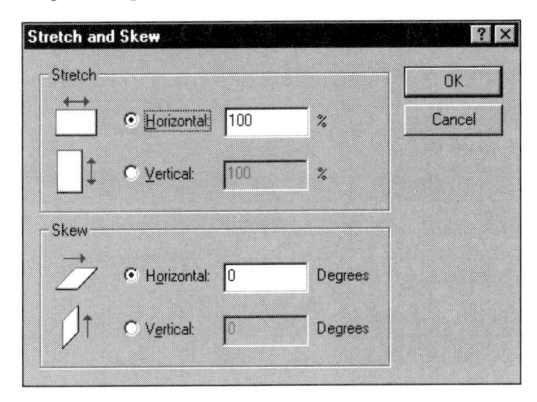

Invert Colors reverses colors, or changes them to their complementary color.

Attributes allows you to change the Width and Height of the object, to specify how it is measured (in Inches, Centimeters, or Pels), or to specify colors or just black and white.

Clear Image removes the image from the screen. If it is not saved, it will be lost.

Options Menu

Edit Colors allows you to define custom colors.

Get Colors allows you to look in another computer, disk, or folder for a color to use in the object.

COMMAND AND FEATURE REFERENCE

Save Colors saves a custom color to a file.

Draw Opaque allows you to switch between opaque and transparent drawing. An opaque drawing covers the existing picture, while a transparent object allows the underlaying picture to show through.

Passwords

Passwords make your computer and networks more secure by requiring users to enter a password before gaining access to a protected resource.

For single users of a non-networked computer, a Windows 95-level password can be set to protect others from logging on to your computer. This does not protect against someone booting the machine from a floppy, but it does prevent casual trespassers from accessing your files and folders. Other levels of security normally do not make sense for a single-user, non-networked computer. To set the Windows 95-level password, follow these steps:

1. Select Start ➤ Settings ➤ Control Panel, and double-click on Passwords. Select the Password tab.

2. Click on the Change Passwords tab if it is not already displayed, and then click on the Change Windows Passwords button.

3. Type the Old password (asterisks will appear as you type), New password, and then retype the new password to confirm it.

4. Click OK twice to finalize the new password.

For multiple users of a non-networked computer, you can set up a separate definition for the system each user will log onto. Each user would have their own password; access to files, folders, and other system resources; and each could even have their own system defaults defined, such as Desktop icons and programs included in the Startup folder, Start Menu, and Program groups. Follow these steps to define a separate system for each user:

1. To allow users to set up different system parameters, select Start ➤ Settings ➤ Control Panel, and double-click on Passwords. Click on the User Profiles tab, and then on Users can customize their preferences and Desktop settings. You may click on either Include Desktop icons and Network Neighborhood contents in user settings or Include Start Menu and Program groups in user settings, or both. You'll have to reboot the system for the changes to be applied.

2. To change the display settings for a user, select Start ➤ Settings ➤ Control Panel, and double-click on Display. Click on the Screen Saver tab. Select the screen saver you want, and if you want to protect users from gaining access to your system, click on Password protected. Click on the Appearance and Settings tabs to change the appearance of the screen display to suit you. When you are satisfied, click on OK.

There are some additional precautions you may take to secure networked computers. You can determine whether you want to restrict access to resources or to individuals using the computers. You can set up passwords for access to your computer as a whole, or to specific files and folders (referred to as resource or Share-level access control). Or, you can allow all persons having the correct password on your network to access your files, or just persons contained in a list who would be required to pass a name and password filter before gaining access (referred to as User-level access control). (See *Network Control Panel* for instructions on how to set these passwords.)

COMMAND AND FEATURE REFERENCE

Passwords can be set for the following resources:

Dial–up Connections To change passwords, double-click on My Computer, double-click on the Dial-Up Networking icon, and select Connections ➤ Dial-Up Server. Click on Allow Caller Access to enable Change Password.

Disks To set and change passwords, click the right mouse button on the disk and select Sharing from the popup menu.

Folders To change the password or sharing status, open Explorer or My Computer, select the folder, select File ➤ Properties, and then click on the Sharing tab.

Printers To change the password or sharing status, open the Printers folder from either Explorer, My Computer, or the Control Panel. Then click on the printer with the right mouse button and select Sharing from the popup menu. You can also select the printer, then select File ➤ Properties, and then click on the Sharing tab.

Mailbox To set or change passwords for gaining access to your mailbox, select Start ➤ Settings ➤ Control Panel and double-click on Mail and Fax. Then from the Services tab, select the Personal Folders. Click on the Properties button and then click on the Change Password button. To set or change the password for access to a mailbox, select Microsoft Mail as the information service and then click on Properties. Select the Logon tab, and then click on the Change mailbox password button.

Network Access Change passwords from the Change Other Passwords button in the Password control panel. Change shared status from the Access Control tab in the Network control panel.

Network Administration Set password access to shared devices from the Access Control tab in the

Network control panel. Also select Change Other Passwords in the Passwords control panel. (You must be logged onto the network to change it.)

Remote Administration Change passwords to allow remote administration from the Remote Administration tab in the Password control panel.

Screen Savers You can use a password to protect others from gaining access to your files when a screen saver is active. To change a password, select Start ➤ Settings ➤ Control Panel and double-click on Display. Select the Screen Saver tab and click on Password protected and then on the Change button.

Shared Resources To change the password or sharing status, open Explorer or My Computer, select the resource, choose File ➤ Properties, and select the Sharing tab. If the resource is shared, you can change the password. You can also change the sharing status from the Access Control tab in the Network control panel.

User Profiles Open the Passwords control panel and select the User Profiles tab to change the ability to restrict or allow separate access for multiple users. To establish User-level access control (that is, access determined by user name), open the Network control panel, select the Access Control tab, and choose between the Share-level access control and User-level access control options.

Windows 95 To change the Windows 95 password, open the Passwords control panel, select the Change Passwords tab, and click on the Change Windows Password button.

NOTE: *You must know the current password in order to change it.*

COMMAND AND FEATURE REFERENCE

Paste Command

Paste copies the contents of the Clipboard into the current document. It is available from the Edit menu and some popup menus that are displayed when you press the right mouse button.

SEE ALSO: *Copying Files and Folders*

Path

A path is the address of a file on the computer, and includes the identification of the disk drive, folder, subfolder, and file name. For example, the path for the FreeCell game might be C:\Windows\Freecell.exe, where C: is the disk drive, \Windows is the folder, and \Freecell.exe is the file name. The "\" separates the different parts of the address. To create a path, follow these steps:

1. Type the drive name followed by a colon, such as C:.

2. Next type a backslash to separate the drive from a folder or filename.

3. Then type the sequence of folders until you reach the file name (including the extension), using backslashes to separate each one.

TIP: *If the name of a file is more than eight characters in length or includes blanks or spaces, enclose the full path in quotation marks, such as "C:\FinanceTechnology StocksQuotes.xls".*

TIP: *For a path to a folder or file on another computer, where the computer disk drive is not mapped to a drive name on your computer, specify the computer name* *with two backslashes, such as in this example, where Marty is the computer name: \\Marty\Doc\Budget.doc.*

TIP: *For a path to a file or folder on another computer that is mapped to a drive name on your own computer, type the path as you would for your own disk drive, such as in this example, where the networked disk drive is mapped to your computer as drive H: H:\Doc\Budget.doc.*

Patterns

SEE: *Display Control Panel*

Personal Address Book

SEE: *Address Book*

Phone Book

SEE: *Address Book*

Phone Dialer

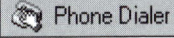

Phone Dialer places phone calls from your computer using a modem. To access it, select Start ➤ Programs ➤ Accessories and click on Phone Dialer. The Phone Dialer window will be displayed.

COMMAND AND FEATURE REFERENCE

The Phone Dialer Window

The menus in the Phone Dialer window contain standard options, as described in *Folder Window*, except for the Edit menu, which contains Speed Dial, and the Tools menu, which contains some special options as described below.

Edit Menu

The Edit menu contains only one unique command, **Speed Dial**. This option displays a dialog box listing previously entered phone numbers that can be immediately dialed by clicking on the appropriate button.

Tools Menu

The Tools menu contains three unique commands:

Connect Using allows you to specify which modem or telephone line is to be used for dialing out when you have more than one. Click on Line Properties to change modem properties. If you want the Phone Dialer to be used for all voice call requests, even if another program initiates it, click on Use Phone Dialer to handle voice call requests from other programs.

Dialing Properties displays the Dialing Properties dialog box in which you can set options such as area code, country, calling card, call waiting disabling, tone vs. pulse dialing, and so on.

Show Log displays a list of calls that have been dialed.

To Dial Using Phone Dialer

To dial a number, you must enter a number into the Number to Dial type box. This can be done in three ways:

- Click directly on the numbers in the phone pad and then click on Dial.

- Type a number in Number to Dial and then click on Dial.

- Click on a Speed Dial button. If the Speed Dial number has already been set up, it will be entered into Number to Dial and then automatically dialed for you. If the Speed Dial number is not set up, you can create it by clicking on a blank button. A Program Speed Dial dialog box will be displayed. Enter the Name and phone number of the person, and then click on Save or Save and Dial.

PIF Editor

The PIF Editor used in earlier versions of Windows has been replaced by the Properties dialog box.

SEE: *Properties*

COMMAND AND FEATURE REFERENCE

Playing Audio CDs

SEE: *CD Player*

Plug and Play

Plug and Play is a feature of Windows 95 that allows it to detect and accommodate hardware installed on the computer system without user intervention. Some hardware is designed especially for the Plug and Play feature. You only have to plug in one of these devices to be able to play it. The Add New Hardware control panel uses the Plug and Play feature as it installs all your hardware components. Windows 95 tries to recognize and determine the characteristics of all your installed hardware. If a device is not labelled Plug and Play, it may not be totally successful. In this case, you may have to change some of the hardware properties for the device to work properly.

SEE ALSO: *Add New Hardware*

Popup Menus and Labels (Context Menus)

Popup menus, also called Context menus, offer quick ways to see options that apply to a device, file or folder. Simply click on a device, file, or folder with the right mouse button, and its popup menu will be displayed. Popup labels are often displayed when you place the pointer on a toolbar button.

Ports

Ports connect devices for inputting and outputting information on your computer. Usually, only one port can be dedicated to a device. You assign ports to a device in the Add New Hardware control panel when the device is installed on your computer.

There are two kinds of ports: serial and parallel. Serial ports, labeled COM1 through COM4, are used for such devices as modems, mice, and, infrequently, printers. Parallel ports, labeled LPT1 through LPT4 (although most computers have only one), are almost exclusively used for printers.

To List Ports in Use

It is useful to consult a list of ports already being used by other devices when you start to add new hardware. To see such a list, follow these steps:

1. Select Start ➤ Settings ➤ Control Panel, and double-click on System.

2. Select the Device Manager tab, and click on View devices by connection. The device list will be listed with ports shown in parentheses.

COMMAND AND FEATURE REFERENCE

3. To print the list, click on the Print button.

> **SEE ALSO:** *Accessibility Options (for alternative input devices);Printing*

Printers Folder

The Printers folder is the only place where you can handle all functions related to printers. From here you can add a new printer, check on a job in the print queue, change the active printer, or modify a printer's properties.

The Printers Folder Window

To access the Printers folder, select Start ➤ Settings ➤ Control Panel, and then double-click on the Printers folder icon. The Printers window will be displayed. (The Printers folder is also available from My Computer.)

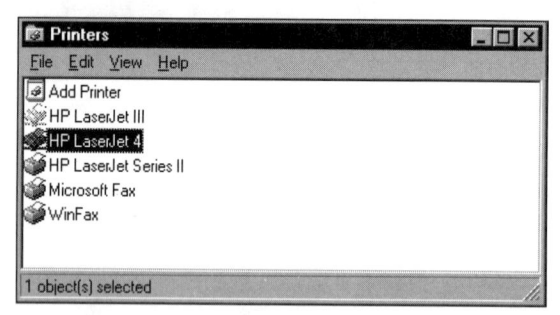

```
Printers
File  Edit  View  Help
  Add Printer
  HP LaserJet III
  HP LaserJet 4
  HP LaserJet Series II
  Microsoft Fax
  WinFax

1 object(s) selected
```

The Printers window lists all the printers connected to your computer or available on the network, including fax "printers." One of the icons in the folder, Add Printer, guides you through the process of adding a new printer to your system. The Printers menus contain standard Windows folder options, as described in *Folder Window*, except for the following unique options:

The **File** menu contains the following unique options:

- **Work Offline** is available for network printers. This option stores a print file temporarily to a disk file called a *spooler*, where it will be printed independently from your computer's other tasks.

- **Properties** will display a dialog box containing several tabs for setting such characteristics as sharing status, fonts used, paper specifications, and so on, as described under "Printer Properties", below.

TIP: *You can also get the File menu printer commands from the popup menu by clicking the right mouse button on a printer icon.*

The **View** menu contains Options, which displays a dialog box containing the following three tabs:

- **Folder** allows you to choose whether to view folders in cascading view or one window at a time.

- **View** displays file types currently registered on your computer. You can choose to hide certain file types, or to show all the files. You can also choose whether to display the full MS–DOS path in the title box, or to hide MS–DOS extensions for registered file types.

- **File Types** lists the registered file types and allows you to add or remove some from the list.

COMMAND AND FEATURE REFERENCE

Printer Queue

From the printer queue, you can view documents being printed or waiting to be printed, and cancel, pause, or change the order in which documents are printed. If you double-click on one of the printers in the Printer window, the printer queue dialog box will be displayed. It lists the name of the document being printed or waiting to be printed, the status of the document, the owner of the document, its progress, and when it entered the print queue. The Status Bar at the bottom of the dialog box contains the number of jobs in the queue. Except for the Printer and Document menus, the menus contain standard options.

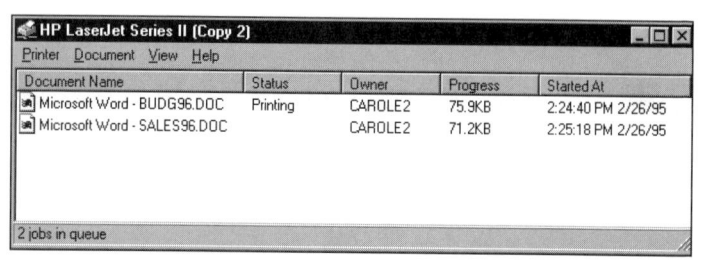

Document Name	Status	Owner	Progress	Started At
Microsoft Word - BUDG96.DOC	Printing	CAROLE2	75.9KB	2:24:40 PM 2/26/95
Microsoft Word - SALES96.DOC		CAROLE2	71.2KB	2:25:18 PM 2/26/95

2 jobs in queue

TIP: *The Printer Queue dialog box is also displayed when you double-click on the printer icon that appears in the Taskbar when a print job is initiated.*

The **Printer** menu contains these specialized options:

- **Pause Printing** is a toggle switch that temporarily interrupts the print job until it is restarted by being clicked on again.

- **Purge Print Jobs** deletes all print jobs from the print queue.

- **Set As Default** sets the printer as the default for the computer.

- **Properties** displays the Properties dialog box for the printer, which contains settings for such characteristics as sharing status, fonts used, paper specifications, and so on, as described below under "Printer Properties."

The **Document** menu contains the options for starting and stopping printing:

- **Pause Printing** is a toggle switch that temporarily interrupts the print job until it is selected again.

- **Cancel Printing** removes a document from the print queue.

NOTE: *To change the order of documents in a print queue, click on the document and drag it to the desired position in the print queue. You cannot change the order of documents in a network printer.*

Printer Properties

While in the Printers window, select File ▶ Properties, or click the right mouse button and select Properties to display the Printer Properties dialog box. It will contain several tabs for controlling the attributes and options for your particular printer. The number of tabs and the options they contain depends on the printer. A printer may be a device other than a printer. For instance, you can "print" to a disk file or a fax device. Some common tabs and the types of options they offer are as follows.

TIP: *To get a quick explanation of what each option in a dialog box does, click on the Help question mark icon and then click on the option. A popup label will be displayed explaining the option and how to use it.*

COMMAND AND FEATURE REFERENCE

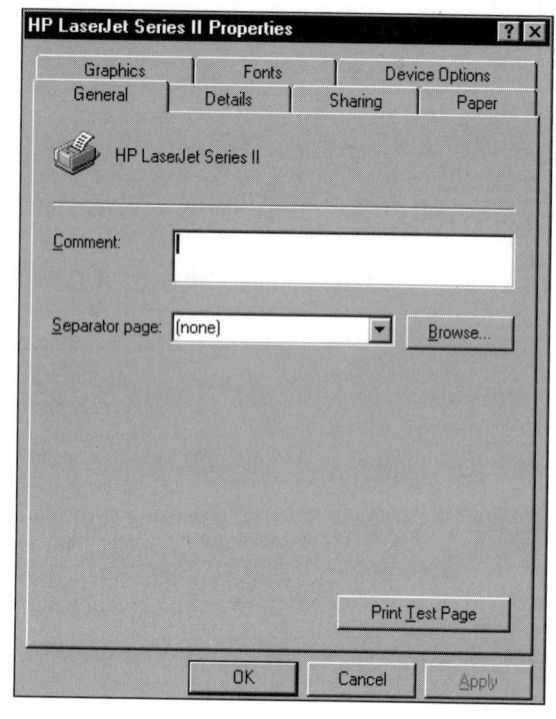

The **General** tab contains options that allow you to enter comments, specify what kind of separator page is used between print jobs, and print a test page.

The **Details** tab contains options to establish and manage printer ports and drivers. You can also set timeout limits for how long Windows is to wait for a printer to be online, or ready, before it displays an error message. From here you can also set options for the print spooler, where documents are kept in a queue until they are printed.

The **Sharing** tab allows you to indicate whether a printer is to be shared or not, and what the shared name and password will be.

The **Paper** tab contains options pertaining to the size and orientation of the paper. It may contain layout options, page source, and the default number of copies.

The **Graphics** tab contains options relating to graphics quality. Settings include graphic image resolution; dithering (blending of colors into patterns) or halftoning; and intensity of image (how light or dark it is).

The **Fonts** tab enables you to manage fonts, including identifying the font cartridge you want to use, how TrueType fonts are printed, and whether to install additional fonts.

The **Device Options** tab contains options such as whether to identify the amount of printer memory available, and whether the printer should attempt to print when printer memory is low.

Additional tabs may be displayed, which will differ depending on the device type.

Adding a New Printer

To add a new printer, select Start ➤ Settings ➤ Printers. The Printers folder will be opened, where you will find the Add Printer icon. Double-click on Add Printer and the Add Printer Wizard will guide you through installing a new printer on your system. Follow these steps:

1. Click on Next to begin installing the printer.

2. Choose whether the printer is a Local Printer attached to your computer or a Network Printer connected to another computer. Click on Next.

3. If the printer is a Network printer, fill in the Network path or queue name. Use Browse to search for the printer if you are not sure of the path. If you will be using any MS-DOS programs, click Yes for Do you print from MS-DOS based programs. If you clicked Yes, you may have to identify a printer port

COMMAND AND FEATURE REFERENCE

for MS–DOS printing. Click Next and skip to Step 5. If the printer is connected to your own computer, select the Manufacturers and Printers (the model) being installed from the lists displayed. If you are manually installing a printer that is not listed, click on Have Disk and follow the instructions. After selecting the manufacturer and model, click Next.

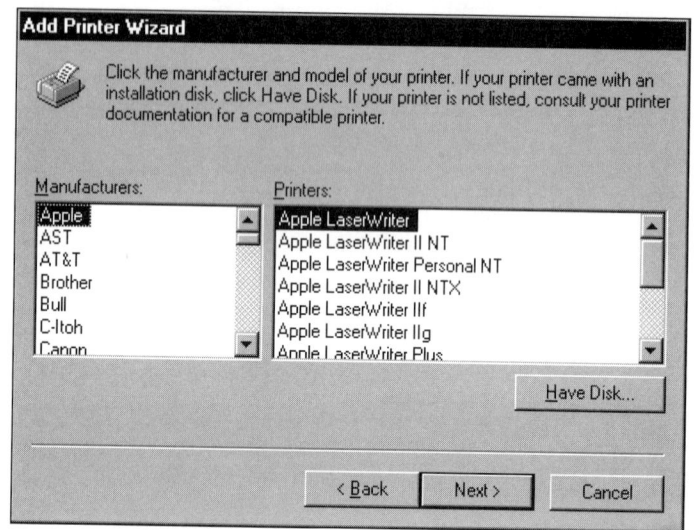

4. Click on the port to be used for the printer. For a normal printer, it would usually be LPT1. It will differ for a disk file, modem, fax or other type of device. Click on Configure Port to verify that the settings are what you want. Click on Next.

5. Enter a name for the printer that you will be sure to remember, and then select whether you want to set this printer as the default printer. Click Next.

6. To print a test page, click Yes. Otherwise click No, and then click Finish. The printer will be added to the contents of the Printers folder.

SEE ALSO: *Associating Files; Registry*

Printing

A Print job may consist of a document to be printed, faxed, or written to disk, using a printer either connected to your computer or on the network to which you are connected. The definition of a printer is somewhat vague. You can think of it as anything that has a name, a port address, and a driver program.

To Interrupt Printing

Occasionally, you may need to interrupt a print job. You may do so in two ways:

- Click on the printer icon on the Taskbar, and when the Printer Queue dialog box is displayed, select Pause Printing or Cancel Printing from the Document menu.

- Select Start ➤ Settings ➤ Printers. Next double-click on the printer icon you want to interrupt, and the Printer queue will be displayed. Select Document ➤ Pause Printing, or Document ➤ Cancel Printing.

- Using either the printer icon or the Printers folder, go to the Printer Queue dialog box, place the pointer on the document you want to interrupt, click the right mouse button for the popup menu, and select Pause Printing or Cancel Printing.

To Initiate Printing

Once your document is open, you can initiate printing in three ways:

- Select File ➤ Print.
- Click on the printer icon in the toolbar.
- Drag a document file to a printer icon.

COMMAND AND FEATURE REFERENCE

After initiating printing, you will see the Print dialog box. Depending on the application, it will contain options such as the following:

Print What describes what is to be printed. The options will vary depending on the application.

Copies displays the number of copies that will be printed (the default is 1 copy). Type the number you require.

Page Range determines whether the whole document, the current page, or a range of pages will be printed.

Printer displays another dialog box where you can change the printer.

Options displays another dialog box with options pertaining to the document you are printing, such as the quality of printing and whether hidden characters are to be printed.

Print allows you to choose Odd, Even, or All pages.

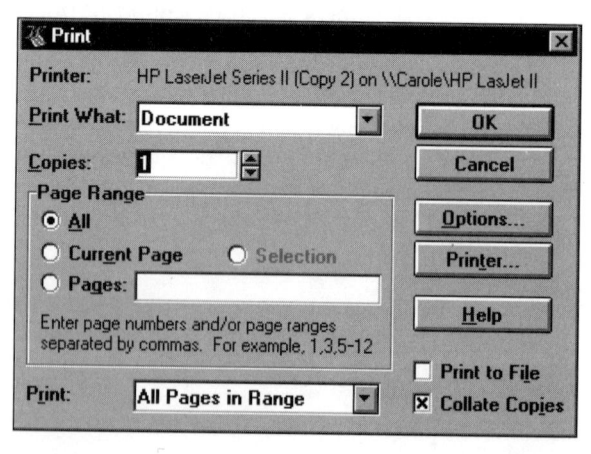

TIP: *If your print dialog box differs, refer to the application for specific instructions.*

PRINTING

To Change a Printer Port

To change a printer port, follow these steps:

1. Select Start ➤ Settings ➤ Control Panel, and then double-click on Printers.

2. Find the printer for which you want to change the port, place the pointer on it, and click on the right mouse button for the popup menu.

3. Click on Properties.

4. Select the Details tab, and find the port you want on the Print to the following port list box.

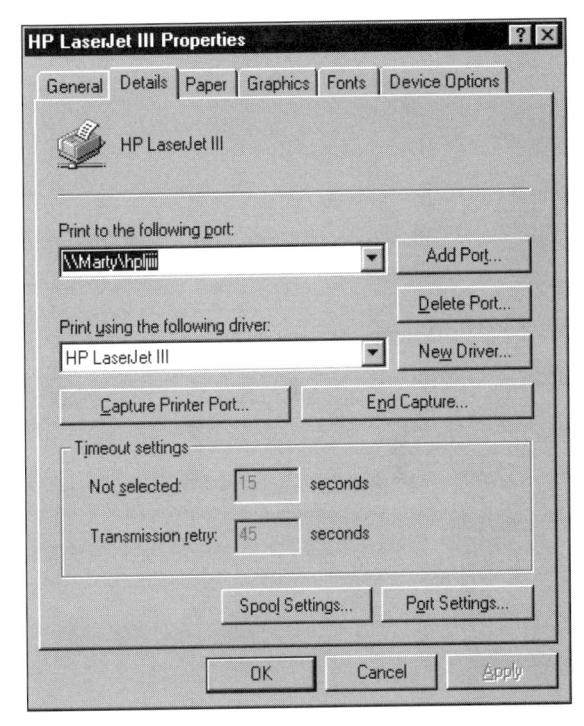

5. Select the new port and click OK.

COMMAND AND FEATURE REFERENCE

Profiles

Windows 95 maintains both hardware and user profiles. Profiles contain the characteristics of the object or user, and relevant defaults. (See *Mail and Fax* for how to set up a Microsoft Exchange profile.)

Hardware Profile

The Hardware profile can be seen on the Hardware Profiles tab in the System control panel. It lists the hardware profiles that are available in your system. You can create additional profiles to enable or disable certain hardware devices on your system. If you do so, you will be prompted when Windows 95 is booted to choose which profile to use in the current session.

Follow these steps to create another Hardware Profile:

1. Select Start ➤ Settings ➤ Control Panel, and then double-click on System. The System Properties dialog box will be displayed. Click on the Hardware Profiles tab.

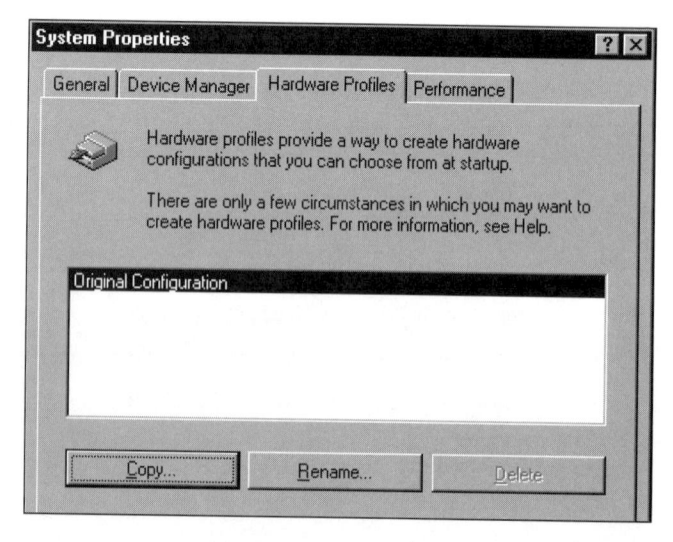

2. Select the hardware profile to be modified, and then click on Copy to create a duplicate of the profile.

3. Enter a name for the copy and click on OK. A new hardware profile will appear in the Hardware Profiles list.

4. To change the copied profile to enable or disable hardware drivers, click on the Device Manager tab.

5. Click on the plus sign next to the device type to see the devices under it.

6. Double-click on the hardware device you want to change. A properties dialog box will be displayed with the hardware profiles listed under device usage.

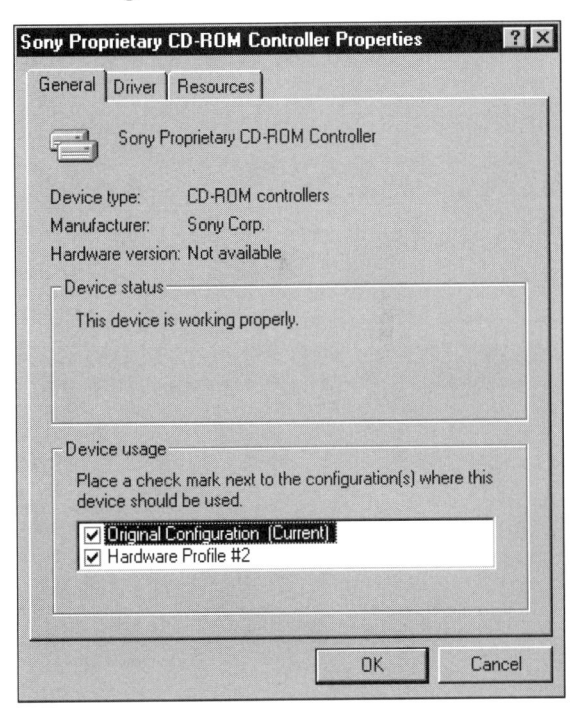

COMMAND AND FEATURE REFERENCE

7. Place a check mark next to the profile to enable the device, or remove it to disable it. Click OK twice.

The next time you bring up Windows 95, you will be asked which hardware profile to use.

User Profiles

User Profiles are used to allow multiple people to have their own customized Desktop settings and passwords. When you log on after establishing your own user profile, Windows uses your settings until another user logs on. Follow these steps to set up the User Profiles:

1. Select Start ➤ Settings ➤ Control Panel, and then double-click on Passwords. The Passwords Properties dialog box will be displayed.

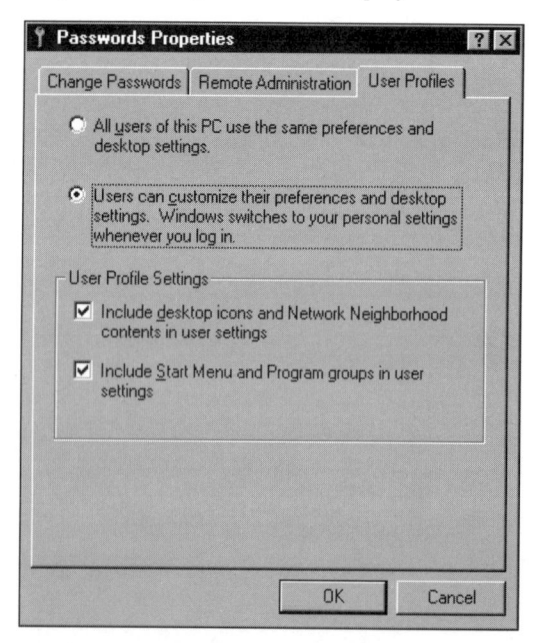

2. Click on the User Profiles tab. The following options will be available to you:

- **All users of the PC use the same preferences and desktop settings** This option is used if no customized user profiles are to be established.

- **Users can customize their preferences and desktop settings. Windows switches to your personal settings whenever you log in** Use this option to set up customized desktop settings for multiple users. When this option is selected, two other User Profile Settings options become available: **1) Include desktop icons and Network Neighborhood contents in user settings**. These options specify that desktop icons and Network Neighborhood contents be customized for an individual user. This can include desktop colors, fonts, and passwords. **2) Include Start Menu and Program groups in user settings**. This option specifies that the contents on the Start menu and the options in the Program submenu are customized to a user. (See *Passwords* for additional information.)

3. Click on the options you want, and then click OK.

SEE ALSO: *Display Control Panel; Passwords; Shut Down; System*

Program Groups, Adding to the Programs Menu

To add new program groups to the Programs menu, first create a folder, and then add a program to it. Follow these steps:

1. Click on the Start button with the right mouse button. The popup menu will be displayed.

2. Click on Open. The Start menu folder will be displayed.

3. Double-click on the Programs folder.

4. Select File ➤ New ➤ Folder. A folder named New Folder will be added to the Programs folder.

5. Type the name that you want the new folder to have, and then press Enter. You now have an empty folder in the Programs menu into which you will add a program or item.

6. Double-click on the new folder just created.

7. Select File ➤ New ➤ Shortcut. The Create Shortcut Wizard will be displayed to help you add the program to the new folder.

8. Type the path and name of the item you want to add to the Programs menu in the Command Line text box, or use Browse to find and select it. Click on Next.

9. Type a shortcut name for the program, and click on Finish.

The next time you bring up the Programs menu, you will see the new folder. When you select that folder, you will see the item that has been added to it.

Program Manager

The functions performed by the Windows 3.x Program Manager have been replaced by the Program menu. If you really like the Program Manager and want it back, follow these steps:

1. From the Explorer, click on the \Windows folder in the left pane.

2. In the right pane, scroll down until you find Progman.exe, the Windows 3.x Program Manager program.

3. Double-click on it to activate it.

> **SEE ALSO:** *Program Groups, Adding to the Programs Menu; Shortcuts*

Programs Menu

The Programs menu lists the programs available in Windows 95, either as stand-alone programs or in a program group (such as Microsoft Office or Microsoft Multimedia). Windows programs are added to the Programs menu automatically as they are installed—you are generally asked to verify in which folder or program group the new program is to be placed. Some programs, such as DOS programs, may not be automatically installed in the Programs menu. These programs can be added using the Add/Remove Programs control panel.

Follow these steps to start a program from the Programs menu:

1. Select Start ➤ Programs. The current list of program groups will be listed.

COMMAND AND FEATURE REFERENCE

2. Select a program group, and the programs it contains will be listed.

3. Click on a program to start it.

SEE ALSO: *Add/Remove Programs; Program Groups, Adding to the Programs Menu; Start Button*

Properties

Properties are charactistics of a computer, device, file, or folder, and are displayed in the Properties dialog box. The properties for any item will vary depending on what it is. To open any Properties dialog box, follow these steps:

1. In Explorer or My Computer, click on the item.

2. Select File ➤ Properties.

TIP: *You can also see the properties by clicking the right mouse button and selecting Properties from the popup menu.*

Quick View

Quick View allows you to view a document without fully opening it. It is available only on the CD-ROM and must be specifically installed using the Custom installation or Add/Remove program. The Quick View command is available from the File menu in either Explorer, My Computer, or Network Neighborhood. If the command is not available on the File menu, then the document cannot be viewed in this way. Follow these steps:

1. Select Start ➤ Programs ➤ Explorer, or double-click on the My Computer or Network Neighborhood icon on the Desktop.

REBOOTING YOUR COMPUTER

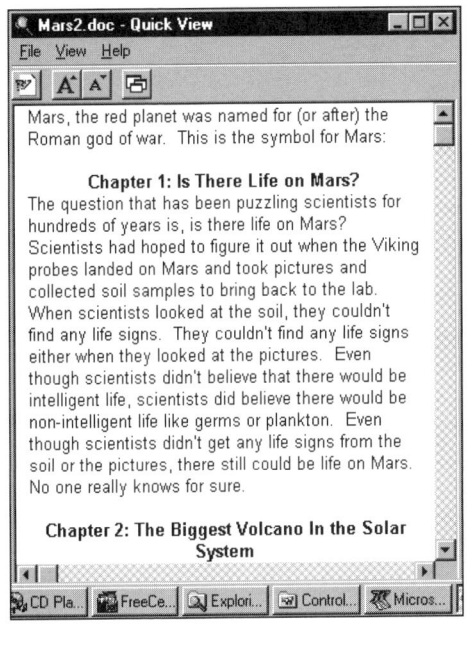

2. Find the file you want to view, and select it.

3. Select File ➤ Quick View. (If Quick View is not available, you cannot do this with the selected document.) A window will open with the selected document or picture in it.

TIP: *You can also select Quick View from the popup menu that is displayed when you right-click on a file.*

Quitting

SEE: *Closing Files or Windows; Shut Down*

Rebooting Your Computer

SEE: *Shut Down*

COMMAND AND FEATURE REFERENCE

Recording Sound Files

SEE: *Sound Recorder*

Recycle Bin

The Recycle Bin, represented on the Desktop by a wastebasket icon, is a folder that temporarily stores deleted files. When it is emptied, the files are purged from the computer all at once. Files are copied to the Recycle Bin both directly and indirectly. You can simply drag a file there, or you can cause it to be placed there by using the Delete function, either from the keyboard or the menu.

TIP: *If the Recycle Bin contains deleted files, the icon shows paper coming out the top; if it is empty, no paper shows.*

The Recycle Bin Window

When you double-click on the Recycle Bin icon, the Recycle Bin window will appear, listing all the files within the folder. If View ➤ Details is selected, you will also see the Original Location of the file, the Date Deleted, the Type of file, and its Size.

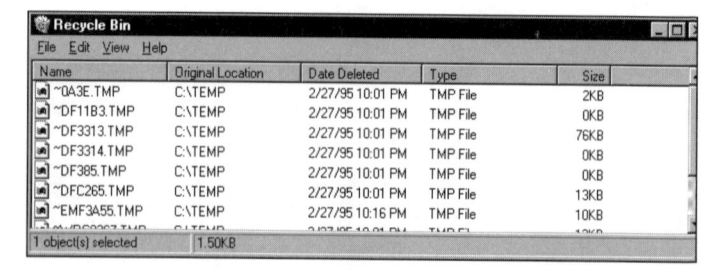

Name	Original Location	Date Deleted	Type	Size
~0A3E.TMP	C:\TEMP	2/27/95 10:01 PM	TMP File	2KB
~DF11B3.TMP	C:\TEMP	2/27/95 10:01 PM	TMP File	0KB
~DF3313.TMP	C:\TEMP	2/27/95 10:01 PM	TMP File	76KB
~DF3314.TMP	C:\TEMP	2/27/95 10:01 PM	TMP File	0KB
~DF385.TMP	C:\TEMP	2/27/95 10:01 PM	TMP File	0KB
~DFC265.TMP	C:\TEMP	2/27/95 10:01 PM	TMP File	13KB
~EMF3A55.TMP	C:\TEMP	2/27/95 10:16 PM	TMP File	10KB

1 object(s) selected   1.50KB

RECYCLE BIN

The Recycle Bin window contains the standard Windows menus and options. The unique options are as follows:

File Menu

Restore becomes available when a file is selected, and moves it back to its originating directory or folder.

Empty Recycle Bin deletes files from the Recycle Bin folder, thus deleting them from the computer.

Edit Menu

Select All selects all the files in the folder.

Invert Selection selects all the files except those currently selected (which become unselected).

View Menu

Options displays an Options dialog box with three tabs:

- **Folder** offers two Browsing options, which affect how selected items are displayed: Browse folders using a separate window for each folder, or Browse folders by using a single window that changes as you open each folder.

- **View** offers options to display all files or to hide files with specific extensions, to display the MS–DOS path in the title bar, and to hide MS–DOS file extensions for registered files.

- **File Types** allows you to add or register a New Type of file (a file with an unregistered extension) or Remove them. You can also Edit the data in the File Type records. (See *Associating Files*.)

COMMAND AND FEATURE REFERENCE

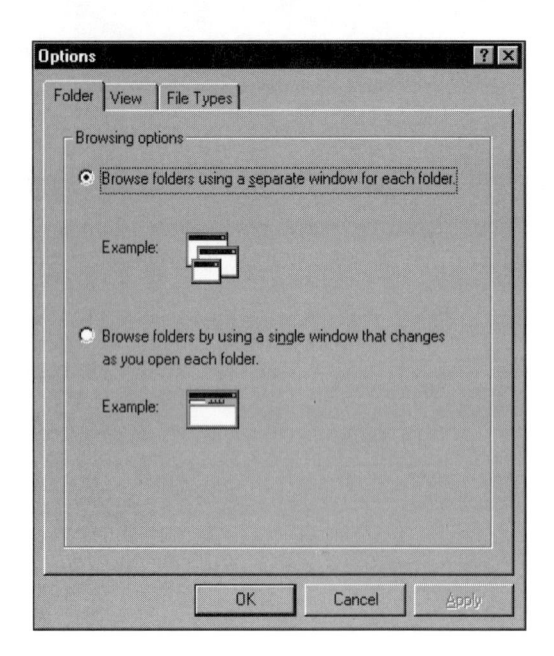

Emptying the Recycle Bin

The disk space dedicated to the Recycle Bin is a constant size. Periodically you'll have to empty the Recycle Bin to release the space taken by the deleted files, making room for additional ones. Follow these steps to empty it:

1. Double-click on the Recycle bin icon. The Recycle Bin folder will be displayed.

2. To empty the whole bin, select File ➤ Empty Recycle Bin. To empty selected files, hold down Ctrl and click on the files to be removed. Then press Del or select File ➤ Delete.

3. Click on Yes to verify that you want to delete the files.

TIP: *You can also empty the Recycle Bin by clicking on the icon with the right mouse button and choosing Empty Recycle Bin.*

Changing the Size of the Recycle Bin

The initial size of the Recycle Bin is automatically set at 10% of the total disk space, but can be changed in the Properties dialog box. You can change the space allocated for the Recycle Bin to be the same for all your disks, or to be individually determined. Follow these steps to change the configuration and size:

1. Click on the Recycle Bin icon with the right mouse button. The right mouse popup menu will be displayed.

2. Select Properties. The Recycle Bin Properties dialog box will be displayed.

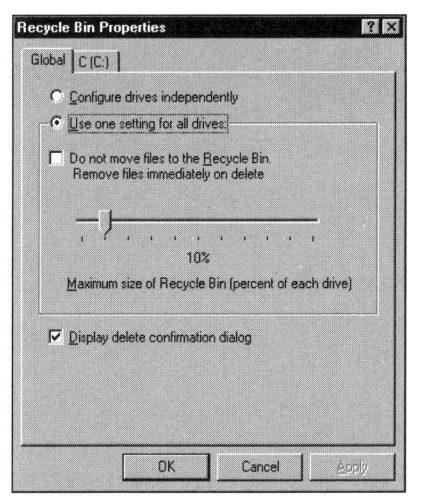

3. To use a common size for all disks, select Use one setting for all drives and then drag the slider to the percentage disk space you want to be allocated for all disks.

4. To determine unique sizes for each of the disks on your system, select Configure drives independently. Click on the tab of the disk for which you want to change sizes. Drag the slider to the percentage you want to allocate to the Recycle Bin on that disk.

5. Click OK.

Recovering Files from the Recycle Bin

To recover files from the Recycle Bin and move them back to their original folders, follow these steps:

1. Double-click on the Recycle Bin icon.

2. Select the files you want to restore, holding down Ctrl for multiple files.

3. Select Restore from the File menu.

You can also drag the file out of the Recycle Bin, or undo the delete by choosing Edit ➤ Undo Delete in any folder or Explorer window or by pressing Ctrl+Z. The undo option is quite powerful, allowing you to undo the last ten things you deleted by selecting the option ten times.

WARNING: *If you delete more files than can be held in the disk space allocated for the Recycle Bin, your earliest deleted files will disappear without warning.*

Bypassing the Recycle Bin

To delete the files immediately without moving them first to the Recycle Bin, follow these steps:

1. Click on the Recycle Bin icon with the right mouse button.

2. Select Properties. The Recycle Bin Properties dialog box will be displayed.

3. On the Global tab, select Do not move files to the Recycle Bin. Remove files immediately on delete.

NOTE: *If you do not move the files to the Recycle Bin, you will not be able to undo or restore any that are accidentally deleted.*

TIP: *If you want to bypass the Recycle Bin for one disk drive only, select Configure drives independently from the Recycle Bin Properties dialog box (on the Global tab), then select the disk drive tab, and finally, select Do not move files to the Recycle Bin. Remove files immediately on delete.*

Regional Settings Control Panel

The Regional Settings control panel allows you to establish the system defaults for language, country, number, currency, time, and date formatting. Follow these steps to access Regional Settings.

1. Select Start ➤ Settings ➤ Control Panel, and then double-click on Regional Settings. The Regional Settings Properties dialog box will be displayed.

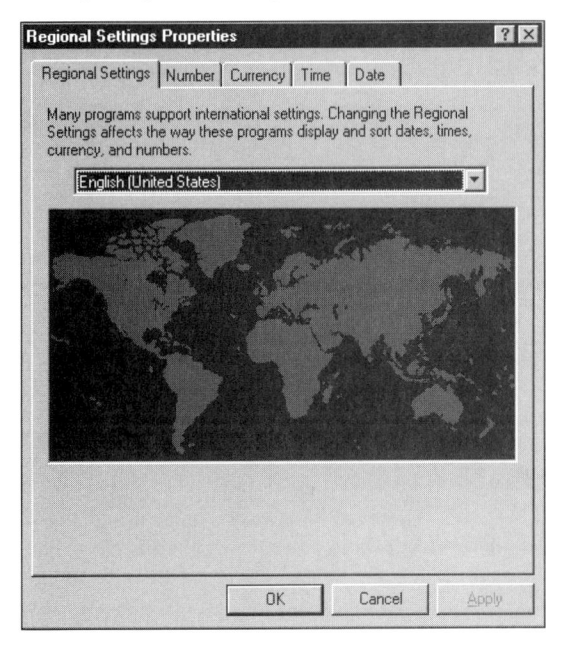

2. On the Regional Settings tab, select a language from the list by clicking on the down arrow and then clicking on the selected country and language.

3. Select the applicable tab for Number, Currency, Time, or Date to change those defaults, if necessary, and then click on OK.

SEE ALSO: *Currency Format; Date/Time, Settings; Number Format; Time Format; Time Zone Default Settings*

COMMAND AND FEATURE REFERENCE

Registry

The Registry is where the system defaults and Properties for all devices, files, folders, and other resources are stored. It is the central source of information for both users and computers. The Control Panel is the primary place where you modify or set the various Registry items.

The Registry replaces the Autoexec.bat, Config.sys, Win.ini, and other .ini files in earlier Windows versions. Those files are still maintained for other programs that use them, but they are not used by Windows 95.

SEE ALSO: *Associating Files; Control Panel*

Registering Files

SEE: *Associating Files*

Remote Access

SEE: *Dial-Up Networking; HyperTerminal*

Renaming Files and Folders

SEE: *Naming Files and Folders*

Resource Meter

The Resource Meter measures the resource use on your computer as you load and use programs. It

RESOURCE METER

measures the use of memory each time a function is performed, such as a program being loaded, a dialog box being displayed, or a menu item being selected. You can install it either with the Add/Remove Programs control panel, or by using the Custom installation procedure in the Windows 95 Setup. Follow these steps to use the Resource Meter:

1. Select Start ➤ Programs ➤ Accessories ➤ System Tools and click on Resource Meter.

2. An introductory message will be displayed telling you what the Resource Meter is all about. Click OK. An icon will appear in your Taskbar next to the time.

3. Double-click on the icon to see the current reading of your system resources.

TIP: You can also see the Resource Meter readout by right-clicking on the icon in the Taskbar and selecting Details from the popup menu.

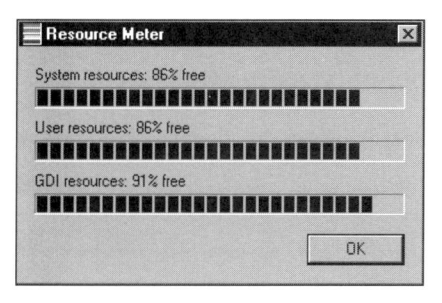

You will see three readings that represent areas in your computer's memory where specialized processing information is stored. The areas are used in varying amounts by different programs. As you run multiple programs, you'll see percentages of use in these areas. These three areas are:

- System resources
- User resources
- GDI resources or Graphic Device Interface resources

4. When you are finished with the Resource Meter, right-click on the icon in the Taskbar and select Exit.

271

COMMAND AND FEATURE REFERENCE

Restoring Files

Files that have been backed up can be restored using the Microsoft Backup utility. Follow these steps:

1. Select Start ➤ Programs ➤ Accessories ➤ System Tools and click on Backup. The Welcome to Microsoft Backup screen will be displayed.

2. After you have read the welcome message, click on OK. After a minute, a message will be displayed about the Full System Backup (see *Backing Up Files and Folders*). Click OK and the Microsoft Backup window will be displayed.

3. Click on the Restore tab.

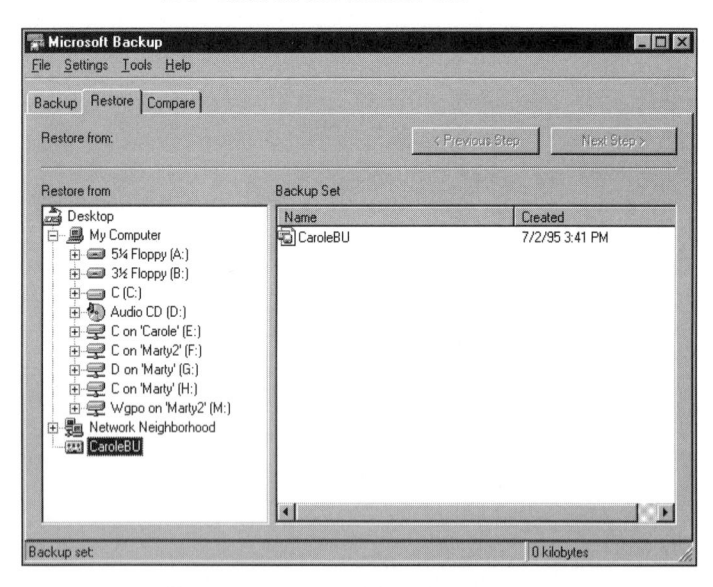

4. Click on the drive where your last backup set was created.

5. In the right pane of the window, click on the backup set you want, and then click Next Step. A list of files will be displayed.

6. To select all files within a folder, click on the empty check box next to the name. To restore selected files, click on the icon in the left pane next to the name of each file or folder you want to restore. As you click on a folder's icon, the files contained within it will be displayed on the right. Click on the empty check box to select them. To restore the complete backup set, click on the backup set name in the right pane.

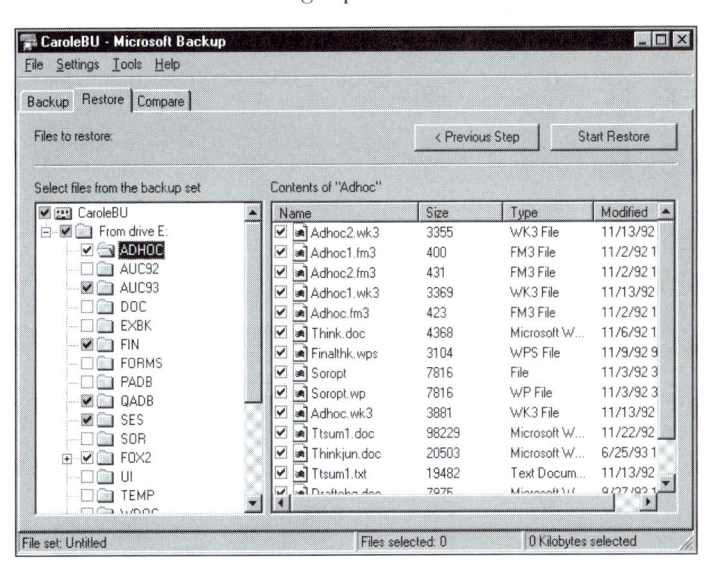

7. Click Start Restore.

NOTE: *A check mark in a gray check box means that only some of the files in a folder have been selected. A check mark in a clear or white box means that all files in a folder have been selected.*

COMMAND AND FEATURE REFERENCE

Right-Clicking

Clicking with the right mouse button gives you two added features:

- If you right click within a dialog box, you can get additional help from the What's This popup label. Click it, and additional information will be displayed. If you then click the right mouse button within the popup information, you'll be able to print or copy the topic.

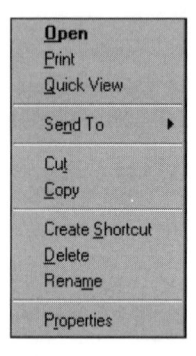

- If you right-click on many objects, like a disk, file, or folder, a popup menu will be displayed that offers a quick way to get at the most commonly used commands for that object. Even right-clicking on the Taskbar or Desktop will display a popup menu.

Run Option

The Run option is used to start a program or open a folder by typing its path and name. Use this approach for setup or install programs on floppy disks or CD-ROMs. Follow these steps:

1. Select Start ➤ Run. A Run dialog box will be displayed.

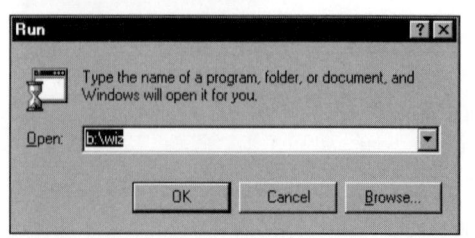

2. If you have Run this program recently, you may find its name in the Open list box. Click on the down arrow and select it, then click OK.

3. If you have not run this program recently, type in the path and program name. (For example, *C:\Folder\Program.*)

4. If you are not sure of the path or program name, use Browse to find and select the program. Then click OK.

Saving Files

Saving your files periodically is an important part of protecting your data from loss caused by accidental deletion or power outage. Many of the Windows 95 windows contain Save and Save As commands in the File menu. Use Save As to assign a name or different folder location to your file. Use Save for files already named and stored in the correct folder. You can select File ➤ Save, or click on the Save icon.

SEE ALSO: *Backing Up Files and Folders*

ScanDisk

ScanDisk allows you to check a disk for errors. Two types of tests can be performed:

Standard tests for file and folder errors.

Thorough tests for the standard items and also scans the disk surface for errors.

The ScanDisk Window

To start ScanDisk, select Start ➤ Programs ➤ Accessories ➤ System Tools, and then click on ScanDisk.

COMMAND AND FEATURE REFERENCE

When ScanDisk is loaded, you will see the following options in the window:

Select the drive you want to check for errors lists the drives available for scanning.

Type of test determines whether to perform a Standard or Thorough test.

Options (available for Thorough tests) allows you to specify which areas of the disk are to be scanned: System and data areas, System area only, or Data area only. You can control whether to test by writing to disk and then trying to read it, and whether repairs of bad sectors in hidden and system files should be performed.

Automatically fix errors will attempt to fix any errors found. If it is not checked, you will be given a choice of repairing the error, deleting the folder, or ignoring the error.

Advanced allows you to specify how the errors will be handled:

- **Display Summary** provides information about the drive being scanned and any errors discovered and repaired.

- **Log file** records the results of a scan in a file named Scandisk.log.

- **Cross-linked files** (files pointing to the same data on a disk) may be deleted, ignored, or copied.

- **Lost file fragments** that cannot be linked to existing files can be deleted or converted to files so you can verify that they are no longer useful. They will be named *File*0000, and so on.

- **Check files for** looks for invalid names, dates, or times, which can cause a file to be unreadable or improperly displayed in sorted data.

- **Check host drive first** checks the uncompressed host drive for errors before checking data compressed with Double-Space or DriveSpace.

After setting the options you want, click on Start to begin scanning the disk.

Screen Saver

The screen saver can be changed or selected in the Display control panel. You can set the speed, shape, density, and color of the screen saver, as well as a password to get back to your work and other settings.

SEE ALSO: *Display Control Panel*

COMMAND AND FEATURE REFERENCE

Searching for Computers, Disks, Files, or Folders

SEE: *Finding Computers; Finding Files and Folders*

Selecting Objects

An object, such as a file in a list, is selected when you click on it. When you select objects, they are highlighted, or shown in reverse video. To select several objects, hold down Ctrl while clicking on them. To deselect one of the objects, again hold down Ctrl while clicking on the object. To select a group of contiguous objects in a list, hold down Shift while clicking on the first and last entries in the list.

Send To Options

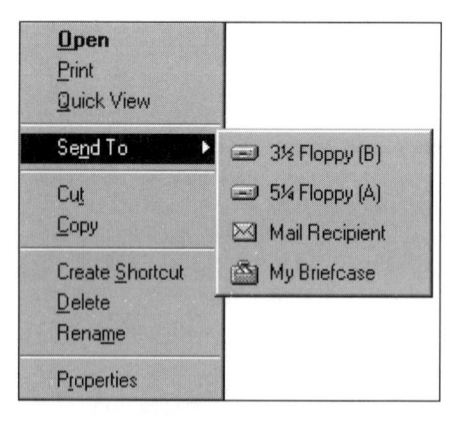

The Send To options on a file or folder's popup menu allow you to send items to common destinations, such as floppy disk drives, a fax, the post-office, or My Briefcase. \SendTo is a folder within the \Windows folder in which Windows automatically places some shortcuts to destinations, and in which you can place shortcuts to send files to other destinations, such as a printer, network drive, or folder. Once the

\SendTo folder is set up with destinations you frequently use, you can send a file quickly to a destination by following these steps:

1. Click on the file with the right mouse button for the popup menu.

2. Select Send To.

3. Click on the listed destination.

TIP: *You can place the \SendTo folder on the Program menu to have access from there as well. (See Program Menu for details on how to do this.)*

SEE ALSO: *Shortcuts*

Setting Up a Printer

SEE: *Printers Folder*

Sharing Resources

SEE: *Network Control Panel; Networks and Networking; Passwords; Properties*

Shortcuts

Shortcuts are quick ways to open or get to a disk, file, folder, printer, computer, or program. Shortcuts can be stored on the Desktop, in a folder, or in the Start menu. They may be identified by an arrow in the lower-left of the icon. When you double-click on a shortcut, the

COMMAND AND FEATURE REFERENCE

file, folder, printer, computer, or program is opened. For example, if you create a shortcut for the printer and drag it to the Desktop, you can then print a file by dragging the file's icon to the printer shortcut icon on the Desktop.

Creating a Shortcut

There are three ways to create a shortcut: using the File menu, popup menus, or drag and copy.

Creating a Shortcut Using Menus

To create a shortcut using menus, follow these steps:

1. Find and click on the item for which you wish to create a shortcut. You may find it using My Computer or Explorer. (In Explorer, the object must be displayed in the right pane.)

2. Select File ➤ Create Shortcut. The shortcut will be instantly created and will appear in the right-hand pane of the window.

3. Drag the shortcut where you want it.

Creating a Shortcut Using a Popup Menu

A quicker way to create a shortcut, which can be done in My Computer, Explorer, or on the Desktop, is to click on the item with the right mouse button and then select Create Shortcut from the popup menu.

Creating a Shortcut Using Drag and Copy

You can create a shortcut by dragging the item for which you want a shortcut to its destination, such as another folder or the Desktop, while pressing Ctrl+Shift. (Pressing Shift only will move a file; Ctrl will copy a file; Ctrl+Shift will create a shortcut for it.) Also, if you drag the item with the right mouse button, you will get a popup menu when you are done dragging from which you can select Create Shortcut.

TIP: *To change the properties of the shortcut, click on it with the right mouse button and click on Properties.*

NOTE: *Deleting a shortcut does not delete the original item. It will still remain on the disk. To delete a shortcut, drag it to the Recycle Bin and release the mouse button. Or just press Delete.*

Placing a Shortcut

A shortcut may be placed in a folder, on the Desktop, or in the Start menu. Create a shortcut, and then follow these steps:

- *To place a shortcut in a folder*, drag the shortcut to the folder and release it.

- *To place a shortcut on the Desktop*, drag the shortcut to the Desktop and release it.

- *To place a shortcut on the Start menu*, create a shortcut and place it on the Desktop, and select Start ➤ Settings, and then Taskbar. The Taskbar Properties window will be displayed. Click on the Start Programs Menu tab and then click on Advanced. Drag the shortcut to the Start Menu folder. You can also drag the shortcut icon directly to the Start Menu folder using Explorer.

TIP: *To remove a shortcut from the Start Menu, select Remove from the Start Menu Programs tab in Taskbar Properties. Then select the item to be removed and click on Remove. You can also find \Windows\Start Menu with Explorer, select the shortcut, and press Delete.*

COMMAND AND FEATURE REFERENCE

> **TIP:** *A quick way to get a shortcut for a program file (one with an extension of .exe, .com, or .bat) in the Start menu, the Desktop, or another folder, is to drag the original file to the destination. The original file will remain in the original folder, and a shortcut will automatically be created at the destination.*

Shut Down (Quitting)

The Shut Down procedure for Windows 95 must be followed if you want to be sure that data is not lost or files corrupted while shutting down your computer. Follow these steps to shut down:

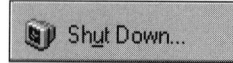

1. When you are ready to shut off the computer, select Start ➤ Shut Down. A Shut Down Windows dialog box will be displayed, containing the following options:

   Shut down the computer prepares the computer to be turned off.

   Restart the computer prepares the computer for shut down, and then starts it up again.

   Restart the computer in MS–DOS mode closes down Windows 95 and restarts the computer in MS–DOS mode, where MS–DOS controls the computer's resources.

   Close all programs and log on as a different user (used for a shared computer) logs you off of the computer so that someone else can use it.

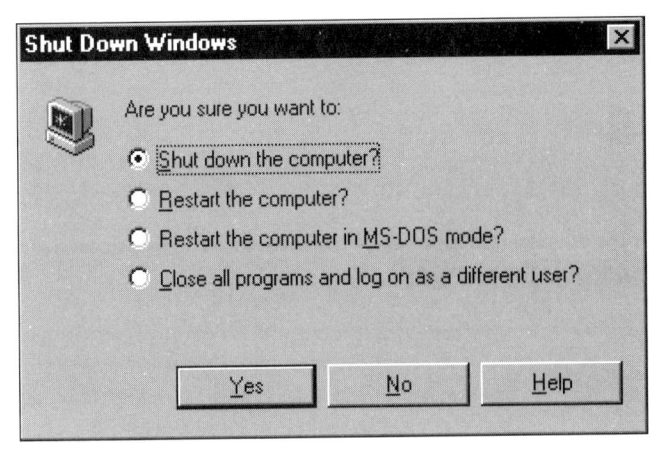

> **Shut Down Windows**
>
> Are you sure you want to:
>
> ⦿ Shut down the computer?
> ○ Restart the computer?
> ○ Restart the computer in MS-DOS mode?
> ○ Close all programs and log on as a different user?
>
> [Yes]   [No]   [Help]

2. Select the option you want by clicking on it, and then click on Yes.

3. Respond to any other questions that may appear, such as whether it is OK to disconnect network users.

Sizing Windows

SEE: *Maximize/Minimize Windows*

Sorting Files and Folders

The Explorer and My Computer windows allow you to list files and folders in order by Name, Type, Size, or Date. To do this, select View Arrange icons, and then click on the order you want.

TIP: *If the Explorer is in Detail view, you can sort a particular column by clicking on the button at the top of the column. On your first click, the column is sorted in*

COMMAND AND FEATURE REFERENCE

ascending order. The second click sorts the column in descending order.

SEE ALSO: *Explorer; My Computer*

Sound Recorder

The Sound Recorder allows you to record sounds on your computer. To use it, you must have an audio input device such as a CD-ROM Player or a microphone installed on your computer, as well as a sound card and speakers.

Sound Recorder   To bring up the Sound Recorder, select Start ➤ Programs ➤ Accessories ➤ Multimedia and click on Sound Recorder. The Sound Recorder window will be displayed.

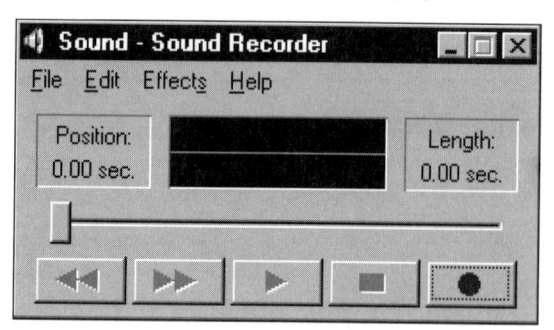

Sound Recorder Toolbars

While you are creating a sound track, you use the tools in the window to control the recording and playback functions. The Sound Recorder contains the following tools:

Position:
0.32 sec.

Position gives the location on the sound track. It is coordinated with the slider, which gives you a visual impression of where the sound track is positioned.

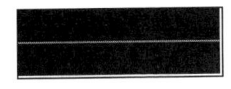

Track Visual Display gives a visual image of the quality of the sound.

Length shows the current length of the sound track.

Slider shows the relative position within the sound track. As the sound records or plays, the slider moves to the right, showing the relative distance within the sound track.

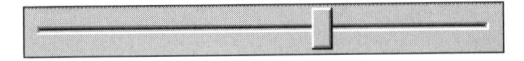

Seek to Start repositions the sound track at the beginning.

Seek to End repositions the sound track at the end.

Play plays the sound track from the current position forward.

Stop interrupts the play or recording.

Record activates the recording function.

The Sound Recorder Menus

The Sound Recorder menus offer special options that aid in the creation of a sound track.

The **File** menu contains the standard options, plus three that deserve special mention:

- **New** allows you to create or record a new sound file. When you click on New, the Record button becomes available, which, when clicked, begins recording.

- **Properties** displays the Properties dialog box for the current sound file.

COMMAND AND FEATURE REFERENCE

- **Revert** removes the changes made to the sound file since the last save.

The **Edit** menu contains these special options:

- **Copy** copies a portion of the file. To use, position the file where the copy is to begin, select Edit ➤ Copy, and then click on Stop when you want the copy to stop.

- **Paste Insert** allows you to insert the copied sound beginning at the current position. It will overlay the current sound.

- **Paste Mix** allows you to mix the copied sound with the sound on the file beginning at the current position.

- **Insert File** allows you to insert a .wav file into the sound track beginning at the current position.

- **Mix with File** combines a sound, beginning in the current location, with those already on the sound track.

- **Delete Before Current Position** deletes the contents of the sound file from the current position to the beginning of the file.

- **Delete After Current Position** deletes the contents of the sound file from the current position to the end of the file.

- **Audio Properties** displays the Audio Properties of the file, which contains information on playback and recordings.

TIP: *If the green line is not seen in the visual display, then the sound file is compressed and cannot be modified.*

The **Effects** menu contains the following options for producing special effects with the sound file: Increase Volume (by 25%), Decrease Volume, Increase Speed (by 100%), Decrease Speed, Add Echo, and Reverse.

Sounds Control Panel

The Sounds control panel allows you to assign sounds to certain events. Select Start ➤ Settings ➤ Control Panel, and then double-click on Sounds. The Sounds Properties dialog box will be displayed, containing the following options:

Events lists the events to which you can assign sounds. If the event has a loud-speaker icon to its left, it already has a sound assigned to it, which you may change.

Sound Name allows you to select the name of the sound that you want to assign to an event. This option becomes available when you click on an event.

Browse allows you to search through the available sounds for the one that you want for a particular event. It is usually a .wav file.

Preview is used to hear the sound, if you have a sound board and speakers, to make sure it is the one you want. When a Sound Name is selected, the Preview becomes available.

Details displays the selected Sound Name's Properties dialog box containing Copyright, Media Length, Audio Format, and other information.

Schemes lists sets of events with particular sounds assigned to the listed events. Windows

COMMAND AND FEATURE REFERENCE

Default is the name of the default scheme. The set of associated sounds are displayed under Events. You can change the sounds associated with the schemes and then save them under a different name, if you want.

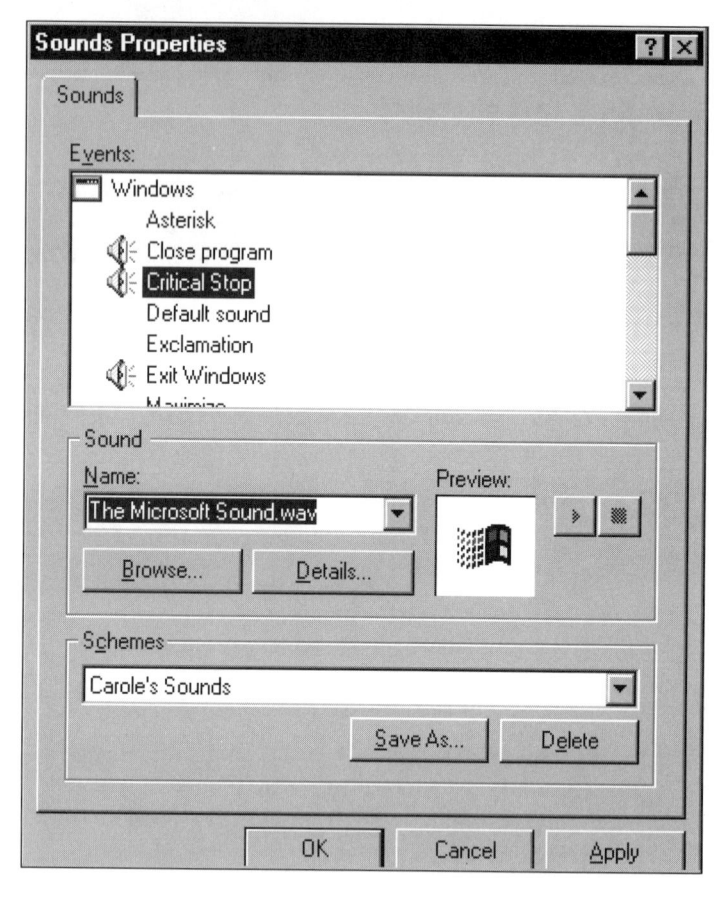

Follow these steps to assign a sound to an event:

1. Select Start ➤ Settings ➤ Control Panel, and then double-click on Sounds.

2. Click on an event to which you want to assign a sound.

3. Add a sound from the Name drop-down list box. If you don't know the sound you want, click on Browse. You will be shown a list of available sounds.

4. Click on a sound, and then click on the Preview arrow to hear it. Continue to select sounds and preview them until you have the sound you want. Click OK twice.

5. Save the set of sounds by clicking on Save As and typing a new name. Click OK.

SEE ALSO: *Accessibility Options (Sound Tab Options); CD Player; Media Player; Multimedia; Sound Recorder*

Start Button

Initially, the Start button is located on the bottom left of your screen on the left-end of the Taskbar. It is the primary way to access files, folders, and programs on your computer. When you click on it, a menu of options will be displayed. Some of the menu options come with Windows 95, but you can add others for quick access.

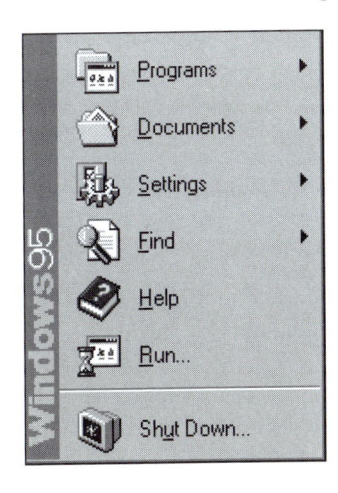

The Start button contains the following options :

Shut down prepares the computer to be shut down or restarted.

Run allows you to run a program or open a folder by typing its path and name.

Help gives you access to system-wide help.

COMMAND AND FEATURE REFERENCE

Find enables you to search for a file, folder, device, computer, or Microsoft network item.

Settings displays the Windows 95 control panels and folders, which control the operation of the vast inventory of features. It is a quick way to access properties and control settings that determine how Windows 95 operates.

Documents lists the last 15 documents that were started by being double-clicked on.

Programs lists the program groups and files available on the system.

TIP: *To add programs and shortcuts to the Start menu, simply drag the file's icon to the Start button.*

SEE ALSO: *Arranging Applications; Startup Applications*

Start Printing

SEE: *Printing*

Startup Applications

A startup application is activated each time Windows is started. If you use certain programs frequently and do not want to initiate them each time you start Windows 95, you can make them Startup Applications. Follow these steps:

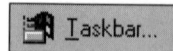

1. Select Start ➤ Settings, and then click on Taskbar. Click on the Start Menu Programs tab.

STARTUP APPLICATIONS

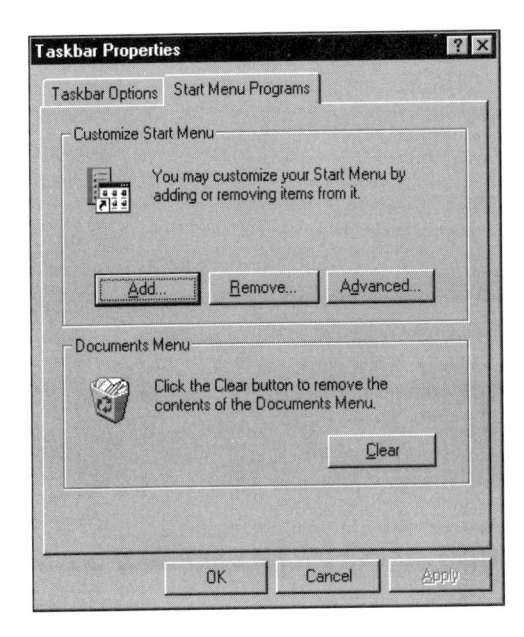

2. Click on Add, and type in the name of the path to the program you want, or click on Browse to find it. Double-click on it to select it and return to the Create Shortcut dialog box. Click on Next.

3. Find the StartUp folder from the list of Start Menu folders, and select it. Click Next.

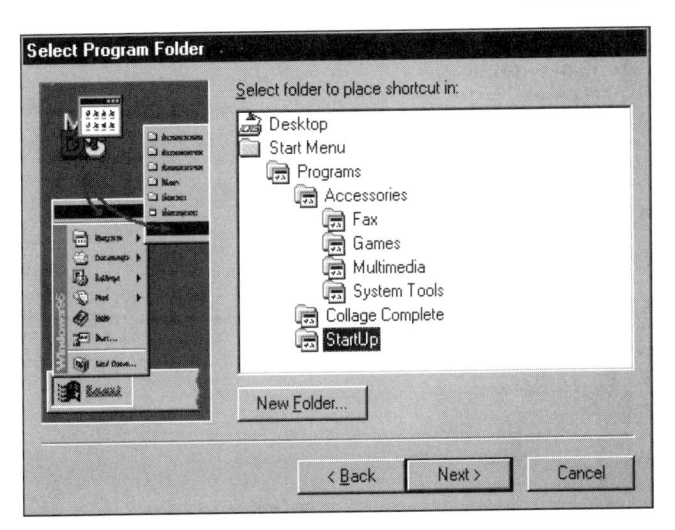

4. Type the shortcut name to appear in the Start Up folder if you don't like the default, and click on Finish.

COMMAND AND FEATURE REFERENCE

5. If you are prompted to choose an icon, click on one, and then click on Finish.

6. Verify that the program has been placed in the StartUp menu by selecting Start ➤ Programs ➤ StartUp.

The next time you start up windows, the program you added to the StartUp folder will be automatically loaded.

NOTE: *If you have the folder open on the Desktop when you shutdown Windows, and its shortcut in the Startup folder, you will get two open copies of the folder the next time you start Windows. Of course, you need only click on the close button to get rid of one copy.*

Stopping Applications

The quickest way to get out of a Windows application is to click the Minimize icon to halt a program temporarily, or the Close icon to close it. If the application is MS–DOS based, you'll have to use the application's procedure for closing, although the window can be minimized.

SEE ALSO: *Closing Files and Folders; Shut Down*

Stop Printing

SEE: *Printing*

Switching Applications, Windows

Switching between applications is facilitated by clicking on the Taskbar, which contains all the active programs. To open an application, click on its icon in the Taskbar. To close an application, click on the Close icon. To place the application's icon on the Taskbar, click on the Minimize icon.

NOTE: *An application does not have to be minimized before another can be opened from the Taskbar.*

TIP: *You can use Alt+Tab to switch between applications that are represented on the Taskbar, or use Alt+Esc to immediately switch to the next application.*

Synchronizing Files

SEE: *My Briefcase*

System Control Panel

The System control panel contains the System Properties for your hardware. It is used both for providing information and for optimizing system performance. However, it should be used with care, since changing the settings without adequate knowledge may degrade your system.

To access the System control panel, select Start ➤ Settings ➤ Control Panel, and then double-click on System. The System Properties dialog box will be displayed, containing the General, Device Manager, Hardware Profiles, and Performance tabs.

General Tab

The General tab contains information about your computer system, which version of Windows 95

COMMAND AND FEATURE REFERENCE

you have, who it is registered to, and the Computer memory size and processor board type.

Device Manager Tab

The Device Manager tab lists all devices on the computer, both shared and directly connected. The following options are available:

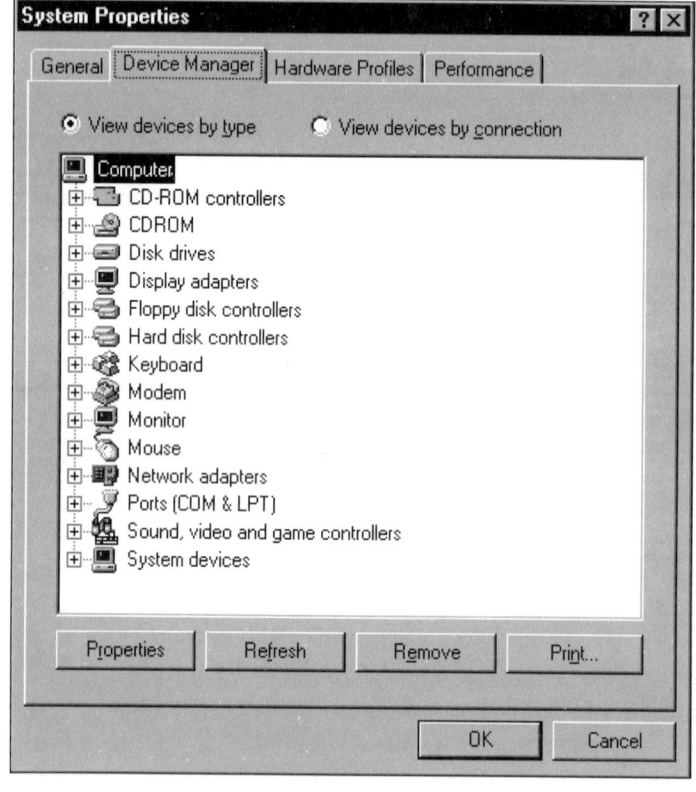

View devices by type lists the devices by type, such as disk drives or Keyboard.

View devices by connection shows with icons how devices are connected to the computer.

Properties displays the properties for the selected device.

Refresh examines the devices on the system and redisplays the list.

Remove deletes a device from the list and the computer. If you delete it, you will have to use Add New Hardware to reinstall it.

Print prints a summary, or a detailed report, of hardware resources on your computer. It can be used for finding hardware problems, for example, by reminding you which devices are connected to which port.

Hardware Profiles Tab

The Hardware Profiles tab allows you to create different hardware profiles containing different devices or resources for your computer system. You might use this for different users, or to prevent access to certain resources. At startup, you select the profile containing the configuration you want to use. You can change the active hardware profile (the profile selected at Startup) on the Device Manager tab. The tab contains three buttons:

Copy allows you to copy a hardware profile so that you make changes to a copy, but not the original.

Rename allows you to rename a hardware profile.

Delete removes a hardware profile from the list.

Performance Tab

The Performance tab displays information about your computer's use of Memory, System Resources,

COMMAND AND FEATURE REFERENCE

Disk Compression, and so on. There are three Advanced Settings buttons:

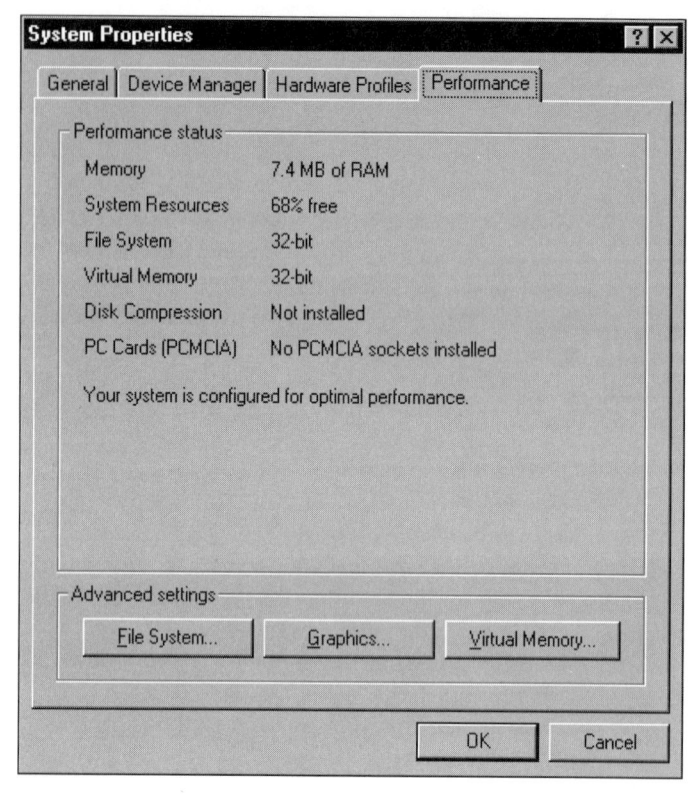

System Properties dialog box — Performance tab:

- Performance status
  - Memory: 7.4 MB of RAM
  - System Resources: 68% free
  - File System: 32-bit
  - Virtual Memory: 32-bit
  - Disk Compression: Not installed
  - PC Cards (PCMCIA): No PCMCIA sockets installed

  Your system is configured for optimal performance.

- Advanced settings: File System..., Graphics..., Virtual Memory...

The **File System** button displays a dialog box with three tabs:

- The **Hard Disk** tab provides options for optimizing hard disk usage. You can specify the Typical role for this machine (Desktop computer, Mobile or docking system as in a portable computer, or Network server), Windows will try to optimize for that use. You can also indicate the Read-ahead optimization when an application requests sequentially stored data. This controls whether Windows should read ahead increments of the data, varying from 0 to 64 kilobytes depending on the position of the slider.

- The **CD-ROM** tab helps Windows to optimize the use of the CD-ROM on your computer by moving the slider from Small to Large to indicate the Supplemental Cache size for the CD-ROM. As you move the slider, a message tells you how much physical memory will be used. To Optimize access pattern for the CD-ROM, select from No-read-ahead, Single-speed drives, Double-speed drives, Triple-speed drives or Quad-speed or higher. Based on this, Windows determines how much memory to set aside for this function.

- The **Troubleshooting** tab provides Settings for advanced users and system administrators. It is primarily used as a diagnostic tool. It allows you to disable several options, such as 32-bit protect-mode disk drivers and synchronous buffer commits so that you can test certain conditions without them.

The **Graphics** button allows you to set the acceleration functions of your display adapters. If your computer has no problems, set the slider on **Full**, the fastest speed. If your computer has severe problems, such as response degradation or unexpected errors in programs, and graphic speed acceleration might be the cause, set the slider first on **None**, and then set it at increasing increments until the problem reoccurs.

The **Virtual Memory** button allows you to specify your own virtual memory settings—the amount of hard disk space used as extra memory—rather than having Windows control it. This should only be done by experienced users.

COMMAND AND FEATURE REFERENCE

System Monitor

The System Monitor tracks the activity of the computer processor (taking a "snapshot" of the processor's activity every five seconds) and presents it in graphic or numeric displays. You can use this for monitoring network activity or heavy resource use at specific times. It can be installed with the Custom installation procedure or Add/Remove Programs.

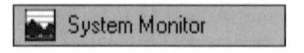

To open the System Monitor, select Start ➤ Programs ➤ Accessories ➤ System Tools, and then click on System Monitor. When you select this, the System Monitor window will be displayed.

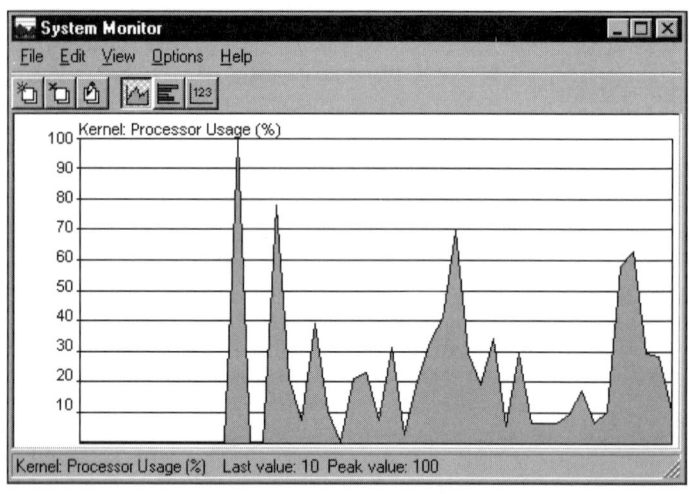

The System Monitor window shows an area chart of the activity on the system as it is occurring. The window contains a number of specific tools and menu items.

The System Monitor Toolbar

The System Monitor toolbar contains tools for changing the presentation of the data, and for adding additional resources to be monitored.

SYSTEM MONITOR

Add Item displays a list of categories of system resources that can be monitored. When you click on a Category, a list of Items within the category will be displayed. When you choose an item to be monitored, a separate monitoring graph will appear in the display area.

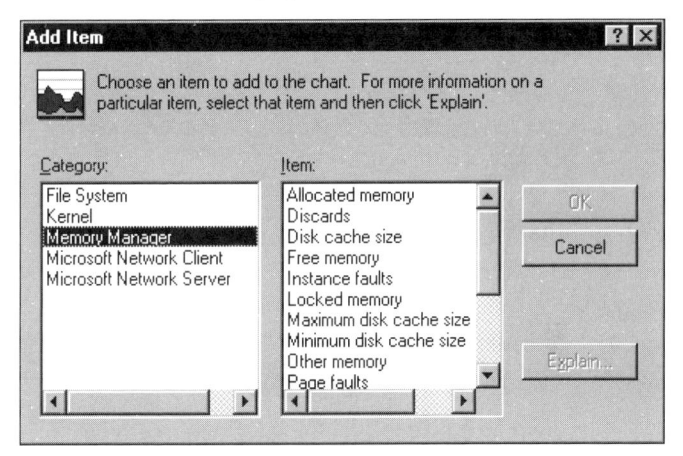

TIP: *To get an explanation of what the item is, click on the item and then click on Explain.*

Remove allows you to remove items from the list of items being monitored.

Edit lists monitoring charts that are currently being displayed. Select the one you want to change, and then click OK. The Chart Options will be displayed where you can change the color and the scale.

Line Charts displays the monitoring data in line chart form.

Bar Charts displays the data in bar chart form.

Numeric Charts displays the data in numeric form.

COMMAND AND FEATURE REFERENCE

System Monitor Menus

The System Monitor menus contain some unique options which allow you to modify the display of data and to select the activity being monitored.

The File Menu

The File menu contains only one unusual command, called **Connect**, which allows you to connect to another computer so that you can monitor its activity.

The Edit Menu

The Edit menu contains four commands. Three are also available from the toolbar: **Add Item**, **Remove**, and **Edit Item**. Look under The System Monitor Toolbar for explanations. (If the toolbar isn't showing, select View ➤ Toolbar.) The fourth, **Clear Window**, clears the information displayed on the window so that you can start again.

The View Menu

The View menu contains the normal **Toolbar** and **Status Bar** commands plus five that are not seen often. Of those, the **Line Charts**, **Bar Charts**, and **Numeric Charts** perform the same function as the toolbar button. **Hide Title Bar** allows you to see only the display of the data rather than the title bar and menus. Double-click on the screen to redisplay the title bar and menus. **Always on Top** ensures that the System Monitor window is always on top. If you should open another window, it will be displayed behind the Systems Monitor window.

The Options Menu

The Options menu offers one command, **Chart**, which allows you to change the frequency of the

Update Interval. As you drag the slider from Faster to Slower, the number of seconds in the update interval is displayed.

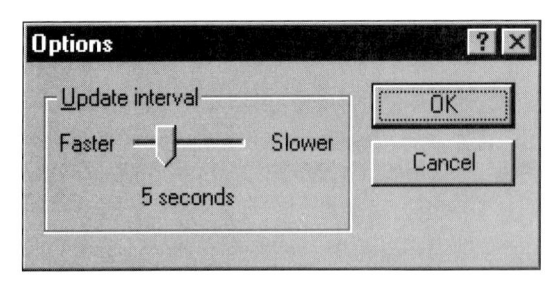

Taskbar

The Taskbar is the primary tool for switching from one program to another and for getting around in Windows 95. It contains commands for finding files and text, initiating or viewing programs and files, and for getting to Help or system settings. The Taskbar contains two types of buttons: one Start button that connects you to your computer's contents, and any number of shortcut buttons for the programs currently active in memory. It also shows the clock and other icons.

The Taskbar is extremely flexible. You can:

- *Resize the Taskbar* by dragging the inside edge
- *Hide the Taskbar* while running an application by selecting Auto hide in the Properties for Taskbar dialog box
- *Allow the Taskbar to be covered* by not selecting Always on top in the Properties dialog box

COMMAND AND FEATURE REFERENCE

To Place an Application on the Taskbar

An application must be active in memory for its icon to be placed on the Taskbar. To place an active application on the Taskbar, click on its minimize button. Then activate the program by clicking on its icon in the Taskbar.

Switching Tasks with the Taskbar

To switch tasks using the Taskbar, choose one of these methods:

- To open a window for an active program on the Taskbar, click on its icon.

- To remove a program's button from the Taskbar altogether, click on the Close icon in the title bar.

- To place an active program's icon in the Taskbar, click on the Minimize button.

To Modify the Taskbar Display

The Taskbar is by default placed on the bottom of the screen, and always displayed on top of other windows so that you can get to it easily. You can change the display by following these steps:

1. Select Start ➤ Settings ➤ Taskbar. The Taskbar Properties dialog box will appear. You can also simply right-click on an empty spot on the Taskbar and select Properties from the popup menu.

2. Place a check mark in the check box next to the options you want:

- **Always on top** will force the Taskbar to remain on top of other windows, ensuring that it is always visible to you.

TASKBAR

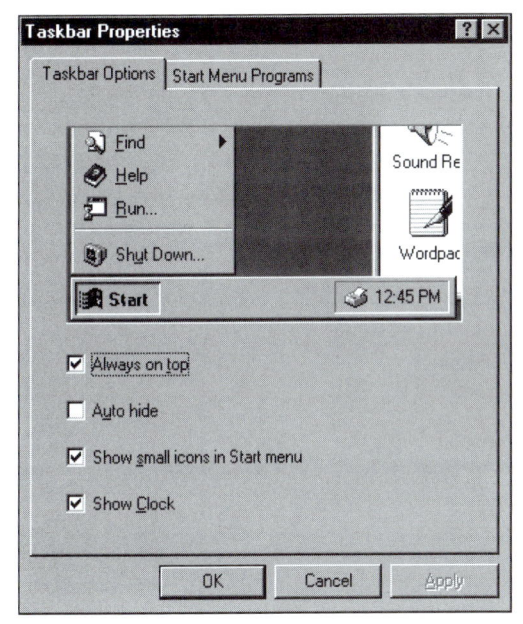

- **Auto hide** displays the Taskbar as a small thin line on the bottom of the screen. To have the thin line show when a full-screen window is displayed, both Always on top and Auto hide must be selected.

- **Show small icons in Start menu** displays a small Start menu with smaller icons.

- **Show Clock** displays the time in the left of the Taskbar. By double-clicking on the clock, you can reset the time or date.

3. Click on Apply to make the changes final, and then click OK.

TIP: *To redisplay the Taskbar when Auto hide has been selected, place the pointer on the thin line on the bottom of the screen, and it will automatically reappear. If Always on top is not also selected, and an application has a full-screen view, minimize the application by clicking on the Minimize button, and the Taskbar will become visible.*

SEE ALSO: *Arranging Applications; Start Button; Date/Time, Settings*

COMMAND AND FEATURE REFERENCE

Text Editor

SEE: *NotePad*

Time Default Settings

SEE: *Date/Time, Settings; Time Format; Time Zone Default Settings*

Time Format

10:10 PM

The current time is displayed according to country and language default formatting, which is established in the Regional Settings control panel. To change the time format, follow these steps:

1. Select Start ➤ Settings ➤ Control Panel, and then double-click on Regional Settings. Select the Time tab. The following options will be available to you:

- **Time Style** determines how the time will be formatted. The Time Sample shows how the current time looks in the current format. Press the down arrow to see a list of available formats.

- **Time Separator** determines which symbol separates the hours from the minutes and seconds (usually a colon).

- **AM Symbol** sets the default for the morning symbol.

- **PM symbol** sets the default for the afternoon symbol.

2. Select the time format you want, and then click on Apply and then OK to activate the time changes, or choose Cancel.

Time Zone Default Settings

The Time Zone specifies in which time zone the computer's clock is set. Follow these steps to set the Time Zone:

1. Double-click on the time display in the Taskbar, or click your right mouse button on it for a popup menu, and select Adjust Date/Time. The Date/Time Properties dialog box will be displayed.

2. Click on the Time Zone tab.

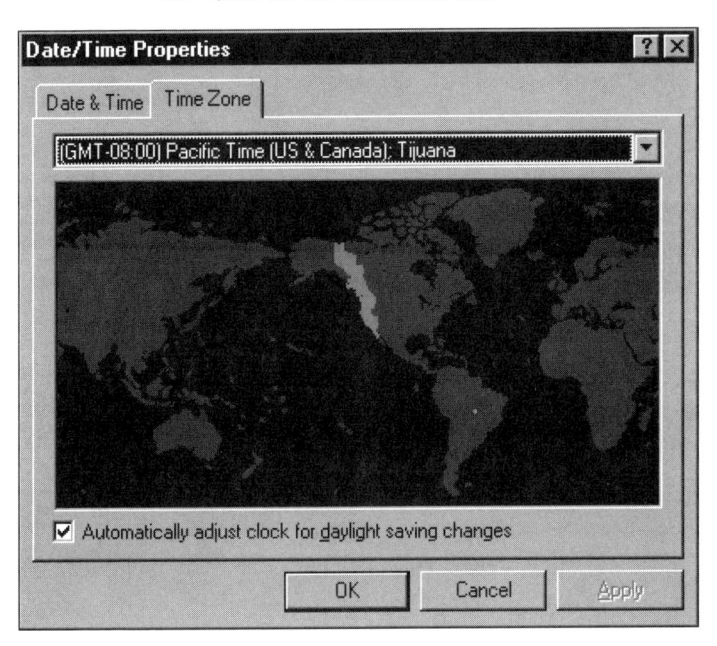

COMMAND AND FEATURE REFERENCE

3. Either click on a spot of the map to set the time zone, or select the zone you want from the drop-down list box by clicking on the down arrow.

4. If you want to automatically adjust for daylight saving changes, place a check mark in that check box.

Toolbar

The toolbar is usually placed immediately below the title bar, and contains buttons for frequently used commands. These buttons make your work easier and more efficient. If a toolbar is not showing on a window, select View ➤ Toolbar. (See *Folder Window* for a definition of the standard toolbar buttons used in Windows 95 folders.)

SEE ALSO: *Folder Window*

Transferring Files

SEE: *Hyperterminal; Microsoft Network (MSN)*

Undelete

Deleted files are stored in the Recycle Bin by default, unless you turn it off. Until you empty the Recycle Bin, deleted files can be retrieved. To do so, follow these steps:

1. Double-click on the Recycle Bin icon.

2. Click the files you want to restore.

3. Select File ➤ Restore.

TIP: *To select multiple files, hold down Ctrl while you click.*

SEE ALSO: *Recycle Bin*

Undo

The Undo command cancels or "undoes" the previous action. It is normally available from the Edit menu. If it is unavailable, the previous action cannot be undone or cancelled. To Undo an action, select Edit ➤ Undo.

NOTE: *Windows 95 allows you to Undo the last ten deletes, moves, copies, or renames.*

Uninstalling Applications

The Uninstall program removes all traces that an application was ever installed. It removes all references to the program in the windows directories and subdirectories. To be uninstalled, an application must have been installed under Windows 95–it cannot be a DOS application, for instance.

The Uninstall feature is found in the Add/Remove Program Properties dialog box. Follow these steps to uninstall a program:

1. Select Start ➤ Settings ➤ Control Panel, and then double-click on Add/Remove Programs. The Add/Remove Programs Properties dialog box will be displayed.

COMMAND AND FEATURE REFERENCE

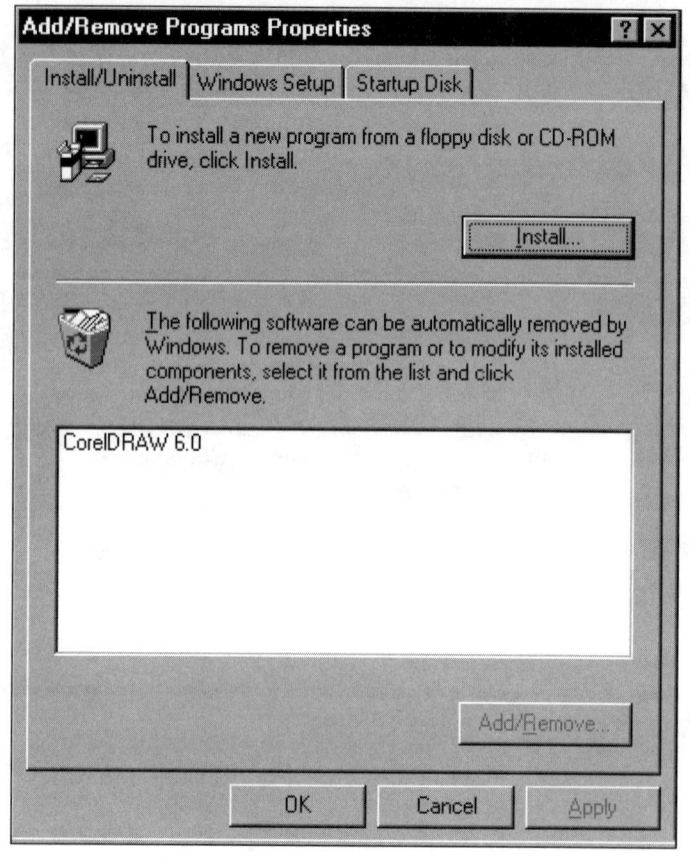

2. If it is not already displayed, click on the Install/Uninstall tab.

3. Select the software you want to remove from the displayed list and click Remove.

Unmapping Network Drives

SEE: *Mapping Network Drives*

User Profiles

SEE: *Profiles*

Viewing Files and Folders

SEE: *Explorer; My Computer; Network Neighborhood*

Views and Windows

SEE: *Folder Window*

Vision Impaired

SEE: *Accessibility Options*

Volume Control

The volume of your sound card and speakers is controlled by the Volume Control accessory. If you have more than one multimedia capability installed, for example, MIDI or Wave handling capability, you can control the volume and balance for each device or capability. Follow these steps to access the Volume Control:

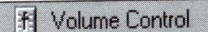

1. Select Start ➤ Programs ➤ Accessories ➤ Multimedia and click on Volume Control. The Volume Control dialog box will be displayed.

COMMAND AND FEATURE REFERENCE

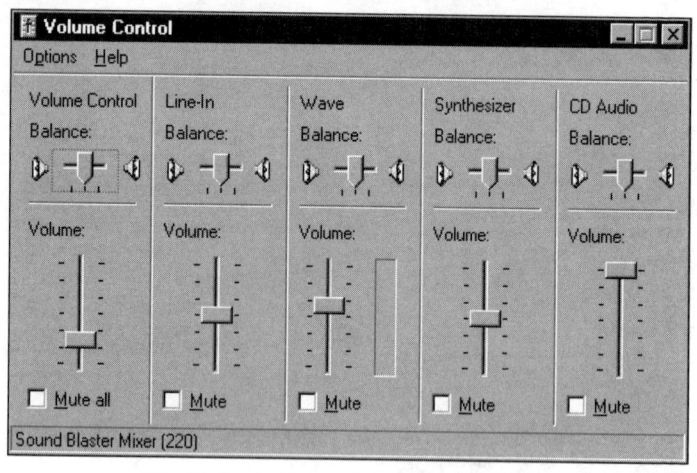

The Volume Control dialog box contains separate features to balance volume for the devices on your computer. Depending on your computer, the following features may or may not appear:

- **Volume Control** is the "master" volume and balance control for sounds coming out of your computer.

- **Line-In Balance** controls the volume and balance for an external device that feeds sound into your computer, such as audio tape or an FM tuner.

- **Wave Balance** controls the volume and balance for playing .wav files as they come into the computer.

- **Synthesizer Balance** controls the volume and balance for incoming sounds from MIDI files.

- **CD Audio Balance** controls the volume and balance for CD-ROM audio files as they come into the computer.

VOLUME CONTROL

- **Microphone** controls the volume and balance for sound coming in via a microphone.

2. To control the volume of the components, move the vertical slider labeled Volume up or down to increase or decrease volume.

3. To control the balance between two speakers, move the horizontal slider labeled Balance to the left or right to move the emphasis to the left or right speaker.

4. Click on Mute All or Mute to silence all or one component's contribution to the sound.

To Vary the Recording Volume

To vary the volume and balance when you are recording, follow these steps:

1. From the Volume Control dialog box, select Options ➤ Properties. The Properties dialog box will be displayed.

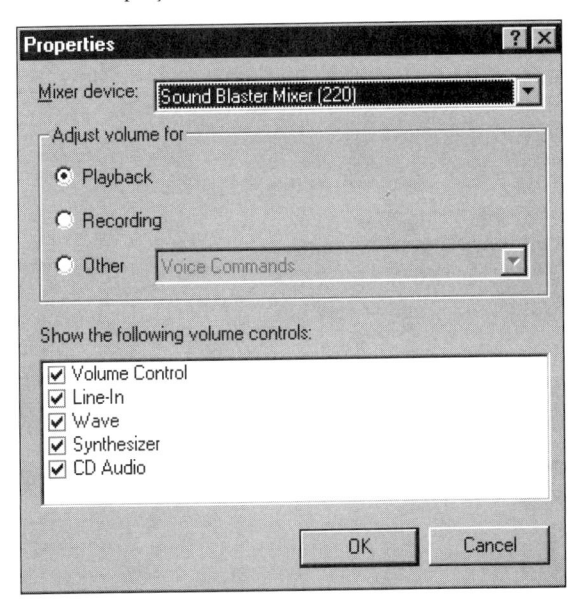

COMMAND AND FEATURE REFERENCE

2. Click on Recording for a list of devices that apply to the recording task.

3. If it is not already checked, click on the check box to select the device you want. Click OK. The Recording Control dialog box will be displayed for the selected devices.

4. Move the Balance and Volume sliders to adjust the volume and balance of the sound.

Adjusting Playback Sound Quality

The Volume Control dialog box displays by default the devices it knows about that pertain to Playback or output of sound. If the device you want to adjust is not on the list, follow these steps to select the device:

1. From the Volume Control dialog box, select Options ➤ Properties.

2. Select Playback, and a list of applicable devices will be displayed.

3. If it is not already selected, click on the device you want, and then click OK. The Volume Control dialog box with the devices that were selected will be displayed.

4. Adjust the Balance and Volume as needed.

> **TIP:** *To control the volume and balance for voice command devices, select Other from the Properties dialog box and then select Voice Commands from the drop-down list box. A list of voice command devices installed on your computer will be displayed in the text display box below.*

What's This

SEE: *Popup Menus and Labels*

Windows 95 Setup

The Windows 95 Setup program installs Windows 95 on your computer. The Setup programs come to you either on a floppy or CD-ROM, and installation takes up to one hour to complete. During the Setup program, you will be asked to choose between four installation types:

Typical recommends choices for optional components and automatically installs them for you.

Portable is for laptop and notebook computers.

Compact is for limited disk space users.

Custom allows you to select the components you want.

Installing Windows 95

The installation procedure for Windows 95 differs only slightly between the four types of installation. This book will guide you through a Typical installation, which is recommended for users with sufficient disk space. It automatically installs the required components and some of the optional ones, although you have an opportunity to select the optional components you want. Follow these steps:

1. Bring up the Windows 95 Setup programs by typing the path to the Setup program. If you are presently using MS–DOS or Windows 3.1 (where you would select File ➤ Run), you would type, for example: **B:\setup**, and press enter, where B: is the drive on which the Windows 95 installation disk will be loaded. At this point, you would click on Enter to enable Windows to perform a routine check on your sytem. This will take some time. Follow the instructions until the Windows 95 Setup screen is displayed.

COMMAND AND FEATURE REFERENCE

2. Click on Continue. Setup will take a few minutes to load the Windows 95 Setup Wizard, which will guide you through the installation procedure.

3. After a few minutes, the license agreement will be displayed. Click on Yes to accept the terms of the agreement. If you have any other programs running, you will be asked to terminate them before continuing. (You can press Alt+Tab to display them and then exit each before returning to Setup.) When Setup is the only program running, click OK. If you are upgrading, Windows will examine your system for old Windows files. If you have deleted them, insert Disk 1 of the old Windows Setup programs into a disk drive and click on Continue. You may have to designate the drive where the disk is located. Then Setup Wizard will begin.

4. After reading about the three steps that make up the installation procedure (Collecting information about your computer, Copying Windows 95 files to your computer, and Restarting your computer and finishing Setup), click on Next.

5. Select the directory in which you want to install Windows. The default is C:\Windows. If you want an alternative, click on Other directory, then click on Next, and then fill in the name. Click on Next. The directory will be prepared, and the system will be checked to see what components are installed and how much space is available.

6. You will be asked to select the type of setup you prefer:

- **Typical** (the default) will automatically install the required Windows 95 components plus some optional components that are commonly used, if you have enough disk space. You will have an opportunity to choose different components.

WINDOWS 95 SETUP

- **Portable** includes options especially selected for portable computers, such as laptops and notebooks.

- **Compact** is used when disk space is low. It will not install the optional components.

- **Custom** allows you to install those Setup components you want. Microsoft advises you to use this only if you are an advanced user or system administrator.

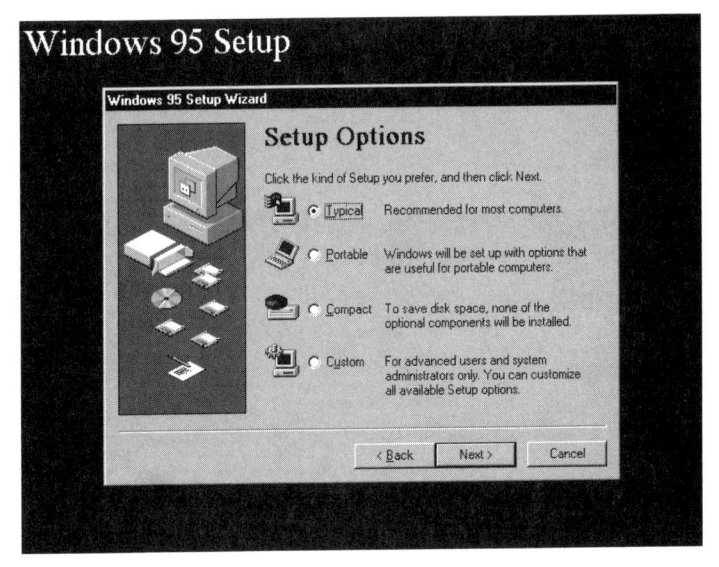

7. Select the option you want, assumed to be Typical in this case, and then click on Next.

8. Type in your name and company name, and then click Next.

9. If you are installing Windows 95 from a CD-ROM, in the Product Identification dialog box, type in your Product ID, a 10-digit CD Key that comes with the product. Click on Next.

10. In the Analyzing Your Computer dialog box, click on the listed hardware components you

COMMAND AND FEATURE REFERENCE

have and then click on Next. Setup will check the hardware on your computer, which will take several minutes. If you are asked if you have specific hardware, answer the question and then click Next.

11. In the Get Connected dialog box, you will now have an opportunity to indicate whether you want to install the The Microsoft Network, Microsoft Mail, and Microsoft Fax components. Click on the services you want, and then click on Next.

12. At this point, in the Windows Components dialog box, you will have an opportunity to choose the optional components to be installed. You can select to have the most common ones automatically installed by clicking on Install. If you do this, click on Next and go to Step 14.

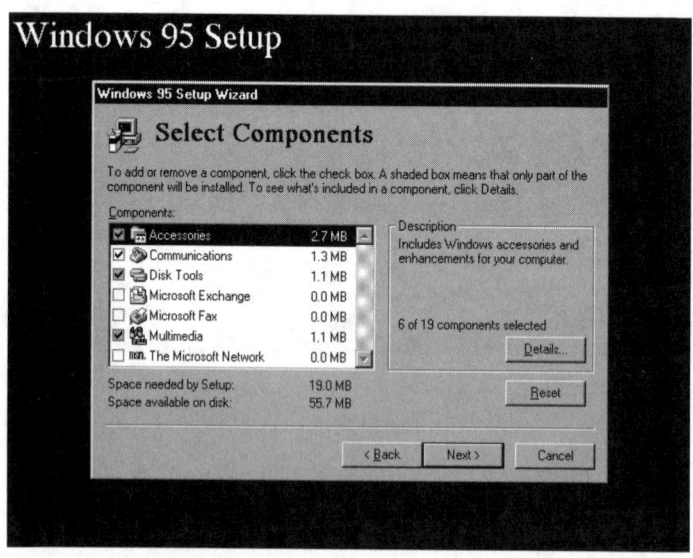

Windows 95 Setup

13. If you want to examine the components and select the ones you want, click on Show me the list of components so I can choose. The Select Components dialog box will be displayed listing the components available to be installed. If a component contains a check mark in the check box, it will be installed; if no check mark appears in the check box, the component will not be installed. If the check box is checked and shaded, only some of the programs that make up the component will be installed. To see the details of what will be installed for any component, select the component and then click on Details. A second screen will be displayed for you to select the individual programs that make up the component. As you do this, Setup will display the impact on disk space. To clear your changes and restore the original selections, click on Reset. When you are done, click on Next.

TIP: *If you do not install an important program now, you can do it later with the Add/Remove Programs control panel.*

14. If you are attached to a network, the Identification dialog box will ask for the Computer name, Workgroup, and Computer Description. These names will be used by other computers on your network to access your computer. After typing the names, click on Next.

15. If you want a startup disk created for booting Windows 95 when you have computer problems (recommended), select Yes, I want a startup disk. This will provide you with the means to start your computer, and special diagnostic aids for you if Windows 95 won't boot off your hard drive. Select your choice and click Next. If you select Yes you will be asked to insert a diskette to copy the Startup files. (A startup disk can also be created later on from the Add/Remove Programs control panel if you don't want to take the time now.)

16. Setup will now ask to begin copying files to the hard disk. This will take some time. Click Next when you are ready.

COMMAND AND FEATURE REFERENCE

17. When the copying step is complete, the Finishing Setup dialog box will be displayed, informing you that the file copy task is complete and that you are ready to restart the computer and finish Setup. Click on Finish.

18. Setup will now reboot your computer. When it starts up again, you may need to enter a network password, if you have one (the default is no password, so just click Cancel and then OK), and then Setup will continue the final installation of the hardware components, the Plug and Play devices, the Control Panel, and other tasks.

19. Verify that your Time Zone and the Date and Time are correct. Click on Close.

20. You will be introduced to a series of Setup Wizards, such as the Inbox Setup Wizard and Add Printer Wizard. Follow the steps as presented, or install the components later.

21. The Welcome to Windows 95 dialog box will be displayed, containing a tip on how to get started, and a button for you to use to register online. You can register, or you can explore Windows 95—perhaps with the Windows 95 Tour, if you installed it. Click on Close to continue. You're on your way!

WinPopup

WinPopup, available in the \Windows folder, allows you to send and receive messages to and from other computers on your network. In order to use WinPopup, it must be active in memory and displayed in the Taskbar of both your computer and the computer with which you are communicating.

When a message is received, the WinPopup window will be enlarged for you to see the message and respond, if necessary. Messages will be stored until you clear one or all of the messages or until you shut down WinPopup or Windows 95.

Loading The WinPopup Window

To load WinPopup into memory so you can receive and send messages to others on your network, follow these steps:

1. With the Explorer, open the Windows folder, find Winpopup.exe (at the end of the folder contents), and double-click on it. The WinPopup window will be displayed.

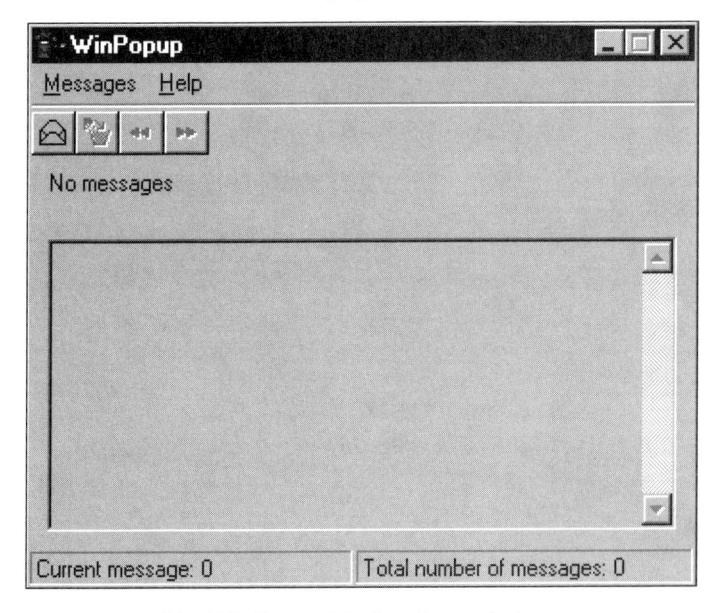

The WinPopup window has only two menu choices: **Messages** and **Help**. The Messages menu provides the following options: **Send** to send a message to another computer, **Discard** to delete a

COMMAND AND FEATURE REFERENCE

received message, **Previous** to look at the previous message, **Next** to look at the next message, **Clear All** to delete all messages, and **Options**, which contains the following choices:

- **Play sound when new message arrives** warns you with sound. If it is not selected, no audio notification is given.

- **Always on Top** makes sure that the WinPopup window is not hidden by other screens.

- **Pop up dialog on message receipt** displays the WinPopup window when a new message is received. If it is not selected, no visual notification will be given.

The WinPopup window contains the following icons:

- **Send** displays a dialog box so that you can send a message.

- **Delete** discards the current message.

- **Previous** displays the previous message.

- **Next** displays the next message.

2. Minimize the window to an icon on your Taskbar by clicking on the Minimize button.

TIP: To make sure you can receive a message from another computer, load WinPopup into memory, set the options for notification, and then minimize it as an icon in the Taskbar. If you want this done automatically, make WinPopup a Startup Application by placing a shortcut to it in the \Windows\Start Menu\Programs\Startup folder. (See Start Up Applications.)

Sending a WinPopup Message

To send a WinPopup Message, follow these steps:

1. Load WinPopup if it is not already in memory.

2. Click on the Send icon, or select it from the Message menu. The Send Message dialog box will be displayed.

3. To send a message to a specific user or computer, click on User or computer. To broadcast a message to all users and computers on your workgroup, click on Workgroup.

4. Type the name of the User or computer or Workgroup in the text entry box.

5. Type your message into the Message area.

6. When your message is ready to send, click on OK. You will be informed that the message has been successfully sent.

WordPad

WordPad is a word processing package that comes with Windows 95. It is unique in that you can create or edit files with varying formats, maintaining

COMMAND AND FEATURE REFERENCE

that format in the process. The formats you can use are: Text, Rich Text, Word 6, and Microsoft Write files. To open WordPad, select Start ➤ Programs ➤ Accessories, and click on WordPad.

WordPad's Menus

When you first open WordPad, you will see a typical word processing window with a menu bar beneath the title bar. Most of the menus contain standard commands, but there are some unique ones, as follows.

File Menu

The File menu contains the following unique commands:

Page Setup displays a dialog box where you can establish the page size, orientation, margins, and source of paper. You can also change the printer by clicking on the Printer button.

Send (only present if you have access to a post office—either on your network, or via a remote connection) loads in Microsoft Exchange so you can send a message to another user or computer.

Edit Menu

The Edit menu contains these unique options:

Links displays a dialog box for managing the maintenance of a linked object. You can Update Now the linked object from the original source, Open or Change the Source, or Break the Link.

Object Properties displays an object Properties dialog box that varies depending on the object in the document.

(Document or Bitmap) Object displays a submenu with Edit and Open usually displayed, although these options vary depending on the object. The submenu commands activate the creating program so that the object can be opened or edited.

TIP: *You can double-click on an inserted object to activate its creating program. To return to WordPad from the other program, click outside the object.*

View Menu

The View menu displays a unique Options command, which contains six tabs: Options, Text, Rich Text, Word 6, Write, and Embedded.

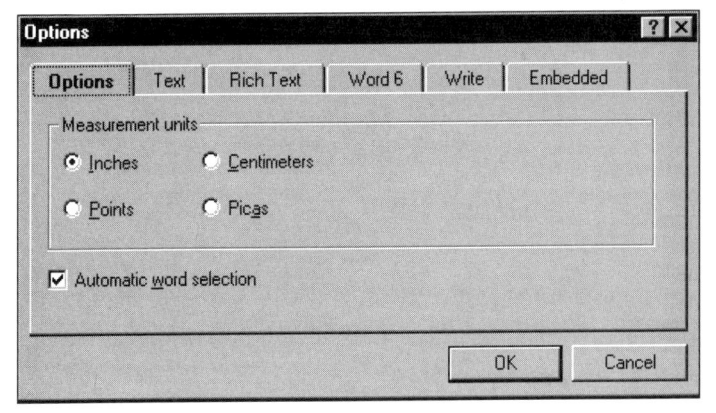

Options sets the standard measurement units to Inches, Centimeters, Points, or Picas. If you select (place a check mark in the check box next to) Automatic Word Selection, WordPad will select a word at a time when you drag the pointer over text. If it is unchecked, only one character will be selected.

Text, Rich Text, Word 6, and **Write** tabs allow you to set the Word wrap and Toolbar defaults for each format type. You can set Word Wrap for No

COMMAND AND FEATURE REFERENCE

wrap, Wrap to window, or Wrap to ruler. You can display the standard toolbar, Format bar, Ruler, and Status bar.

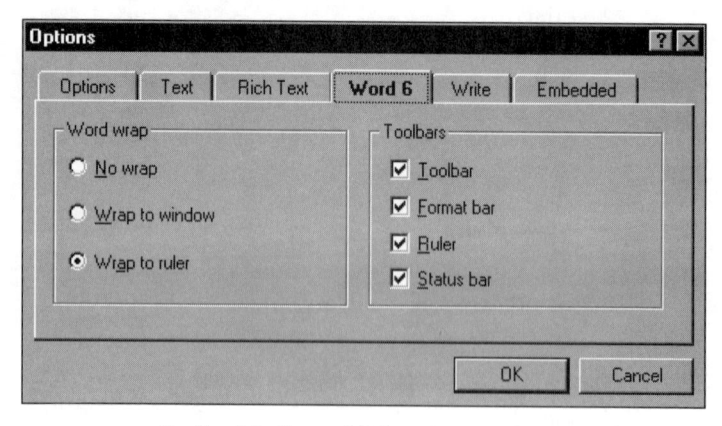

Embedded establishes the Word Wrap and Toolbar defaults for any embedded objects inserted in your document.

Insert Menu

The Insert menu contains the following options:

Date and Time inserts the date and time into your document, according to the format you select.

Object displays a dialog box for selecting the type of object that can be inserted into a document. You have several choices for creating a new object:

- **Create New** allows you to select the type of object to be created. The program for creating it will be activated. For example, if you choose to create a bitmap image, Paint will be activated.

- **Create from File** inserts an object from an existing file. It can be embedded or linked.

- **Link** is displayed when Create from File is selected. When you select Link, the object is linked to the document. In this case, the object will be inserted into the document, but any modifications to the original file will update the picture in the document, as well. When Link is not selected, the file will be inserted into your document as an embedded object. When you edit it, the original, creating program's menus and toolbars will be activated.

- **Display as Icon** inserts an icon into a document, rather than the content of the object itself. When the icon is double-clicked, the object will open.

Format Menu

The Format menu contains formatting options for finetuning a document:

Font allows you to choose the Font, Style, Size, Color, and special effects, such as Strikeout and Underline, to be used in the document.

Bullet Style formats a selected paragraph in a bullet style.

Paragraph allows you to set Indentation and Alignment for a selected paragraph.

Tabs sets the tab stop positions for selected text in the document.

TIP: *You can also set tabs by clicking on the Ruler where you want the tab stop to be placed. To move a tab, simply drag it to a new position on the ruler. To remove a tab, drag it off the ruler.*

COMMAND AND FEATURE REFERENCE

WordPad's Toolbars

WordPad has two toolbars—the standard Toolbar and the Format Bar, which contain the following buttons:

Toolbar

In addition to some of the standard Windows icons, the Toolbar contains these special icons:

New creates a new document. It can be a Word 6, Rich Text, or Text Only document.

Open allows you to select a document to open.

Save saves the document to disk.

Print prints the document.

Print Preview displays the document as it will print.

Find searches for a file containing text or an object.

Date & Time places the date and time in the document where the insertion point is placed, according to the format you select.

Format Bar

Font displays the current font, and when opened, a list of fonts that are available to be used.

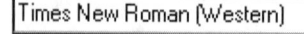

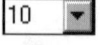

Times New Roman (Western)

Size displays the current size, and when opened, a list of the sizes that apply to the selected font.

Bold makes the selected text boldface.

Italic makes the selected text italic.

Underline underlines the selected text.

Color displays a palette of colors for the font.

Align Left forces either the selected text or the text from the insertion point on to be justified left.

Center centers either the selected text or the text from the insertion point on.

Align Right forces either the selected text or text from the insertion point on to be justified right.

Bullets places the selected paragraphs in a bulleted style.

To Create a Document

To create a WordPad document, you can use several approaches, depending on what you need to do:

◆ **To create a document from scratch:**

1. Click the pointer in the text area and type what you want.

2. Use the toolbars and menus to enhance the text with formatting, color, and other special effects.

3. Save the document by clicking on the Save icon.

◆ **To insert the contents of the Clipboard:**

1. Place the contents into the Clipboard in another application by highlighting the text or graphic and clicking on Copy or Cut.

COMMAND AND FEATURE REFERENCE

2. Bring up WordPad and click the pointer where you want the contents of the Clipboard to be placed.

3. Click on the Paste icon.

- **To insert an object:**

    1. Place the pointer where you want the inserted object to be placed.

    2. Select Insert ➤ Object.

    3. Select File ➤ Create.

    4. Enter the path and name of the object to be inserted. Use Browse if you don't know where the file is located. If the object is to be linked, click on Link. Click on OK.

Index

Note to the Reader:
Throughout this index, **boldfaced** page numbers refer to primary discussions of a topic.

Symbols & Numbers

+ (plus sign), in disk or folder in Exploring window, 116
32-bit protect mode disk drivers, disabling, 297
800 number for MSN sign-up, 179

A

Access Control tab, in Network control panel, 216–217, 223
Access Type, for shared resources, 222
accessibility options, **24–30**
Accessibility Properties dialog box
  Display Tab, 27
  General Tab, 29–30
  Keyboard Tab, 25–26
  Mouse Tab, 28
  Sound Tab, 27
accessories, **21–22**
adapter cards
  configuring for network, 212, 214
  installing, 218
Add, in Keyboard Properties dialog box, 149
Add Item tool, in System Monitor, 299
Add New File Type dialog box, 48
Add New Hardware control panel, **30–32**, 244
  assigning ports in, 245
Add Printer icon, 246
Add Printer Wizard, 251–252
Add share button, in Net Watcher toolbar, 210
Add to Favorite Places (Microsoft Network File menu), 185
Add to Personal Address Book (Address Book File menu), 37
Add/Remove Programs Control Panel, **32–35**, 143, 261, 317
Add/Remove Programs Properties dialog box
  Install/Uninstall tab, 33, 33, 307
  Startup Disk tab, 35
  Windows Setup tab, 34
Address Book
  adding new entry, 38–39
  in Microsoft Exchange, **35–39**, 165
  in Microsoft Exchange Tools menu, 170–171
  order of, 157
Address Book button, in Microsoft Exchange toolbar, 168
Address Book window, 36–37
  toolbar in, 37
Addressing tab
  in Microsoft Exchange Options dialog box, 174
  in Microsoft Exchange Settings Properties dialog box, 157
Adjust Free Space (DriveSpace Drive menu), 105
Administer menu, in Net Watcher, 211
Administrator Account Details, for Microsoft Mail Postoffice, 177
Adobe fonts, 134
Advanced defragmentation method, 89–90
Advanced menu (DriveSpace), 106
Advanced Program Settings dialog box, for MS-DOS mode, 197
Advanced tab (Find: All Files dialog box), 128
Airbrush tool (Paint), 233
Align Left button, in WordPad, 326
Align Right button, in WordPad, 326
Alt key, 26
Always on Top option, for Taskbar, 302
AM Symbol, 304
America Online, 109
Analyzing Your Computer dialog box, 315–316
.ani files, 192
animation, playing, 160–164
Appearance Properties (Display Properties dialog box), 101

INDEX

application files
and backups, 50
   dragging to create shortcut, 44
applications
   adding or removing, **32–35**
   arranging, **39–45**
   autoloading when opening document, 231
   displaying on Start menu, 40–41
   double-clicking icons, 20
   installing, **143**
   placing on Desktop, 42–43
   placing in folders, 43–44
   placing in Startup folder, 45
   placing on Taskbar, 302
   run command for installing, 77
   starting, 4, 20–21
   startup, 45, **290–292**
   stopping, **292**
   switching between, **292–293**
   Taskbar button for running, 2
   uninstalling, 33, **307–308**
Arrange Icons command, in View menu, 131, 195
arranging
   applications, **39–45**
   folders, **45**
   windows, **46–47**
arrow downward, for Inbox Importance code, 166
ASCII file format, Notepad for, 226
associating files, 19–20, **47–49**
Attached, for Inbox contents, 167
attaching file to fax, 124
Attributes, in Paint Image menu, 235
Audio Properties, in Sound Recorder Edit menu, 286
Auto hide option, for Taskbar, 303
Autoexec.bat file, 270
Automatic Word Selection, 323

B

background, **58**
   creating for Desktop, 231
Background Properties tab (Display Properties dialog box), 99–100
backing up
   drag and drop for, 58
   files and folders, **49–58**
   passwords for, 56
backslashes (\\), for computer name in path, 241
Backup tab (Microsoft Backup window), 50
bad sectors, 136
   repairs to, 276
Bar Charts tool, in System Monitor, 299
Billing, in Microsoft Network Tools menu, 187
binary number system, in scientific calculator mode, 63
bitmap image, as fax, 119
Bold button, in WordPad, 326
bootable disk, creating, 35, 136–137, 317
Briefcase folder, 202. *See also* My Briefcase
broadcasting, **59**
Browse, in Sounds Control Panel, 287
browsing files, **59–60**
Brush tool (Paint), 232
bullet style, in WordPad, 325
bulletin boards, 178
Bullets button, in WordPad, 326
Buttons tab, in Mouse Properties dialog box, 190–191

C

C on calculator, 61
cable, 218
CAD, in Statistics box, 64
Calculator, **60–64**
Calendar type, for Date format, 87
Call command, in HyperTerminal, 142
Call Preferences, for modem, 189
call waiting, disabling, 121
calling card, for phone calls, **65–66**
Cancel command buttons, 9
canceling
   last action, **66–67**
   printing, 147, 253
Caps Lock, beep for, 26
capturing screen image, **67**
Cascade (Taskbar pop-up menu), 46

INDEX

case sensitivity, in file searches, 129
CD, in Statistics box, 64
CD Audio Balance, in Volume Control dialog box, 310
CD Player, 22, **67–72**
  Disc menu, 69
  Options menu for, 70
  tools for, 70–71
  View menu, 70
  volume for, 71–72
CD-ROM, installing Windows 95 from, 315
CD-ROM drive, ejecting disk from, 161
CD-ROM tab, in File System dialog box, 297
CE on calculator, 61
Center button, in WordPad, 326
Center option, for wallpaper patterns, 100
Change Calling Card dialog box, 65–66
Change Letter (DriveSpace Advanced menu), 106
Change Ratio (DriveSpace Advanced menu), 106
Character Map, **72–73**
  enlarging characters on, 73
characters
  changing display size, 74
  international, **144**
chat forums, 178
check boxes, 8–9
  clicking, 34
Check Names icon, in Inbox-Microsoft Exchange, 111–112
Clear Image, (Paint Image menu), 235
clicking, xiv
client software, configuring for network, 212, 213–214
client-server network, 217
Clipboard, **74–75**
  capturing window image to, 67
  copying media clip to, 162
  inserting contents in WordPad document, 327
  Notepad to view contents, 226
  pasting contents, 240
Clipboard Viewer, **75–76**

clock, on Taskbar, 2, **87–88**, 303
Close button, 6, 7, 292
  in dialog boxes, 10
  in Net Watcher toolbar, 210
Close command, in folder File menu, 131
closing
  files, **76**
  windows, **76**, **229**
.clp files, 75
CODECs, 80
Color button, in WordPad, 326
color palette
  in Paint, 234
  setting for display, 102
Column (Microsoft Exchange View menu), 169
COM ports, 245
command buttons, 9
Command Line (Run), 5, **77**
Command Prompt Only, for starting Windows, 200
communications, 22
Compact installation, for Windows 95, 313, 315
Compare tab (Microsoft Backup window), 50, 78
comparing files, **78–80**
  after backup, 53
Compose menu (Microsoft Exchange), 175
  ➤ New Message, 110
Compose New Fax wizard, 123
Compress (DriveSpace Drive menu), 105
Compress a Drive dialog box, 107
compressed sound files, 286
Compressed Volume File, 104
  connecting to drive, 106
compression, **80**
  DriveSpace for, **104–108**
CompuServe, 15, 109, 179, 218
computer
  connecting to other, **80–81**
  direct cable connection to other, **95–96**
  finding, **126**
  floppy disk for booting, 35
  restarting, 199
  tracking processor activity, 298–301

INDEX

Computer Name
 in Network control panel Identification tab, 216
 in path, 240–241
Config.sys file, 270
 for MS-DOS mode, 198
configuration files, changes for new hardware, 30
Configuration tab, in Network control panel, 212–215, 223
Connect button, in HyperTerminal toolbar, 141
Connect To dialog box, 95
Connect Using (Phone Dialer Tools menu), 242–243
connecting to other computers, **80–81**. *See also* Dial-Up Networking
 direct cable connection for, **95–96**
 in HyperTerminal, 141
 passwords for dial-up, 238
Connection Description dialog box, 141
Connection Settings, in Microsoft Network Tools menu, 187
Connection tab, for Modem Properties dialog box, 189
Contents tab, in Help Topics: Windows Help dialog box, 138–139
context menus, **244**. *See also* popup menus
context-sensitive help, 140
Continuous Play, for audio CDs, 68
Control menu, 6, 7
 ➤ Close, 76
Control Panel, 4, 13, **81**, 270
Copy button, in folder toolbar, 133
Copy command, 74, 83
 in folder Edit menu, 131
 in Notepad, 226–227
 in Sound Recorder Edit menu, 286
Copy system files, as format type, 136
copying
 to create new profile, 157
 disks, **82–83**
 drag and drop for, 103
 file to Briefcase, 203–204
 files in Explorer, 17–18
 files and folders, **83–84**
cover page for fax, 124
 creating, 120
 default for, 119
Create Empty (DriveSpace Advanced menu), 106
Create Shortcut command, in folder File menu, 131
Create Shortcut Wizard, 260
credit card
 for Microsoft Network registration, 179
 for phone calls, **65–66**
cross-linked files, 277
Ctrl key, 26
 for multiple file selection, 194
 for multiple object selection, 278
.cur files, 192
Curve tool (Paint), 233
Custom installation, for Windows 95, 313, 315
Cut command, in Notepad, 226–227

D

Dat button, in calculator, 63–64
data areas, testing disk for errors in, 276
Data bits, for modem, 189
data compression, during backup, 54
date
 displaying on Taskbar, 88
 inserting in WordPad document, 324
 setting system clock, 87–88
Date & Time icon, in WordPad, 326
date format, **86–87**
Date Modified tab (Find: All Files dialog box), 127, 128
Date separator, 87
Date/Time Properties dialog box, 88, 305–306
daylight savings time, adjusting for, 306
decimal number system, in scientific calculator mode, 63
decimal symbol
 for currency, 86
 setting default, 228
Default Cover Page, for fax, 119

332

INDEX

default settings, for time zone, **305–306**
defragmenting disks, **89–90**
Delete (DriveSpace Advanced menu), 106
Delete After Current Position, in Sound Recorder Edit menu, 286
Delete Before Current Position, in Sound Recorder Edit menu, 286
Delete button
  in folder toolbar, 133
  in Microsoft Exchange toolbar, 168
Delete (folder File menu), 131
deleted files, temporary storage of, 264
Deleted items folder, in Microsoft Exchange, 167
deleting
  all print jobs, 248
  devices, 295
  folders, **90–91**
  hardware profile, 295
  Microsoft Exchange options for, 172
  shortcuts, 281
  shortcuts from Start menu, 41
deleting files, 18, 20, **90–91**
  without using Recycle Bin, 268
Deliver Now (Microsoft Exchange Tools menu), 170
Deliver Now Using (Microsoft Exchange Tools menu), 170
Delivery tab
  in Microsoft Exchange Options dialog box, 173–174
  in Microsoft Exchange Settings Properties dialog box, 157
Depends on Password Access Type, 222
Desktop, 5, **91–92**
  creating background for, 231
  placing applications on, 42–43
  resolution of, 102
  user-customized settings, 258
Desktop popup menu
  ➤ New, ➤ Folder, 44
  ➤ Properties, 135
Detail view, in Explorer, 115
Details (Sounds Control Panel), 287
Details (View menu), 195

Details button, in folder toolbar, 133
Details command, in folder View menu, 131
Details tab, in Printer Properties dialog box, 250
Device Manager tab (System Properties dialog box), 245, 294–295
Device menu, in Media Player, 162
Device Options tab, in Printer Properties dialog box, 251
Diagnostics tab, in Modem Properties dialog box, 189–190
dialing calls
  properties for fax, 120
  rules for, 66
  using Phone Dialer, 243
Dialing Properties (Phone Dialer Tools menu), 243
Dialing Properties dialog box, 65
Dialing tab (Microsoft Fax Properties dialog box), 120–121
dialog boxes, 3, 5–6
  Browse button, 60
  Find File button, 60
  Help icon in, 140
  parts of, *front cover*, 8–10
  right clicking within, 274
dial-up adapters, configuring for network, 212
dial-up connections, passwords for, 238
Dial-Up Networking, **92–94**, 218
  to access Internet, 144, 146
  creating new connection, 93–94
  established connection dialing, 94
  first time use, 93
Dial-Up Networking folder, in My Computer, 208
differential backup, 53
Digit Grouping symbol, 228
direct cable connection, **95–96**
Direct Cable Connection program, 80
directory, **97**. *See also* folders
  for Windows 95, 314
Disc menu (CD Player), 69
Disc Settings dialog box, 69
Disc Time Remaining, for audio CDs, 68

INDEX

Disconnect button, in HyperTerminal toolbar, 141
Disconnect Net Drive, in folder toolbar, 132
Disconnect Network Drive dialog box, 159
Disconnect user button, in Net Watcher toolbar, 210
disconnecting network drives, **159–160**
disk drives
  compressing or uncompressing, 107–108
  free space and capacity of, 98
  icons for, 13
disk file, printing to, 249
disk Properties dialog box, 208
disk tools, **98**
disks
  accessing, **30**
  copying, **82–83**
  defragmenting, **89–90**
  formatting, **136–137**
  label for, 137
  naming, **208**
  passwords for, 238
  permitting sharing of specific, 221
  space on, **97–98**
  testing for errors, 275
display adapters, acceleration functions of, 297
Display as Icon, for object in WordPad document, 325
Display Control Panel, **99–102**
Display menu, in Clipboard, 76
Display Properties dialog box, 99
  Appearance tab, 101
  Background Properties tab, 99–100
  font settings in, 135
  Screen Saver tab, 100–101
  Settings tab, 102
Display Summary, from ScanDisk, 277
Display Tab (Accessibility Properties dialog box), 27
display of Taskbar, 302–303
dithering, 251
Document or Bitmap Object, in WordPad Edit menu, 322–323
document files, associating with application, 47

document icons, double-clicking, 20
Document menu
  ➤ Cancel Printing, 253
  ➤ Pause Printing, 253
document window, 6
documents
  creating in WordPad, 327–328
  linking and embedding information in, **150–153**
  starting, **102–103**
Documents list, 103
Documents option, on Start menu, 4, 21, 102, 230–231, 290
DOS programs
  adding to Programs menu, 261
  running, 196
Double-click speed, for mouse, 191
double-clicking, xiv
  to start backup, 58
  starting applications by, 14
DoupleSpace, 104
drag and drop, **103**
  to copy, 83
  to create shortcut, 280–281
  file or folder to Recycle Bin, 91
  to move or copy file, 117
  to move files and folders, 193
  to move icons, 195
  windows, 46
Drag and Drop (Microsoft Backup Settings menu), 52
dragging, xiv
Draw Opaque (Paint Options menu), 235
Drive menu (DriveSpace), 105–106
  Compress, 107
drives, mapping network, **158–160**
DriveSpace, 80, **104–108**
  window, 105–106
drop-down list box, 9

E

Edit Colors (Paint Options menu), 235
Edit menu
  for calculator, 61
  in Clipboard, 76
  ➤ Copy, 83

INDEX

for folder, 131
in Media Player, 162
in Microsoft Exchange, 169
in Microsoft Network, 186
to move files and folders, 194
➤ Paste, 83
➤ Paste Special, 151–152
in Phone Dialer, 242
for Recycle Bin, 265
in Sound Recorder, 286
in System Monitor, 300
➤ Undo, **66–67**, 91, 307
in WordPad, 322–323
Edit Pattern, for background display, 99
Edit Play List, for audio CDs, 68
Edit tool, in System Monitor, 299
Editable fax message, 118–119
editing
  embedded objects, 153
  linked files, 152
Editor. *See* NotePad; WordPad
Effects menu, in Sound Recorder, 287
Eject button, in Media Player, 161
electronic mail, 15, **109–113**, 178
  on Internet, 146
  replying to, **112–113**
  sending, **110–112**
Ellipse tool (Paint), 233
ellipsis (...), in Start button menu, 3
embedded objects
  inserting, 151–152
  modifying, 153
  WordPad defaults for, 324
Empty Recycle Bin (Recycle Bin File menu), 265
Enable indicator on taskbar, in Keyboard Properties dialog box, 149
End Selection button, in Media Player, 161
Erase Tape (Backup Tools menu), 54
Eraser/Color Eraser tool (Paint), 232
erasing, before backups, 54
even pages, printing, 254
event log, for Microsoft Exchange, 169
events, **114**
  assigning sounds to, 287

exclamation mark, for Inbox Importance code, 166
Exclude File Types (Microsoft Backup Settings menu), 52
Exit and Logoff (Microsoft Exchange File menu), 169
Explore command, in folder File menu, 130
Explorer, 16–17, **114–117**
  access when working with Start menu, 41
  to add folder, 84
  arranging icons in, 46
  to associate files, 48
  to change Programs folder, 42
  to copy files, 83
  to copy floppy disks, 82
  Detail view in, 115
  disk space in status bar, 97
  double-click to start document, 103
  to find computer, 126
  to find file set for backup, 58
  to find files or folder, 116–117
  icon size in, 133
  to map network drives, 158–159
  moving icons in, 195
  naming disk in, 208
  preventing host drive display on, 108
  sorting files in, 283–284
  toobar in, 115
extensions for file names, 125

F

Fast Forward button, in Media Player, 161
Favorite Places, in Microsoft Network, 185, 186
Fax accessory, 22
fax device, printing to, 249
fax profile
  changing properties in, 157–158
  setting up, 155–157
faxes, 15, **117–125**. *See also* Mail and Fax
  creating, 123–124
  listing those scheduled for sending, 124

335

INDEX

retrieving remote, **122–123**
File Filtering (Microsoft Backup Settings menu), 51
file fragments, lost, 277
File Manager, 11–12. *See also* Explorer
File menu
  in Address Book, 36–37
  in Clipboard, 75
  ► Close, 76
  ► Delete, 20, 91
  ► Empty Recycle Bin, 266
  ► Exit, 229
  for folder, 130–131
  in HyperTerminal, 142
  ► Install New Font, 134
  in Media Player, 162
  in Microsoft Backup, 51
  ► Open File Set, 55
  in Microsoft Exchange, 169
  in Microsoft Network, 185
  ► New ► Folder, 84, 260
  ► New ► Shortcut, 260
  ► Open, 230
  in Paint, 234
  in Printer folder, 247
  ► Properties, 97
  Sharing tab, 221, 238
  ► Quick View, 262–263
  for Recycle Bin, 265
  ► Restore, 268
  in Sound Recorder, 285–286
  in System Monitor, 300
  in WordPad, 322
file names, 208–209
  changing, 209
  length, 18
  quotation marks for long, 240
File and Print Sharing dialog box, 215, 221
file sets
  for backup, 51, 54–55
  Full System Backup, 55
  name for, 57
File System button, in System Properties Preferences tab, 296–297
File Transfer Status, in Microsoft Network Tools menu, 187
file types, **125**
  searches for files by, 128
  selecting to include or exclude from backup, 51
File Types (Microsoft Backup Settings menu), 51–52
File Types (Recycle Bin View menu), 265, 266
File Types (View option for Printer folder), 247
File Types tab, for Microsoft Network options, 186
files
  accessing, **30**
  associating, 19–20, **47–49**
  attaching to fax, 124
  backing up, **49–58**
  browsing, **59–60**
  closing, **76**
  comparing, **78–80**
  copying, **83–84**
  deleting, 18, 20, **90–91**
  finding with Explorer, 116–117
  finding with My Computer, **207**
  moving, **193–194**
  naming, **208–209**
  opening, **230–231**
  permitting sharing of specific, 221
  popup menu for, 117, 207
  restoring, **272–273**
  saving, **275**
  selecting for backup, 56
  selecting multiple, 83
  sorting, **283–284**
  synchronizing between computers, 17, 202–205
  working with, 17–20
Fill With Color tool (Paint), 232
FilterKeys feature, 24, 26
Find (Address Book Tools menu), 37
Find: All Files dialog box, 127
Find command
  in folder File menu, 130
  in Microsoft Exchange Tool menu, 171
  in Microsoft Network Tools menu, 187
  in Start menu, 4, 290
Find icon, in WordPad, 326
Find Setup Wizard, 140
Find tab, in Help Topics dialog box, 139–140

INDEX

finding
  computers on network, **126**
  file or folder in My Computer, **207**
  files and folders, **126–129**
  files or folders with Explorer, 116–117
Flip/Rotate (Paint Image menu), 235
floppy disks. *See also* disks
  for booting computer, 35, 136–137, 317
  with compressed-volume file, 106
  copying, **82–83**
Folder option, in Recycle Bin View menu, 265, 266
Folder tab, for Microsoft Network options, 186
Folder View, in Microsoft Exchange, 167
Folder (View option for Printer folder), 247
folders, 12, **129–130**
  accessing, **30**
  arranging, **45**
  backing up, **49–58**
  copying, **83–84**
  creating/adding, **84–85**
  deleting, **90–91**
  finding with Explorer, 116–117
  finding with My Computer, **207**
  for fonts, 134–135
  for incoming files, 143
  moving, **193–194**
  naming, **208–209**
  passwords for, 238
  permitting sharing of specific, 221
  placing applications in, 43–44
  popup menus in Explorer, 117
  sorting, **283–284**
  toolbar for, 132–133
  window, **130–133**
  working with, 17–20
Folders (Microsoft Exchange View menu), 169
Font list, in WordPad, 326
fonts, **134–136**
  for screen display, 101, 102
  size for display, 74
  in Windows 95, 135–136
  in WordPad, 325
Fonts folder, 134–135

Fonts tab, in Printer Properties dialog box, 251
Format menu, in WordPad, 325
Free-Form Select tool (Paint), 232

G

Games, **137**
GDI resources, monitoring use, 271
General tab
  in Keyboard Properties dialog box, 150
  in Microsoft Exchange Options dialog box, 172
  for Microsoft Network options, 186
  in Modem Properties dialog box, 188–189
  in Mouse Properties dialog box, 192–193
  in Printer Properties dialog box, 250
  in System control panel, 293
Get Colors (Paint Options menu), 235
Get Connected dialog box, 316
global sharing, 220–221
Go to different folder, drop-down list box in toolbar for, 132
Graphic Device Interface resources, monitoring use, 271
Graphics button, in System Properties dialog box, 297
Graphics tab, in Printer Properties dialog box, 251
Gregorian Calendar, 87
guest computer, 96

H

halftoning, 251
hard disk response time, Disk Defragmenter program and, 89
Hard Disk tab, in File System dialog box, 297–298
hardware, detecting and accomodating, 244
hardware profile, **256–258**
Hardware Profiles tab, in System Properties dialog box, 295
headphones, volume control for, 71

337

INDEX

Hearts, 137
Help, **138–140**, 289
  for Calculator, 63
  context-sensitive, 140
  with MS-DOS commands, 199
  on Start menu, 4, 138
Help button, 9–10
  in dialog boxes, 140
  in Microsoft Exchange toolbar, 168
Help menu, for folders, 132
Help Topics dialog box, 138
  Contents tab, 138–139
  Find tab, 139–140
  Index tab, 139
hexadecimal number system, in scientific calculator mode, 63
hidden host drive, for compressed data, 104
hiding Taskbar, 301
High Contrast feature, 24, 27
highlighting of selected objects, 10
horizontal scroll bar, 6, 8
host computer, 96
host drive
  letters for, 108
  ScanDisk for, 277
HyperTerminal, 22, 81, **140–143**, 218
  creating new connection, 141
  menus for, 142
  window for, 141–143

I

icons, 5
  arranging, **46**
  for files and association with programs, 49
  moving/arranging, **195–196**
Identification tab, in Network control panel, 215–216, 223
Image menu, in Paint, 235
Image Quality, for fax, 119
Import Mail Data (Microsoft Exchange File menu), 169
Importance code, for Inbox contents, 166–167
importance level, for e-mail, 111
Inbox, 109, **143**, 168. *See also* Microsoft Exchange (Inbox)
  displaying contents, 166
  option in Microsoft Network to open, 183
Inbox Setup Wizard, 156
Inbox-Microsoft Exchange dialog box, 110
  default settings for, 118
incoming files, folder for, 143
incoming messages, collection by Microsoft Exchange, 165
Index tab, in Help Topics dialog box, 139
individual sharing properties, 221
information, types of, 12–17
information services, 179
.ini files, 270
input devices, alternative in serial port, 29
Insert File
  in Inbox-Microsoft Exchange dialog box, 111
  in Sound Recorder Edit menu, 286
Insert menu, in WordPad, 324
inserting
  Clipboard contents in WordPad document, 327
  objects in WordPad, 328
Install New Modem Wizard, 93
installing
  Connection components, 316
  fonts, 134
  modem, 188
installing applications, **143**
  automatic addition to Programs menu, 261
  run command for, 77, **274**
installing Windows 95, **313–318**
  and Microsoft Exchange components, 165
  selecting optional components, 316
International characters, **144**
Internet, 15, 109, **144–146**
  access to, 179
  Address Book information for, 39
  address format, 146
  Dial-Up Networking to access, 144, 146
  Microsoft Network to access, 144, 145–146
Internet Control Panel, 146

INDEX

Internet Explorer, 146
Internet mail, 146
Internet Setup Wizard, 146
interrupting printing, **147**, 253
Intro Play, for CD Player, 69, 70
Invert Colors (Paint Image menu), 235
Invert Selection command, in Recycle Bin Edit menu, 265
Italic button, in WordPad, 326

K

keyboard, **11**
Keyboard control panel, **147–150**
Keyboard Tab (Accessibility Properties dialog box), 25–26
key-encrypted faxes, 125

L

label, for disk, 137
LAN (Local Area Network), 35
Landscape Orientation, for fax, 119
language, system default for, 269
Language Properties dialog box, 149
Language tab, in Keyboard Properties dialog box, 149
Large Icons button, in folder toolbar, 133
Large Icons command, in View menu, 131, 195
Last Modified Date (Microsoft Backup Settings menu), 51
leading zeroes, displaying, 228
left mouse button, 10–11
left-handedness, and mouse buttons, 11, 191
Length tool, in Sound Recorder, 284
libraries, 179
license agreement, 314
Line Charts tool, in System Monitor, 299
Line-In Balance, in Volume Control dialog box, 310
Line tool (Paint), 233
Line Up Icons command, in folder View menu, 131
linked files, editing, 152

linking and embedding information, **150–153**, 229
Links, in WordPad Edit menu, 322
links to files. *See* shortcuts
List (View menu), 195
list boxes, 9
List button, in folder toolbar, 133
List command, in folder View menu, 131
List Fonts by Similarity view, 135
listing, ports in use, 245–246
LOAD, in Statistics box, 64
local area networks, 217
log, creating system while rebooting, 199
log file, 277
logging on, password to prevent others from, 236
Long date style, 87
lost file fragments, 277
LPT port, 245

M

M+ on calculator, 61
Magnifier tool (Paint), 232
mail arrival, options for, 172
Mail and Fax, **154–158**
mail profile
 changing properties in, 157–158
 setting up, 155–157
mailbox, password for, 238
mailbox.pab, 155
mailbox.pst, 155
Make New Connection folder, 93
Map Network Drive, in folder toolbar, 132
mapping network drives, 13–14, **158–160**
path for, 241
Mark as Read (Microsoft Exchange Edit menu), 169
Mark as Unread (Microsoft Exchange Edit menu), 169
Maximize button, 6, 7
maximizing windows, **160**
maximum speed, for modem, 189
MC on calculator, 61, 62
measurement system, 228
measurement units, in WordPad, 323

INDEX

Media Player, **160–164**
  menus in, 162–163
memory
  in calculator, 61, 62
  measuring use of, 271
menu items, description on Explorer status bar, 115
menus
  to create shortcut, 280
  for folder, 130–132
  font for, 135
  in HyperTerminal, 142
  in Media Player, 162–163
  in Net Watcher, 211
  in Paint, 234–236
  in Sound Recorder, 285–287
  in System Monitor, 300–301
  in WordPad, 322
message boxes, font for, 135
Message format, for fax, 118
Message tab (Microsoft Fax Properties dialog box), 118–119
Messages menu, in WinPopup, 319–320
messaging center. *See* Microsoft Exchange (Inbox)
messaging session, profile to define, 154
metric measurement system, 228
microphone, 284
  in Volume Control dialog box, 311
Microsoft Backup window, 50–51, 57
  closing after completion, 52, 53
  Compare tab, 78
  comparing files with, 78–80
  restoring files with, **272–273**
Microsoft Exchange (Inbox), 15–16, 59, 109, **164–175**, 218
  Address book in, **35–39**
  advantages of, 165
  menus in, 169–175
  setup for, 165–166
  shortcut for, 143
  start options and display appearance, 166
  toolbar, 168
  window, 166–167
MicroSoft Exchange Settings Properties dialog box, 155, 157
Microsoft Fax, **117–125**, 154
  installing, 316
Microsoft Fax Properties dialog box
  Dialing tab, 120–121
  Message tab, 118–119
  Modem tab, 121
  User tab, 121
Microsoft Fax Tools (Microsoft Exchange Tool menu), 171
Microsoft Mail, 109, 154
  Address Book information for, 38
  installing, 316
  postoffice, **176–178**
Microsoft Mail Tools (Microsoft Exchange Tool menu), 171–172
Microsoft Network, 35, 109, 154, **178–187**
  to access Internet, 144, 145–146
  Address Book information for, 38
  installing, 316
  registering to use, **179–182**
  signing off, 184
  signing on to, 182–184
  toolbar for, 185
Microsoft Network base window (MSN Central), 183, **184–187**
Microsoft Plus!, 146
Microsoft Windows 95 Startup Menu, 199
Microsoft Workgroup Postoffice Admin dialog box, 176
Minesweeper, 137
Minimize All Windows (Taskbar pop-up menu), 43
Minimize button, 6, 7, 292
minimizing windows, **160**
  for backup, 52
Mix with File, in Sound Recorder Edit menu, 286
mixing sound, 286
modem, 80, 93
  installing, 188
  port for, 245
Modem tab (Microsoft Fax Properties dialog box), 121
Modems Control Panel, **187–190**
monitoring users of shared resources, 209–211
Motion tab, in Mouse Properties dialog box, 192

INDEX

Mount (DriveSpace Advanced menu), 106
mouse, **10**
  port for, 245
Mouse Control Panel, **190–192**
mouse pointer
  appearance of, 191
  trail for, 192
Mouse Tab (Accessibility Properties dialog box), 28
MouseKeys feature, 24, 28
Move Item button, in Microsoft Exchange toolbar, 168
moving files or folders, **193–194**
  with drag and drop, 103
  in Explorer, 17–18
moving/arranging icons, **195–196**
MR on calculator, 61, 62
MS on calculator, 61, 62
MS Exchange Settings, 154
MS-DOS environment, **196**
  installing Windows 95 from, 313
MS-DOS mode, **196–198**
  restarting computer in, 282
MS-DOS programs, switching between full-screen and window, 198
MS-DOS prompt, 196, **198–199**
MS-DOS Startup menu, **199–200**
Msdos.sys file, 200
MSN. *See* Microsoft Network
MSN Central, 183, **184–187**
MSN Central (Microsoft Network File menu), 186
Multimedia control panel, **200–201**
multimedia fields, playing, 160–164
Multimedia Properties dialog box, 201
multiple file selection, 83, 194
multiple users
  customized desktop settings for, 259
  on non-networked computer, passwords for, 236–237
My Briefcase, 17, **202–205**
  copying file to, 203–204
My Computer, 13–14, **206–208**
  to add folder, 84
  arranging icons in, 46
  to copy files, 83
  to copy floppy disks, 82
  ➤ Dial-Up Networking, 208
  ➤ Connections ➤ Dial-Up Server, 238
  disk space in status bar, 97
  double-click to start document, 103
  to find file or folder, **207**
  to format disk, 136
  to map network drives, 158–159
  moving icons in, 195
  naming disk in, 208
  preventing host drive display on, 108
  sorting files in, 283–284

N

Name & Location tab (Find: All Files dialog box), 127
names
  for disks, **208**
  for files and folders, **208–209**
  for shared resource, 222
NE1000 compatible adapter, 219
NE2000 compatible adapter, 219
NE3200 compatible adapter, 219
negative numbers
  default for displaying, 227–228
  format for currency, 86
negative sign symbol, 228
Net Watcher, **209–211**, 218
network, **217–223**
  finding computer on, **126**
  list of installed components, 213
  password for, 238
  printers on, 246, 251
  security for computers on, 237
  sending messages to multiple people on, 59
  sending and receiving messages on, 59, **318–321**
  setting up hardware, 218–219
  and Windows 95 install, 317
Network Administration, password access to, 238–239
Network control panel, **212–217**
  Access tab, 223
  Configuration tab, 212–215, 223
  Identification tab, 215–216, 223

INDEX

network drives, 13
  mapping, **158–160**
  unmapping or disconnecting, **159–160**
Network Neighborhood, 15, **224–225**
  for mapping network drives, 158–159
  moving icons in, 195
Network Properties dialog box, 219
network software, setting up, 219–220
networking cards, 81
New (Sound Recorder File menu), 285
New button, in HyperTerminal toolbar, 141
New Entry (Address Book File menu), 36, 38–39
New Fax (Microsoft Exchange Compose menu), 175
New Hardware Wizard, 30
New icon, in WordPad, 326
New Message (Address Book File menu), 37
New Message (Microsoft Exchange Compose menu), 175
New Message button, in Microsoft Exchange toolbar, 168
new product information, 179
New Window (Microsoft Exchange View menu), 169
Newsgroups, on Internet, 146
Next Mark button, in Media Player, 161
Notepad, **226–227**
Notification, for Accessibilities options, 29
notification area, in Taskbar, 2
Num Lock, beep for, 26
number of copies, printing, 254
number format, **227–228**
  system default for, 269
Numeric Charts tool, in System Monitor, 299
numeric entry box, 9
numeric keypad, MouseKeys to define, 28–29
NUMLOCK, and calculator entry, 61

O

Object Properties, in WordPad Edit menu, 322
objects
  inserting in WordPad, 324, 328
  selecting, 10, **278**
octal number system, in scientific calculator mode, 63
odd pages, printing, 254
OK command buttons, 9
OLE (Object Linking and Embedding), **150–153**, 229
online registration, **229**
online service. *See* Microsoft Network
opaque drawing, 236
Open dialog box, 230
Open icon, 230
  in WordPad, 326
opening
  files, **230–231**
  windows, **229**
optimizing hard disk usage, 296
Options, in WordPad, 323
Options menu
  in Paint, 235–236
  in System Monitor, 300–301

P

Page Range, for printing, 254
Page Setup, in WordPad File menu, 322
pages in dialog box, tab to select, 8
Paint, **231–236**
  color palette in, 234
  menus in, 234–236
  toolbox for, 232–233
Paper tab, in Printer Properties dialog box, 250–251
paragraph options, in WordPad, 325
parallel port, 245
  for direct cable connection, 95
parent window, 14
parity, for modem, 189
partial backups, **56–58**
passwords, **236–239**
  in backups, 56

INDEX

to clear screen saver, 100–101
for direct cable connection, 96
for Microsoft Network, 179, 182–183, 187
for network resources, 216
for postoffice, 155, 177
for resource sharing, 221
user-customized settings, 258
Passwords Properties dialog box, User Profiles tab, 258–259
Paste button, in folder toolbar, 133
Paste command, 74, 83, **240**
  in folder Edit menu, 131
  in Notepad, 226–227
Paste Insert, in Sound Recorder Edit menu, 286
Paste Mix, in Sound Recorder Edit menu, 286
Paste Shortcut command, in folder Edit menu, 131
Paste to Host, in HyperTerminal, 142
pasting screen image, 67
path, **240–241**
  to computer postoffice, 155
  for file search, 127
Pattern, for background display, 99
pause, in Disk Defragmenter, 90
Pause Printing, 248, 253
payment method dialog box, for Microsoft Network, 181
peer-to-peer network, 217
Pencil tool (Paint), 232
Performance tab, in System Properties dialog box, 295–297
Personal Address Book, 35, 165, 170
Personal Distribution List, Address Book information for, 39
Personal Folders, in Microsoft Exchange, 167
Phone Dialer, 22, **241–243**
phone number, to access Microsoft Network, 181–182
physically challenged persons, computer adjustments for, **24–30**
Pick Color tool (Paint), 232
PIF Editor, 243
Play button, in Media Player, 161
Play tool, in Sound Recorder, 284
playback, adjusting sound quality, 312

plug and play, **244**
plus sign (+), in disk or folder in Exploring window, 116
PM Symbol, 304
Pointers tab, in Mouse Properties dialog box, 191–192
pointing, xiv
pointing devices, 10. *See also* mouse
Point-to-Point Protocol Account, 144–145
Polygon tool (Paint), 233
popup menus, **244**
  Copy command, 84
  to create shortcut, 280
  Cut and Paste from, 194
  for files, 207
  Properties, 262
  Quick View, 263
  right-clicking for, **274**
  Send To options, **278–279**
portable computer
  dialing properties for, 123
  direct cable connection to, 95
  synchronizing files with, 202
Portable installation, for Windows 95, 313, 315
Portrait Orientation, for fax, 119
ports, **244–246**
  for modem, 189
  for printer, 245, 252, 255
Position tool, in Sound Recorder, 284
positive numbers, default for displaying, 227–228
postoffice
  adding new users to, 177–178
  Address list, 35, 170
  Microsoft Mail, **176–178**
  path to, 155
Preview, in Sounds Control Panel, 287
preview box, for Background Display property, 99
Previous Mark button, in Media Player, 161
Previous Version of MS-DOS, starting, 200
Primary Network Logon, 215
Print button
  in Microsoft Exchange toolbar, 168

343

INDEX

in WordPad, 326
Print command
  in folder File menu, 130
  in Microsoft Backup File menu, 51
Print dialog box, 254
Print Preview icon, in WordPad, 326
Printer menu, in printer queue, 248
Printer Properties dialog box, 249–251
printer queue, 248
printers
  adding new, 251
  allowing network access to, 215
  icons in My Computer, 13
  password for, 238
  permitting sharing of specific, 221
  port for, 245, 252, 255
  setting default, 248
Printers folder, **246–252**
printing, **253–255**
  drag and drop for, 103
  interrupting, **147**, 253
  report of hardware resources, 295
  starting, 253–254
  test page, 252
Product Identification dialog box, 315
profile ID, 36
profiles, 154, **256–259**
Progman.exe, 261
program groups
  adding to Programs menu, **260**
  in Windows 3.x, 19
program listings, Notepad to edit, 226
Program Manager, 1, **261**
programs. *See* applications
Programs submenu (Start menu), 4, 21, **261–262**, 290
  ➤ Accessories, Calculator, 60
  ➤ Character Map, 72
  ➤ Clipboard Viewer, 75
  ➤ Dial-Up Networking, 93, 94
  ➤ Direct Cable Connection, 96
  ➤ Fax ➤ Compose New Fax, 123
  ➤ Fax ➤ Cover Page Editor, 120
  ➤ Games, 137
  ➤ HyperTerminal, 141
  ➤ Multimedia, 161
  ➤ Multimedia ➤ CD Player, 68–69
  ➤ Multimedia ➤ Media Player, 163
  ➤ Multimedia ➤ Sound Recorder, 284
  ➤ Multimedia ➤ Volume Control, 309
  ➤ Notepad, 226
  ➤ Paint, 231
  ➤ Phone Dialer, 65, 241
  ➤ System Tools ➤ Backup, 50, 78, 272
  ➤ System Tools ➤ Disk Defragmenter, 89
  ➤ System Tools ➤ DriveSpace, 105, 107
  ➤ System Tools ➤ Net Watcher, 210
  ➤ System Tools ➤ Resource Meter, 271
  ➤ System Tools ➤ ScanDisk, 275
  ➤ System Tools ➤ System Monitor, 298
  ➤ WordPad, 322
  adding new groups to, **260**
  changing, 40, 41–42
  ➤ Microsoft Exchange, 110, 118, 166
  ➤ MS-DOS Prompt, 198
  ➤ Windows Explorer, 115
Properties, **262**
  of Desktop, 92
  of devices, 295
  in DriveSpace Drive menu, 106
  in Keyboard Properties dialog box, 149
  for Modems dialog box, 187–190
  for network components, 215
  in Printer folder File menu, 247
  of shortcuts, 281
  in Sound Recorder File menu, 285
  storage of, 270
Properties button
  in folder toolbar, 133
  in HyperTerminal toolbar, 141
  in Inbox-Microsoft Exchange, 111
Properties command, in folder File menu, 131
Properties dialog box, 98, 243
  General tab, 97, 98

INDEX

Properties menu, in Media Player, 163
protocols, configuring for network, 212, 214
Purge Print Jobs, 248

Q

Quick View, 131, **262–263**
quitting. *See* closing; shut down
quotations marks, for file names greater than 8 characters, 240

R

radio buttons, 8. *See also* option buttons
Random Track Order, for audio CDs, 68
Read Only Access Type, 222
Read Receipt icon, in Inbox-Microsoft Exchange, 111
Read tab, in Microsoft Exchange Options dialog box, 172–173
Read-ahead optimization, 296–297
Receive button, in HyperTerminal toolbar, 141
Received, in Inbox contents, 167
Record tool, in Sound Recorder, 284
Recording Control dialog box, 312
recording volume, varying, 311–312
recovering files, from Recycle Bin, 267–268
Rectangle tool (Paint), 233
Recycle Bin, 20, 91, 133, **264–268**
  changing size, 267
  deleting files without using, 268
  drag and drop to, 103
  emptying, 266
  recovering files from, 267–268
  size and loss of files, 268
  undeleting file from, 306
Redetect Tape Drive (Backup Tools menu), 54
Refresh command
  in DriveSpace Advanced menu, 106
  in folder View menu, 131
  in Microsoft Backup File menu, 51

Regional Settings control panel, 144, **269**
  Currency tab, 85–86
  date format settings, 86–87
  and time format, 304
registering (associating) files, 19–20, **47–49**
registration, online, **229**
Registry, 30, **270**
remote access, 208. *See also* Dial-Up Networking; HyperTerminal
Remote Administration, password for, 239
remote fax, retrieving, **122–123**
Remote Mail (Microsoft Exchange Tool menu), 171
Remove, in Keyboard Properties dialog box, 149
Remove tool, in System Monitor, 299
Rename command, in folder File menu, 131
renaming files, 18
Repeat Delay, in Keyboard Properties dialog box, 148
Repeat Rate, in Keyboard Properties dialog box, 148
Reply to All (Microsoft Exchange Compose menu), 175
Reply to All button, in Microsoft Exchange toolbar, 113, 168
reply to electronic mail, **112–113**
Reply to Sender (Microsoft Exchange Compose menu), 175
Reply to Sender button, in Microsoft Exchange toolbar, 168
Request a Fax dialog box, 122–123
resolution, of Desktop, 102
Resource Meter, **270–271**
resource sharing, **220–223**, 237
  troubleshooting problems, 223
Restore (Recycle Bin File menu), 265
Restore button, 7
Restore tab (Microsoft Backup window), 50
restoring files, **272–273**
RET, in Statistics box, 64
Revert (Sound Recorder File menu), 286
right mouse button
  for popup menus, 244

345

INDEX

for resource sharing, 223
right-clicking, xiv, **274**
Rounded tool (Paint), 233
Run option (Start menu), 77, 143, **274–275**, 289

S

Safe Mode, for starting Windows, 200
Safe-Mode Command Prompt Only, for starting Windows, 200
Save Colors (Paint Options menu), 235
Save command, naming files with, 208–209
Save icon, in WordPad, 326
saving files, **275**
Scale, in Media Player, 163
ScanDisk, 90, **275–277**
Scandisk.log, 277
Scheme
  for events with assigned sounds, 287–288
  for pointer, 192
  for screen appearance, 101
Scientific mode, for calculator, 61, 62–63
screen image, capturing, **67**
Screen Saver tab (Display Properties dialog box), 100–101
screen savers, 92, 237, **277**
  password for, 239
scroll bars, 6, 7, 8
Scroll Lock, beep for, 26
searches, for Help, 140
secondary button on mouse, 11
security, for fax, 124, 125
Seek to End tool, in Sound Recorder, 284
Seek to Start tool, in Sound Recorder, 284
Select All command
  in folder Edit menu, 131
  in Recycle Bin Edit menu, 265
Select Components dialog box, 316–317
Select Network Component Type dialog box, 213, 219–220
Select Program Folder dialog box, 291

Select server button, in Net Watcher toolbar, 210
Select tool (Paint), 232
selecting
  multiple files, 83
  objects, 10, **278**
Send, in WordPad File menu, 322
Send button, in HyperTerminal toolbar, 141
Send tab, in Microsoft Exchange Options dialog box, 173
Send To command, in folder File menu, 131
Send To options (popup menu), **278–279**
sending e-mail, 110–112
  with WinPopup, 321
Sent Items folder, in Microsoft Exchange, 167
separator, for hours and minutes, 304
serial ports, 245
  for direct cable connection, 95
SerialKey Devices feature, 24, 29
server software, 217
service software, configuring for network, 212, 214–215
Services (Microsoft Exchange Tool menu), 172
Services tab
  in Microsoft Exchange Options dialog box, 173
  in MS Exchange Settings Properties dialog box, 155
Set As Default printer option, 248
Set As Wallpaper (Centered), in Paint File menu, 234
Set As Wallpaper (Tiled), in Paint File menu, 234
Settings (DriveSpace Advanced menu), 106
Settings menu in Microsoft Backup, 51–54
  ➤ Options, ➤ Compare, for Backup, 79
Settings submenu (Start menu), 4, 290
  ➤ Control Panel, 13, 81, 87, 134
    ➤ Accessibility Options, 25
    ➤ Add New Hardware, 30

346

INDEX

- Add/Remove Programs, 25, 307–308
- Date/Time, 88
- Display, 74, 99, 237
- Display, ➤ Screen Saver, 239
- Keyboard, 147
- Mail and Fax, 155, 157
- Mail and Fax, ➤ Services tab, 238
- Microsoft Mail Postoffice, 176
- Modems, 187
- Mouse, 190
- Multimedia, 71, 201
- Network, 212, 219, 220
- Passwords, 236, 258
- Passwords, ➤ User Profiles, 236
- Printers folder, 246, 255
- Regional Settings, 88, 269
- Regional Settings, Number Tab, 227–228
- Regional Settings, ➤ Time, 304
- Sounds, 287
- System, 245, 256, 293
- Printers, 253
- Taskbar, 40, 302
- Start Menu Programs tab, 290–291

Settings tab (Display Properties dialog box), 102
setup
  Run option for, 274
  Windows 95, **313–318**
Setup Wizards, 318
shared computer, shut down to log on different user, 282
shared resources, **220–223**
  hard disk in My Computer, 13
  on host computer, 96
  monitoring who is accessing, 209–211
  name for drives, 158
  password for, 239
  postoffice folder as, 177
  viewing network drives, 206
Share-level access control, 216, 237
Sharing command, in folder File menu, 131
Sharing tab, in Printer Properties dialog box, 250

Shift key, 26
  to select multiple files, 194
  to select multiple objects, 278
Short date style, 87
shortcut buttons, on Taskbar for active programs, 301
shortcut keys, *back cover*
shortcuts, 18–19, **279–282**
  creating, **280–281**
  creating for Explorer, 115
  deleting, 281
  deleting from Start menu, 41
  on Desktop, 42
  locations for, 39
  placing, 281
Show files button, in Net Watcher toolbar, 210
Show Grid (Paint View menu), 234
Show/Hide Folder List button, in Microsoft Exchange toolbar, 168
Show Log (Phone Dialer Tools menu), 243
Show shared folders button, in Net Watcher toolbar, 210
Show Thumbnail (Paint View menu), 234
Show users button, in Net Watcher toolbar, 210
ShowSounds feature, 24, 27
shut down, 3, 5, **282–283**
Shut down (Start button), 289
Sign In (Microsoft Network File menu), 185
Sign Out (Microsoft Network File menu), 185
Size, file in Inbox contents, 167
size of file, as search restriction, 128
Size list, in WordPad, 326
sizing handle, 6, 7
slider, 9
  in Media Player, 162
  in Sound Recorder, 284
Small Icons button, in folder toolbar, 133
Small Icons (View menu), 131, 195
Solitaire, 137
Sort (Microsoft Exchange View menu), 169
sorting, files and folders, **283–284**

347

INDEX

sound
  attaching to events, 114
  for new WinPopup message, 320
  playing clips, 160–164
sound card, volume of, 309
Sound Recorder, 22, **284–287**
  menus in, 285–287
Sound tab (Accessibility Properties dialog box), 27
Sounds Control Panel, 114, **287–289**
SoundSentry feature, 24, 27
speaker icon, 72
speaker volume, 309
  for modem, 189
special characters, adding to document, 72–73
Speed Dial (Phone Dialer Edit menu), 242, 243
Speed tab, in Keyboard Properties dialog box, 148
spinner, 9
Sta button, in calculator, 63–64
standard deviation, from calculator, 63–64
Standard mode, for calculator, 61, 62
Start button, 2, **3**, **289–290**
Start menu
  adding to, 5
  creating shortcut on, 115
  displaying applications on, 40–41
  ➤ Documents, 4, 21, 102, 230–231, 290
  ➤ Find,
    ➤ Computer, 126
    ➤ Files or Folders, 126
  ➤ Help, 138
  ➤ Programs. *See* Programs submenu (Start menu)
  ➤ Run, 77, 143, **274–275**, 289
  ➤ Settings. *See* Settings submenu (Start menu)
  ➤ Shut Down, 76, 282
  ➤ Restart the Computer, 199
Start Menu folder
  dragging shortcuts to, 281
  opening, 260
Start Selection button, in Media Player, 161
starting applications, 4, 20–21
  by double-clicking, 14

starting documents, **102–103**
starting Windows, options for, 199–200
startup applications, **290–292**
startup disk, creating, 35, 317
Startup folder, 21
  placing applications in, 45
  placing Inbox in, 157
  WinPopup in, 320
statistical functions, 63–64
Status bar
  in Explorer, 115
  Paint tool description in, 232
Status Bar command, in folder View menu, 131
Step-by-Step confirmation, when starting Windows, 200
StickyKeys feature, 24, 26
Stop bits settings, for modem, 189
Stop button, in Media Player, 161
Stop sharing button, in Net Watcher toolbar, 210
Stop tool, in Sound Recorder, 284
stopping applications, **292**
Stretch/Skew (Paint Image menu), 255
subfolders, searches in, 127
Subject, in Inbox contents, 167
subject line, for fax, 119
sums, from calculator, 63–64
Supplemental Cache size, for CD-ROM, 297
Switch Languages, in Keyboard Properties dialog box, 149
switching applications, **292–293**
  with Taskbar, 302
synchronizing files between computers, 17
Synthesizer Balance, in Volume Control dialog box, 310
system areas, testing disk for errors in, 276
System control panel, **293–297**
system defaults, storage of, 270
system log, creating while rebooting, 199
System Monitor, **298–301**
System Properties dialog box, Hardware Profiles tab, 256–257
system resources, monitoring use, 271

INDEX

T

Tabs
  in dialog boxes, 8
  in WordPad, 325
tape backups, formatting when needed, 54
Taskbar, **2–5**, 92, **301–303**
  clock on, 2, **87–88**, 303
  displaying date on, 88
  language indicator on, 149–150
  modifying display, 302–303
  placing application on, 302
  Print icon, 147
  switching tasks with, **292–293**, 302
Taskbar pop-up menu
  Cascade, 46
  Minimize All Windows, 43
  Tile Horizontally, 46
  Tile Vertically, 47
Taskbar Properties dialog box, 40–41, 302–303
telephone calling card, **65–66**
Terminal (Windows 3.x), 22
test page, printing, 252
testing, disk for errors, 275
text box, 9
text file editor. *See* Notepad; WordPad
text objects, font for, 135
Text tool (Paint), 233
Tile Horizontally (Taskbar pop-up menu), 46
Tile option, for wallpaper patterns, 100
Tile Vertically (Taskbar pop-up menu), 47
Time
  inserting in WordPad document, 324
  setting system clock, 87–88
time format, **304–305**
Time to send, for fax, 118
time zone, default settings, **305–306**
timeout limits, for printer, 250
Title bar, 6, 8
  dragging to move window, 46
  font for, 135
ToggleKeys feature, 24, 26
toll prefixes, for fax, 120
tool tips, for CD Player toolbar, 70
Toolbar, 6, 8, **306**
  for Address Book window, 37
  for CD Player, 68
  for Explorer, 115
  for folders, 132–133
  for HyperTerminal, 141–142
  for Inbox–Microsoft Exchange dialog box, 111
  for Microsoft Exchange, 171
  for Microsoft Network, 185
  for MS-DOS window, 199
  for My Computer, 206–207
  for Net Watcher, 210–211
  for Sound Recorder, 284–285
  for System Monitor, 298–299
  for WordPad, 326–327
Toolbar command, in folder View menu, 131
toolbox, for Paint, 232–233
Toolkit Properties dialog box, 222
Tools menu
  in Address Book, 37
  ▶ Disconnect Network Drive, 160
  ▶ Map Network Drive, 160
  in Microsoft Backup, 54
  in Microsoft Network, 187
Tools menu (Explorer), ▶ Find ▶ Files or Folders, 126
Tools menu (Microsoft Exchange), 170–174
  Address Book, **35–39**
  ▶ Microsoft Fax Tools, 118
  ▶ Advanced Security, 125
  ▶ Request a Fax, 122
  ▶ Show Outgoing Faxes, 124
Tools menu (Phone Dialer), 242–243
  ▶ Dialing Properties, 65
Track Time Elapsed, for audio CDs, 68
Track Time Remaining, for audio CDs, 68
Track Visual Display tool, in Sound Recorder, 284
trackballs, 10
Transfer menu, in HyperTerminal, 142
transparent drawing, 236
triangle, in Start button menu, 3

349

INDEX

Troubleshooting tab, in File System dialog box, 297
TrueType fonts, 134
Type of Item, for Inbox contents, 167
Typical installation, for Windows 95, 313, 314

U

Uncompress (DriveSpace Drive menu), 105
Undelete, 20, **306–307**
Underline button, in WordPad, 326
Undo button, in folder toolbar, 133
Undo command, **307**
 in folder Edit menu, 131
uninstalling applications, 33, **307–308**
unmapping network drives, **159–160**
Unmount (DriveSpace Advanced menu), 106
Unread messages, 169
Up One Level
 in folder toolbar, 132
 in Microsoft Exchange toolbar, 168
user interface, 1
User-level access control, 216, 237
user name, for Microsoft Network, 182
user profiles, **258–259**
 passwords in, 239
user resources, monitoring use, 271
User tab (Microsoft Fax Properties dialog box), 121
users
 display settings for, 237
 list of permissions for, 221

V

verifying backups, 53
vertical scroll bar, 6, 7
video, playing, 160–164
View Bitmap (Paint View menu), 235
View menu
 ➤ Arrange Icons, 46
 for calculator, 61
 for CD Player, 70
 for folders, 131–132
 in Paint, 234
 in Printer folder, 247
 for Recycle Bin, 265
 in System Monitor, 300
 in WordPad, 323–324
View menu (Explorer), ➤ Options, 48
View menu (Fonts), 135
 Hide Variations, 135
View option
 for Printer folder, 247
 in Recycle Bin View menu, 265, 266
View tab, for Microsoft Network options, 186
Virtual Memory button, in System Properties dialog box, 297
vision impaired. *See* Accessibility options
voice call requests, Phone Dialer to handle, 243
volume control, **309–312**
 for CD Player, 71–72
 in Media Player, 163

W

Wallpaper, for background display, 99
wastebasket icon, 264. *See also* Recycle Bin
.wav file, 287
 inserting, 286
Wave Balance, in Volume Control dialog box, 310
Welcome to Windows 95 dialog box, 318
Wgpo0000 folder, 176–177
Win.ini file, 270
Window frame, 6, 7
windowed MS-DOS programs, switching to full-screen, 198
Windows 3.1, installing Windows 95 from, 313
Windows 95, xi
 adding and removing components, 34
 choosing optional component to install, 316

INDEX

file structure, 12
fonts used in, 135–136
password for, 239
screen, **1–11**
setup, **313–318**
Windows 95 Setup Wizard, 314
Windows 95 Startup Menu, 199
windows, 5–6
  adjusting size, 7–8
  closing, **76**
  dragging, 46
  maximize or minimize, **160**
  opening and closing, **229**
  parts of, *front cover*, 6–8
  previous versions of, 196
  switching between, **292–293**
Windows Components dialog box, 316

\Windows\SendTo folder, 278–279
\Windows\Start Menu\Programs\Startup folder, 21, 45
  placing Inbox in, 157
  WinPopup in, 320
WinPopup, 59, **318–321**
  loading window, 319
  sending message, 321
word wrap, in Notepad, 226
WordPad, 22, **321–328**
Work Offline (Printer folder File menu), 247
Write, 22

Z

Zoom (Paint View menu), 234

Shortcut Keys in Windows 95

Keystroke	Purpose
Alt+Enter	Switches the active document between full-screen and operating in a window
Alt+Esc	Switches among the folders and the programs on the Taskbar
Alt+F4	Closes the active window
Alt+Print Screen	Captures the image of the active window and places it in the Clipboard
Alt+Spacebar	Opens the Control menu for the active window or selected Taskbar object; same as clicking on the far left of the active window's title bar or right-clicking on a Taskbar program or folder
Alt+Tab	Switches among programs and folders on the Taskbar using the Task Switcher dialog box
Arrow keys	Moves the selection in the direction of the arrow
Backspace	Activates the parent folder of the active window
Ctrl+A	Selects all the objects in a window
Ctrl+C	Copies selected objects to the Clipboard
Ctrl+V	Pastes the contents of the Clipboard at the current insertion point
Ctrl+X	Cuts (removes) the selected objects and places them in the Clipboard
Ctrl+Z	Undoes the last copy, move, delete, paste, or rename operation performed
Ctrl+Esc	Opens the Start menu
Delete	Moves the selection to the Recycle Bin for eventual deletion
Enter	Activates the selected object or menu option in the way that clicking or double-clicking would; also closes the active dialog box, implementing any changes that were made
End	Moves the selection to the last object
Esc	Closes the active menu or the active dialog box without making a selection